FOG, SMOG,
AND POISONED RAIN

Dangerous Weather

Fog, Smog, and Poisoned Rain

Michael Allaby

ILLUSTRATIONS by Richard Garratt

Facts On File, Inc.

Fog, Smog, and Poisoned Rain

Facts On File, Inc.
132 West 31st Street
New York NY 10001

Library of Congress Cataloging-in-Publication Data

Allaby, Michael.
   Fog, smog, and poisoned rain / Michael Allaby; illustrations by Richard Garratt.
      p.   cm. — (Dangerous weather)
Includes bibliographical references and index.
   ISBN 0-8160-4789-8 (acid-free paper)
   1. Fog. 2. Smog. 3. Acid rain. I. Title.
QC929.F7 A48 2003
363.739′2—dc21   2002153844

Facts On File books are available at special discounts when purchased in bulk quantities for businesses, associations, institutions, or sales promotions. Please call our Special Sales Department in New York at (212) 967-8800 or (800) 322-8755.

You can find Facts On File on the World Wide Web at
http://www.factsonfile.com

Text design by Erika K. Arroyo
Cover design by Nora Wertz
Illustrations by Richard Garratt

Printed in the United States of America

VB Hermitage 10 9 8 7 6 5 4 3 2 1

This book is printed on acid-free paper.

For Ailsa
—M.A.

To my late wife, Jen, who gave me inspiration
and support for almost 30 years
—R.G.

Contents

Preface

What are fog, smog, and poisoned rain?

Have you ever flown in an airplane through cloud? Beneath you the ground falls away as your plane climbs. Then, as you enter the base of the cloud, fragments of cloud begin to cover the ground, which disappears from view a few patches at a time until you lose sight of it altogether. Through the window you can see the wings and engines of the plane quite clearly, but beyond the wingtips there is simply a pale gray nothing. You are looking at the inside of the cloud, and if the cloud were on the ground and you were standing in it you would call it fog.

Fog is nothing more than a cloud that touches the ground. Both are made from tiny droplets of water. These are so small you can breathe perfectly easily in the fog, inhaling the droplets and then breathing them out again. They are colorless, odorless, tasteless, and completely harmless. You are unaware of breathing them, but you know the air is full of water because it quickly wets your clothes and hair. In addition, of course, it obscures your view. If you are in the open countryside where there is no road or path to guide you, a fog can soon disorient you by hiding all the landmarks. It is easy to lose your way.

Fogs are not confined to land. They also form at sea, and before ships had radar that could see through them they caused many collisions. Ships had to slow down and sound their whistles so the crews of other ships would know where they were. Lighthouses on the shore had foghorns sounding coded signals, like their lights, to warn ships away from dangerous rocks and shallow water.

A fog that reduces visibility but is not dense enough to hide landmarks completely is called mist or, if it is even thinner than that, haze. A mist consists of water droplets, but a haze is caused by tiny solid particles that hang in the air, too small and light to fall to the ground. Sometimes water vapor condenses onto them, and the haze then changes to mist.

Smog

Fog, mist, and haze are usually harmless, but not always. Years ago, several times in most winters, fogs that were far from harmless used to form in most of the industrial cities of northern Europe. They were so dense the streetlights came on in the middle of the day. Cars and buses crawled along with their lights on and often ran across the road or right off it because their drivers could not see where they were. There were many collisions, but they caused little damage because the vehicles were all moving very slowly. Walking on foot was a little easier if there were a wall or curb to follow, but even then it was easy to become hopelessly lost. Schools, factories, shops, and city offices closed early because it took so long for people to find their way home. This was a mixture of fog and smoke called smog. London became famous—or notorious—for smog of this kind, but many other cities were affected just as badly. Breathing it was painful for anyone and dangerous for asthma sufferers and those with bronchitis or any other respiratory ailments. Smog could and did kill.

Smog of this type occurred only in northern cities, but cities farther south did not escape. They suffered from a different kind of smog that colored the air yellow or brown. It did not reduce visibility seriously, but breathing it could make people ill.

This book is about fog and both types of smog. It is also about air pollution—what it is, what causes it, the harm it does, and what we can do to reduce it. Smog is only one of the forms pollution can take. Years ago, before clean air laws made them more careful about the wastes they pumped into the air, you could identify factories by their smell or by the air around them. Steel mills, breweries, and chemical works had distinctive smells, and the glue factories, where animal bones were melted down, and tanneries that made leather created the worst smells of all. Woolen mills and blanket factories did not smell, but they filled the air with fibers that blew everywhere, tangled together in clumps, and clung to trees and bushes.

Acid rain and the ozone layer

Unfortunately, trying to clean the air did not end air pollution. It brought improvements, but it also exchanged some types of pollution for others. In rural areas many miles from industrial centers, the air became more acid. The acid clung to surfaces, dissolved in mist, rain, and snow, and fell to the ground, where it altered the chemistry of soils and some lakes. It was called acid rain, although rain was only one of the forms it took and was not the most harmful.

Fog and smog touch the ground, and acid rain falls to the ground. Pollution also occurs high above the ground, higher even than the cruising altitudes of modern airliners. High in the upper air is the ozone layer, a region where ozone accumulates. Ozone is a serious pollutant at ground level, but in the upper atmosphere it absorbs some kinds of harmful radiation. Scientists discovered that chemical substances manufactured and used on the ground were finding their way into the upper air and destroying ozone.

Natural pollution

It is easy to suppose that all pollution is our own fault, that our activities are the only source of harmful airborne substances. This is wrong. Nature itself is a polluter on a grand scale.

Volcanoes are the most spectacular polluters. Big eruptions make the TV news. We marvel at the glowing rivers of molten rock and the balls of fire hurled into the sky. We also see huge clouds of hot dust and gas. Sometimes these clouds are so big they alter the weather by shading the ground.

Even ordinary trees cause pollution. In the countryside, gases they release are the principal cause of haze and smog. Wildfires also pollute the air, and when the fires are large their effects are felt hundreds of miles away.

Making air safe to breathe

Happily, we are able to improve the quality of the air we breathe. Many advances have been made already and there will be more in years to come. This book closes with an outline of the ways in which pollution is being brought under control.

Introduction

Several years have passed since the publication of the first edition of the Dangerous Weather series of books. Much has happened during that time, and my friends at Facts On File and I felt it would be appropriate to revise all the books in the series to bring them up to date.

As we began to prepare the new editions, it occurred to us that none of the books so much as mentioned air pollution. Pollution is clearly a matter of great concern, and omitting it from a series of books about the atmosphere might make it seem that we were either ignorant or uncaring. First, though, we had to decide whether the subject would fit into the overall concept of the series. Is it "dangerous weather"?

Air pollution affects our health and well-being, so it is reasonable to describe it as "dangerous." This means it fits the first part of the series title. It is "dangerous," but is it "weather"? The most dramatic example of air pollution—and one I remember very well from personal experience, indeed familiarity—is smog. The smog I knew was a mixture of fog and smoke trapped beneath a temperature inversion, which gave rise to the word *smog*. Both fog and temperature inversions are meteorological phenomena. They are very definitely "weather." Pollution modifies them, but it also depends on them. Without the fog and the inversion there could be no smog. More recently, we have watched anxiously as industrial gases have made rain more acid. Again, our cars and factories add the acid, but air movements carry it to distant places, and it is rain that brings it to the ground. Air movements and rain are parts of our weather. Bright sunshine is also part of our weather, and if we worry that too much exposure to it may be harmful because certain chemicals we release into the air have reduced the amount of ozone in the stratosphere, then ozone depletion must also be considered a meteorological phenomenon.

Air pollution therefore qualifies as "weather." This is reflected in the title of this addition to the Dangerous Weather series: *Fog, Smog, and Poisoned Rain*.

In order to understand how pollution occurs we need to know something of the way weather happens. You will read here about air masses, weather fronts, and how movements of the air and oceans transport heat from the equator into high latitudes. You will learn about how fog develops, the various forms it takes, and how clouds grow and why rain falls.

Sidebars throughout the book provide more detailed explanations of technical matters. You will find sidebars on such topics as temperature inversions, adiabatic cooling and warming, the photolytic cycle involved in the formation of photochemical smog, steam cars, and much more.

Most of the book deals directly with pollution, however. It describes the causes and effects of both "pea-soup" and photochemical smog, as well as acid rain, and it tells the story of the depletion of the ozone layer.

The book explains what fossil fuels are and what happens when they burn. Fuel combustion is the principle source of air pollution. Factory and power plant emissions enter the air through tall stacks. The book describes the way stack emissions travel and mix with the surrounding air. It also lists the primary and secondary pollutants that result from vehicle emissions.

Not all pollution is the fault of factories and automobiles. Volcanoes are major air polluters, and, perhaps surprisingly, plants, and especially trees, release chemicals that are a significant cause of photochemical smog. Wildfires occur naturally—although some are set deliberately—and a big forest fire can pollute a wide area. The book describes all of these, with examples of major eruptions and major fires.

The pollution that results from our activities can be reduced or, in some cases, eliminated. A substantial part of the book discusses how certain forms of pollution have been greatly reduced over the years and how further improvements in air quality are likely to be achieved in years to come. You will read about alternatives to the internal combustion engine in "New Cars for Old," about renewable energy in "Sun and Wind," and about nuclear and thermonuclear power in "Heat without Fire."

Measurements are given in familiar units, such as pounds, feet, miles, and degrees Fahrenheit, throughout the book, but in each case I have added the metric or scientific equivalent. All scientists now use standard international units of measurement. These may be unfamiliar, so I have added them with their conversions as an appendix.

You will find suggestions for further information listed at the end of the book. The sources include a number of books you may find useful, but a much larger number of web addresses. If you have access to the Internet, these will allow you to learn more about pollution, its causes, and its remedies quickly and free of charge.

The book is illustrated with diagrams and maps. My friend and colleague Richard Garratt prepared all of these. As always, I am deeply grateful to Richard for his skill in translating my crude drawings into such accomplished artwork. I am grateful, too, to Frank K. Darmstadt, my editor at Facts On File, for his hard work, cheerful encouragement, and patience.

If *Fog, Smog, and Poisoned Rain* encourages you to pursue your interest in atmospheric science, it will have achieved its aim and fulfilled my highest hopes for it. I hope you enjoy reading the book as much as I enjoyed writing it for you.

— Michael Allaby
Tighnabruaich
Argyll, Scotland
www.michaelallaby.com

WATER IN THE AIR

Air masses and fronts in summer and winter

When air is polluted the effect is not confined to the immediate area. Airborne pollutants can travel, sometimes for a very long way. In the 1960s, for example, British factories were blamed for polluting lakes and forests in southern Sweden, and factories in the industrial regions of eastern Europe were suspected of causing pollution in what was then West Germany. It turned out that the cause of the pollution was not so straightforward as people first thought, but there was no doubt that substances entering the air could be carried for hundreds or even thousands of miles.

In April 1997 a Russian space rocket released a cloud of soot from burned kerosene as it climbed through the atmosphere following its launch either from the Baikonur Cosmodrome in Kazakhstan or from Plesetsk, Russia. (It is uncertain which of two rockets launched a few days apart released the soot.) The soot was detected a little over a week later 6,000 miles (9,650 km) away as a cloud 100 miles (160 km) long and 300 feet (90 m) thick in the sky 12 miles above California. Too thin to be visible or to cause any harm, the soot cloud was detected by highly sensitive instruments. Its presence showed just how far pollutants can travel given favorable conditions.

Dust from the Sahara Desert is occasionally washed to the ground by rain in northern Europe. It coats everything with a thin red film, so the rain is called "blood rain." The dust even turns up in America, and this happens every year. Clouds of dust drift westward from Africa, cross the Atlantic Ocean, and arrive in Florida. The dust contains iron oxides—which is why it is red—and it fertilizes single-celled algae in the water off Florida. The algae, which are poisonous, then multiply into a bloom, called a red tide, that kills fish and sometimes birds and mammals as well and that can make humans ill.

Factory smoke, soot, and desert dust do not travel *through* the air, they travel *with* it. The air itself moves. Think of a hot-air balloon. It rises into the sky and then drifts. It moves because the air in which it floats is moving. When solid particles and tiny liquid droplets become airborne they travel in the same way. We feel air movement, of course, and call it "wind," but air moves on a much larger scale than this. The air around the wind also moves because the Earth is rotating on its axis.

Moving air

If you watch TV weather forecasts regularly, you may have noticed that while weather systems can move in any direction, between about latitudes

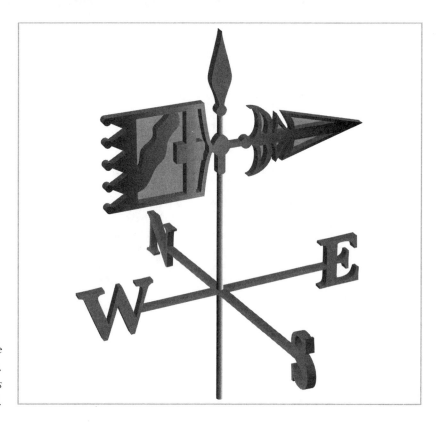

Weather vane. Because of the way it is made. the vane always points into the wind.

30°N and 60°N they very often move from west to east. These are called the mid-latitudes, and in mid-latitudes the prevailing winds are from the west. (Wind direction is always reported as the direction from which the wind is blowing, not the direction into which it is blowing. This is because weather vanes, fixed to the tops of church steeples and other tall buildings to tell people the wind direction, point into the wind.)

Air movements transport heat from the equator to the poles and return cold air to the equator to be warmed. This is known as the general circulation of the atmosphere (see sidebar).

Whenever air moves, it tends to start turning in a circle. Water does the same, which is why it usually forms a spiral when it runs out of a bathtub. The spiral is called a vortex, and the tendency of a moving fluid to follow a circular path is called vorticity. It is as though the air consists of countless tiny particles all spinning around their vertical axes, so that together they make the entire body of air turn. When air flows into an area because the pressure there is lower than it is outside, its vorticity causes the air to curve to the left in the Northern Hemisphere and to the right in the Southern Hemisphere. When it flows out of an area of higher pressure, its vorticity turns it in the opposite direction.

The Earth turns in an easterly direction, and this imparts an apparent swing to all moving objects not fixed to the surface. Because the Earth is

General circulation of the atmosphere

The Sun shines more intensely at the equator than it does anywhere else, and movements of the air transport some of the warmth away from the equator. Near the equator the warm surface heats the air in contact with it. The warm air rises, and near the tropopause, at a height of around 10 miles (16 km), it moves away from the equator, some heading north and some south. As it rises the air cools, so the high-level air moving away from the equator is very cold—about −85°F (−65°C).

This equatorial air subsides around latitude 30° N and S, and as it sinks it warms again. By the time it reaches the surface it is hot and dry, so it warms this region some distance from the equator. At the surface, the air divides. This is a region of calm winds, sometimes called the horse latitudes. Most of the air flows back toward the equator, and some flows away from the equator. The air from north and south meets at the Intertropical Convergence Zone (ITCZ), and this circulation forms a number of Hadley cells.

Over the poles the air is very cold. It subsides, and when it reaches the surface it flows away from the poles. At about latitude 50–60° N and S, air moving away from the poles meets air moving away from the equator. The colliding air rises to the tropopause, in these latitudes about seven miles (11 km) above the surface. Some flows back to the poles, forming polar cells, and some flows towards the equator, completing Ferrel cells.

Follow this movement and you will see that warm air rises at the equator, sinks to the surface in the subtropics, flows at a low level to around 55° N and S, then rises to continue its journey towards the poles. At the same time, cold air subsiding at the poles flows back to the equator.

If it were not for this redistribution of heat, weather at the equator would be very much hotter than it is, and weather at the poles would be a great deal colder.

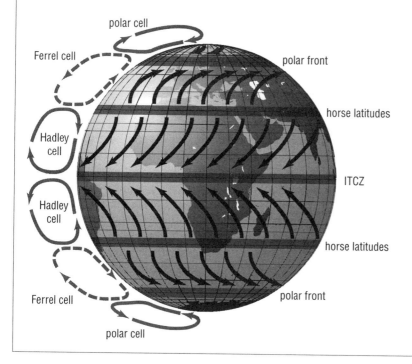

General circulation of the atmosphere. Air movements carry heat away from the equator.

approximately spherical, a point on the equator moves faster than one in a high latitude. Both points take 24 hours to complete one full rotation, but the point on the equator has farther to travel, so it must move faster. Consequently, when air (or water) moves toward the equator, it is traveling eastward at the speed of the latitude where it began its journey, but the closer it gets to the equator the faster the surface beneath it is traveling. The result is that the fluid follows a path that curves toward the west in relation to the surface, because in reality the surface is moving to the east beneath it. If the fluid moves away from the equator the opposite happens, and its path is deflected to the east. The French physicist Gaspard Gustave de Coriolis (1792–1843) was the first person to describe this effect, in 1835, so it is known as the Coriolis effect (abbreviated as CorF, because it was formerly known as the Coriolis force). The magnitude of the CorF is zero at the equator and increases to a maximum at each pole. It is also directly proportional to the speed of the moving body. The CorF sometimes acts in the same direction as vorticity, so the two reinforce each other, and sometimes in the opposite direction, so the resulting deflection is weaker.

Three-cell model

The diagram of the general circulation of the atmosphere shows there are three cells in each hemisphere. This is called the "three-cell model" of the circulation; it is very approximate, but a useful guide. It shows that air rises over the equator. This produces a region of permanent low pressure. Air descends on the poleward side of the Hadley cells, creating a belt of high pressure, and flows back toward the equator. The returning air is moving away from an area of high pressure, so its vorticity swings it to the right in the Northern Hemisphere and to the left in the Southern Hemisphere. Because it is moving toward the equator, the CorF reinforces this swing, turning the air toward the west in both hemispheres. As the air approaches the equator the CorF weakens, with the result that instead of blowing parallel to the equator, which is what would happen if the CorF were stronger, the winds blow from the northeast in the northern hemisphere and from the southeast in the southern hemisphere. These are the most reliable winds in the world, and because they always follow the same track, for which the Old German word was *trade*, they are known as the "trade winds."

Over the poles subsiding air produces regions of permanent high pressure. Air moves out of these areas, producing northeasterly and southeasterly winds. In midlatitudes, however, air is moving away from the equator. Consequently, it is swung in the opposite direction to produce generally westerly winds.

The strongest westerlies occur at a height of about seven miles (11 km), near the tropopause, where they form a band of very fast wind called the jet stream. The jet stream snakes to the north and south and sometimes breaks up into several patches where it blows in circles, but its generally eastward movement drags weather systems with it. That is why the weather in mid-latitudes usually moves from west to east, although sometimes it moves north or south and sometimes remains stationary for days or even weeks on end.

Together, the three circulation cells produce tropical easterly winds, mid-latitude westerlies, and polar easterlies. The strength of the easterlies and westerlies is fairly equally matched. It must be, because winds push against the surface—think of what it feels like when you ride a bike on a windy day. If they pushed harder in one direction than the other, the Earth would either accelerate, so the days would become shorter, or slow down, so they would become longer. In fact, days remain the same length. (Actually, they do vary because of the winds, but by a very tiny amount that cancels in the long run.)

Air masses

Air is constantly on the move. As it moves it is affected by the surfaces it crosses. It is warmed from below by contact with the surface, so air that crosses hot ground becomes warm, but air crossing an ice sheet becomes cold. If the air crosses water, water will evaporate into it, and the air will become moist.

The influence of surface conditions is important only where the surface itself is vast and uniform. An ocean provides a suitable surface and so does a fairly level plain that extends over most of a continent. As air moves slowly over such a surface it will form a body of air covering about 500,000 square miles (1.3 million km²) or more to a depth of several miles. Within it the temperature, pressure, and humidity vary little from place to place at any given height. Such a body of air is called an air mass.

Not many surfaces are big enough to turn air crossing them into air masses. This makes it possible to classify air masses into just a few types. The first division is between air masses that form over continents, called continental air masses (abbreviated c) and those that form over the ocean, called maritime (m). The second division distinguishes between polar (P), arctic (A) or antarctic (AA), tropical (T), and equatorial (E) air. These types can then be combined to produce maritime polar (mP), continental polar (cP), maritime tropical (mT), continental tropical (cT), and maritime equatorial (mE) air. Maritime arctic (mA) and continental equatorial (cE) are not included because arctic air is too cold to be anything but very dry and almost all the equatorial region is ocean, so these types seldom, if ever, develop.

Air masses form as they spend several days moving slowly across a surface. As they move away from that surface and across a different one, their characteristics begin to change. A cP air mass that forms over North America and then crosses the Atlantic will be mP by the time it reaches Europe.

Several air masses form over North America. There is cA air to the north, with cP air to the south of it over the center of the continent, and mA air to the northwest, over the Pacific, and northeast, over the Atlantic. To the south cT air forms over Mexico and Texas and mT over the oceans to the west and east. When they move from the regions where they form, air masses bring very characteristic weather. A southerly migration of cA

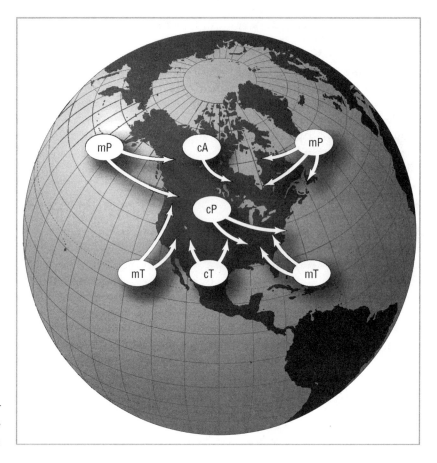

North American air masses and the directions they move in

air from the far north will bring extremely cold, dry weather, and a northwesterly movement of mT air from the Caribbean will bring hot, humid conditions, often with rain.

If air becomes polluted, the pollutants will be carried by the air mass. North American pollution will cross the ocean toward Europe and European pollution will drift eastward over Russia and then Asia. This does not mean Europe suffers from American pollution or Asia from pollution far to the west. Air cleans itself. Pollutants dissolve into cloud droplets and are washed to the ground by rain or snow. Particles cling to solid surfaces. If polluted air travels far enough, it will rid itself of the pollutants. The Russian soot that drifted to America was very much an exception. Western Europe receives very clean air that has crossed the Atlantic, even though that air may have been polluted when it left American shores.

When a cold air mass moves over a warmer surface, the air is heated from below. This makes the surface air rise. It cools as it rises, its moisture condenses, and rain or snow falls, cleansing the air. When warm air crosses cold ground, the opposite happens. The air settles, and the lowest layer is chilled by contact with the ground, so a layer of cold air lies beneath air that is warmer. This is an inversion (see sidebar, page 8). Rising air cannot penetrate the inversion, and so pollutants accumulate beneath it. This is because air in the inversion layer is less dense, because it is warm, than air heated at the surface and rising through the lower layer.

Fronts

Air masses lie next to one another. Obviously, they must do so, because there can be no gaps between them. Warm air and cold air do not mix very readily. Their densities are different, and this makes them tend to separate, the denser air sinking beneath the less dense air. If the colder air mass moves faster than the adjacent warm air mass, the cold air is pushed beneath the warm air, lifting it clear of the surface. If the warm air moves faster, it rides up and over the cold, denser air.

The boundary between two air masses is quite distinct. It appears on weather maps as a "front." The name dates from World War I, when armies opposed each other along fronts. At Bergen in Norway, a team of scientists led by Vilhelm Bjerknes (1862–1951) was studying climate and discovered air masses and the boundaries separating them. The air masses were so different they likened them to the armies they read about in the newspapers every day and the boundaries to fronts. The name stuck.

The high-level jet stream is at the top of the front, called the polar front, between polar and tropical air. The jet stream itself is a "thermal wind," so called because what causes it is the sharp difference in temperature, and therefore air density, on either side of the front. It blows at an average 65 MPH (105 km/h), but in winter, when the temperature contrast is greatest, it sometimes reaches 310 MPH (500 km/h).

Depressions

The jet stream does not blow in a straight line. It follows a wavy path, and the waves move slowly around the world. Over a period of a few weeks, slight undulations along it grow bigger until air takes short cuts across the ends of waves, like a river breaking through meanders to form oxbows. Remember that the jet stream runs along the polar front. Its undulations are also undulations in the front, so as they pass a point on the surface people there experience alternating polar and tropical air.

At the surface waves along the polar front appear as waves in the fronts on weather maps. If the air behind the front is warmer than the air ahead of it, the front is said to be "warm," and it is a "cold front" if the air behind the front is cooler than air ahead of it. At the crest of the wave between a warm and cold front, an area of low surface pressure develops. Meteorologists call this a "cyclone" because air circulates around it cyclonically—counterclockwise in the Northern Hemisphere. It is better known as a "depression." The cold front moves a little faster than the warm front, so the warm air is steadily lifted from the ground. When this happens the

Temperature inversions

Ordinarily, temperature decreases with height, but sometimes there is a layer above ground level where the air is warmer than the air below. This is an inversion.

There are three principal ways an inversion can develop.

On clear, still nights the ground cools rapidly by radiating away its warmth. Air next to the ground is chilled by contact, but this cooling extends only a few hundred feet above the surface. Above the surface layer of cool air there is a layer of air that has not been chilled and is warmer. In the morning the Sun warms the ground, the low-level air is also warmed, and the inversion breaks down.

Frontal inversions form where warm, stable air moves above a layer of cooler air at a weather front. The warm air lies like a blanket above the cool air.

An inversion can also form near the center of an anticyclone, where air is subsiding. As it sinks, the air warms by compression. If the air near the ground is moving, with gusts and eddies of wind, the subsiding air cannot sink through it, so it lies above the turbulent layer. The inversions that are so common over Los Angeles are usually caused by subsiding air at the eastern edge of the semipermanent anticyclone over the Pacific Ocean. Cool air moving from the ocean over the land intensifies these inversions by lifting the warmer air and forming a cool layer beneath it. The mountains to the east of Los Angeles prevent the pool of cool air from moving farther inland and weakening the inversion.

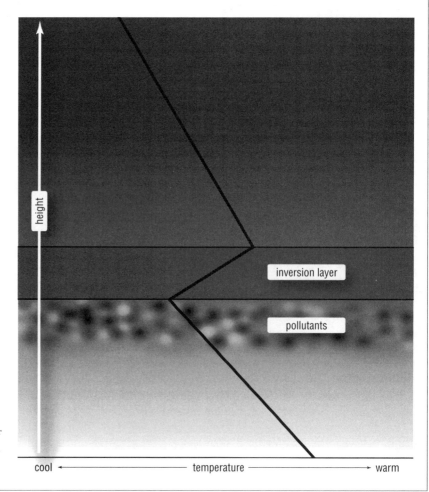

Inversion. A layer of warm air overlies cooler air.

fronts are said to be "occluded" or to form an "occlusion." Finally, the warm air is completely clear of the surface, air moves in to fill the low pressure, and the fronts disappear, only to be replaced by a new frontal system.

Because the waves along the polar front move from west to east, so do the depressions at surface level, and because the waves follow one another, depressions often occur in families. One follows another. This pattern is particularly marked in winter, when the jet stream is strongest. It is what makes midlatitude weather so changeable and difficult to forecast.

Depressions along fronts—frontal depressions—usually bring cloudy, wet weather. Rain and snow cleanse the air of pollutants, and so dismal weather is a very effective antipollution mechanism.

Frontal systems can also trap pollutants, however. The fronts do not rise vertically from the surface, but slope gently. A warm front slopes at about 0.5–1° and a cold front at about 2°. These are gradients of 1:115–1:57 for a warm front and 1:30 for a cold front. Warm air lies between the two fronts in what is called the "warm sector," with cold air ahead of the warm front and behind the cold front. The warm air lies above both fronts, and so warm air overlies colder air for a considerable distance ahead of the warm front and behind the cold front. This forms two frontal inversions. If the air is fairly dry, so the fronts produce little or no rain or snow to cleanse the air, pollutants can accumulate beneath the inversions.

Fronts can either reduce air pollution or make it worse. It all depends on how much weather they produce.

Evaporation and condensation

Water cleanses the air. It washes the air in the same way it washes our clothes and dishes, but it also has an additional trick that we do not use at home. We use liquid water for all our washing. Air contains liquid water, but it also contains water vapor, which is a gas, and water vapor scavenges airborne pollutants.

Water is hydrogen oxide, H_2O. A water molecule consists of two hydrogen (H + H) atoms linked by covalent bonds to a single atom of oxygen (O). A covalent bond is one in which two atoms share one or more outer electrons.

Air also contains ozone. This is a variety of oxygen with three atoms in its molecule (O_3) rather than the two atoms (O_2) of ordinary oxygen. Ozone is produced mainly in the stratosphere (see "Spray Cans and the Ozone Layer," page 104), but a small amount sinks through the tropopause and into the troposphere, the lower atmosphere, where we live, birds fly, and the weather happens. In addition to the stratospheric ozone that descends from above, the burning of hydrocarbon fuels, principally gasoline, produces the ingredients from which a sequence of chemical reactions also releases ozone (see "Photochemical Smog," on page 55).

Ozone readily forms compounds with other substances. Some of these are pollutants, so ozone helps cleanse the air. It is not very efficient, however, because the ozone molecule is not very stable. All it takes is a photon of sunlight with just the right amount of energy, and one of the atoms is knocked off the ozone molecule: O_3 + photon → O_2 + O. A photon is a "particle" of electromagnetic radiation such as sunlight, and shortwave sunlight provides the energy needed.

Free oxygen atoms are also very reactive. They have a vacancy for electrons and will grab hold of any they bump into. When one encounters a water molecule it combines with it, either splitting the water molecule into two or joining it to form hydrogen peroxide. So the sequence of reactions is:

$$O_3 + \text{photon} \rightarrow O_2 + O$$
$$O + H_2O \rightarrow H_2O_2 \text{ (hydrogen peroxide); then}$$
$$H_2O_2 \rightarrow 2OH; \text{ or directly}$$
$$O + O_2 \rightarrow 2OH$$

OH is known as hydroxyl, and it is so powerfully reactive some people have called it "the vacuum cleaner of the air." It reacts with hundreds of compounds, some of them pollutants, and the products of many of those reactions are substances that are either harmless or soluble, so they dissolve in cloud droplets and are washed to the ground. Hydrogen peroxide has a similar effect, but it does not last long before breaking down into hydroxyl.

It is hydroxyl we can thank for removing from the air a whole range of gases, including methane (CH_4), carbon monoxide (CO), sulfur dioxide (SO_2), hydrogen sulfide (H_2S), methyl bromide (CH_3Br), methyl chloroform (CH_3CCl_3), and many more. The amount of hydroxyl in the air varies depending on the amount of water vapor and ozone, and it is difficult to measure. Certainly, there is not much of it, and, of course, it vanishes as soon as it finds something to react with. Atmospheric chemists who have tried measuring it estimate there are, on average, about 3.3–130 million OH molecules in every cubic inch of air (0.2–8 million per cm^3). The numbers sound big, but in fact this is a very low concentration.

The universal solvent

Water cleans our clothes, dishes, and ourselves because "dirt" dissolves in it, allowing us to remove the dirt with the water. It cleans the air the same way. Polluting substances ("dirt") dissolve in it, and when the water falls to the ground as rain or snow the pollutant comes down with it.

A substance that would dissolve absolutely anything would be a "universal solvent" (and a bit tricky to store, because it would dissolve any container). There is no such thing as a truly universal solvent, but water comes close. Salt, sugar, alcohol, carbon dioxide, oxygen, and a wide range of other substances will dissolve in water—but not fats or oils.

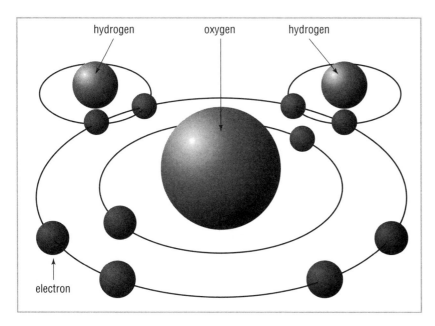

hydrogen   oxygen   hydrogen

electron

Covalent bonding in the water molecule. Each of the hydrogen atoms shares two of the outer electrons belonging to the oxygen atom.

Indeed, water is such a good solvent that pure water never occurs naturally. The clean, clear water you drink from a mountain spring (or buy in a bottle) is in fact a solution (the ingredients are listed on the label). You can buy pure water, called "distilled" water, but it did not occur naturally. It was purified in a factory. Enough seawater to fill an Olympic size swimming pool contains more than 70 tons (63.5 tonnes) of dissolved substances, of which 63 tons (57.5 tonnes) is common salt.

The secret of water's success in dissolving things can be traced to its molecule. This is a covalent compound of hydrogen and oxygen, but if you look at the drawing of the covalent arrangement you will notice that the two hydrogen atoms are both on the same side of the oxygen atom. Draw a line to the center of the oxygen atom from the center of each hydrogen atom and the angle between them is 104.5°. The molecule is V-shaped.

An atom consists of a nucleus surrounded by electrons. The nucleus comprises protons, which are subatomic particles carrying a positive charge, and neutrons, which carry no charge. An electron carries a negative charge precisely equal to the positive charge of the proton. If the atom has enough electrons to balance the charge of its nucleus, it will be electromagnetically neutral. The hydrogen atom, which is the simplest and smallest of all atoms, consists of a single proton and a single electron. When it bonds with oxygen to make a water molecule, it shares its single electron with the oxygen atom. This means its proton is located on the outside of the water molecule. Because the two hydrogen atoms are both on the same side of the oxygen atom, there are two protons on the outside of the molecule on one side and just electrons on the opposite side.

Consequently, although the positive and negative charges in the water molecule balance overall, so it is neutral, there is a positive charge on one side of it and a negative charge on the other. A molecule of this kind is said to be polar because it has two poles, like a magnet.

Many compounds are held together because their constituent atoms carry opposite charges that attract one another. Such compounds are called ionic. Salt is an ionic compound. It is sodium (Na) chloride (Cl). The sodium atom carries a positive charge (Na^+), the chlorine a negative charge (Cl^-), and the atoms arrange themselves in a pattern we recognize as salt crystals. Put the crystals into water, however, and they fall apart. Water molecules move around freely. Their negatively charged oxygen ends are attracted to the sodium, and their positively charged ends hold on to the chlorine. As the water molecules continue to move around, they pull the salt molecules apart, breaking the ionic bonds between sodium and chlorine. The salt is then dissolved.

Water molecules are attracted to one another. The oxygen of one molecule is attracted to the hydrogen of another. They form a bond called a hydrogen bond. This bond is weak, so it is constantly breaking and reforming. In liquid water hydrogen bonds link molecules into small groups. There are some polar covalent substances that can form hydrogen bonds with water. Ethanol (the alcohol in drinks such as beer, wine, and spirits) is one. At one end of an ethanol molecule there are two hydrogen atoms and one oxygen atom, so the oxygen can link to another ethanol molecule by hydrogen bonding, and at the other end the ethanol has three hydrogen atoms, so it is polar. When it mixes with water, hydrogen bonds form between ethanol and water molecules, dissolving the ethanol completely.

Other covalent molecules are so strongly polarized they break apart in water. This process is called ionization, and it leaves the separated parts carrying charges. The covalent bonds break, and the resulting ions (charged particles) attach themselves to water molecules.

Its ability to dissolve such a variety of types of substances makes water a powerful cleaning agent, but in the air it has yet another trick. It can capture solid particles. That is what happens when water vapor condenses.

Condensation

There is always some water in the air, even in the driest desert. It is present as a gas, water vapor, which is invisible and has no smell or taste. Water vapor is not the same thing as the steam you see when you breathe out on a cold day. Steam is made from tiny droplets of liquid water. It is water that has condensed—but why did it do that?

Liquid water consists of groups of water molecules linked together by hydrogen bonds. These groups move around freely, can slide past each other, and they constantly break, but when groups break apart the molecules immediately join others to form new groups. Water vapor, the gas, consists of molecules that are entirely free. There are no hydrogen bonds linking them, and no hydrogen bonds are able to form because the molecules have so much energy they move fast enough to tear themselves free.

The weight of the atmosphere exerts a pressure. This is the atmospheric, or air, pressure that you can measure with a barometer. You can then divide the total pressure into the proportions accounted for by each of the atmospheric constituents. The result is known as the partial pressure for that constituent. Air is 78 percent nitrogen, for example, so if the total pressure is 1,013 millibars (which is the average sea-level pressure), nitrogen exerts 78 percent of that, or 790 millibars (mb). The partial pressure of nitrogen is 790 mb. Water vapor is no different, but the partial pressure of water vapor is called the vapor pressure.

As the amount of water vapor in the air increases, so does the vapor pressure, but there is a limit, known as the saturation vapor pressure, to the amount of water vapor air can hold. It is the vapor pressure at which molecules begin to link by hydrogen bonding—in other words, to condense. Saturation vapor pressure varies according to the temperature. The warmer the air, the more water it can hold. At 40°F (4°C) the saturation vapor pressure is about 8 mb, at 60°F (15°C) it is 17 mb, and at 90°F (32°C) it is 47.5 mb.

The temperature at which water vapor condenses and evaporates is known as the dewpoint temperature. It varies according to the amount of water vapor present in the air—the "wetness" of the air.

Humidity

The "wetness" of the air is called its humidity, and there are several ways to describe it. The "absolute humidity" is the mass of water vapor present in a unit volume of air, measured in grams per cubic meter (usually abbreviated to g/m³ or gm⁻³; 1 gm⁻³ = 0.046 ounces per cubic yard). Changes in the temperature and pressure alter the volume of air, however, and this will alter the amount of water vapor in a unit volume without actually adding or removing any moisture. The concept of absolute humidity takes no account of this, and so it is not very useful and is seldom used.

"Mixing ratio" is more useful. This is a measure of the amount of water vapor in a unit volume of dry air—air with the water vapor removed. "Specific humidity" is similar to mixing ratio but measures the amount of water vapor in a unit volume of air including the moisture. Both are reported in grams per cubic meter.

How much moisture is there in the air? This varies widely. Over a hot, dry desert the amount is close to zero, though it never quite reaches zero. In a warm, moist area water vapor might make up 7 percent of the mass of the air, so 100 pounds of air contains around seven pounds of water.

The term that is most familiar is *relative humidity*. This is the easiest one to measure—it is the measurement you read from hygrometers, either directly or after referring to tables—and it is the one you hear in weather forecasts. Relative humidity (RH) is the amount of water vapor in the air expressed as a percentage of the amount needed to saturate the air at that temperature. When the air is saturated, the RH is 100 percent (the "percent" is often omitted).

Cloud condensation nuclei

When the saturation vapor pressure is reached, you would expect water vapor to start condensing into droplets at once, but it is not quite so simple. In very clean air the saturation vapor pressure can be exceeded, although not by very much; RH rarely exceeds 101 percent. This is because water vapor condenses most readily onto a surface. You can see this when moist air in a warm room condenses onto a cold windowpane or when it condenses onto grass and leaves at night, forming dew. In the air the particles onto which water condenses are called cloud condensation nuclei (CCN).

Not just any particles will do. Water does not condense onto the smallest particles, with diameters of about 0.002 μm (1 μm, called a micrometer, is equal to one-thousandth of a millimeter or one-millionth of a meter, or 0.000046 inch). This is because the saturation vapor pressure is higher over a curved water surface than over a flat one, and it increases as the curvature increases. It is known as the "curvature effect" and arises because the force that binds water molecules to one another is strongest on a flat surface and weakens as curvature of the surface increases. Consequently, water evaporates much faster from a curved surface than from a flat one, and small droplets evaporate much faster than big ones. Droplets that form on the smallest particles evaporate almost immediately.

Giant particles, more than 20 μm across, are also unsuitable. They are heavy enough to fall, so they do not remain airborne long enough for water to condense onto them. The most effective particles are 0.2 μm–2.0 μm in diameter. Air over land contains an average of about 80,000 to 100,000 particles of this size in every cubic inch (5–6 million per liter) and air over the ocean, far from the nearest land, usually contains about 16,000 per cubic inch (1 million per liter).

Hygroscopic substances will dissolve in moisture they extract from the air. Common salt is hygroscopic. Leave it exposed to the air, and before long the crystals will stick together as the salt becomes wet. A little while later the salt turns into liquid—in fact, a concentrated solution. Some CCN are hygroscopic, and as the RH rises they start to gather water from the air. As well as salt, which enters the air from sea spray that evaporates leaving microscopically small salt crystals floating in the air, the hygroscopic nuclei include some kinds of dust, smoke, and sulfate (SO_4), all of which are pollutants. Water can start forming droplets around salt crystals when the RH reaches 78 percent, and the other hygroscopic nuclei absorb water at somewhat higher humidity. When the relative humidity reaches about 90 percent enough vapor may have condensed to form a fine haze that restricts visibility. Once droplets have started to form, more water vapor condenses onto them, so they grow.

Then they merge with one another until they are so heavy they fall from the cloud, taking their CCN with them.

Evaporation

Water enters the air in the first place by evaporating from a surface. As everyone knows, if you leave a bowl of water long enough the water will disappear. It has changed from being a liquid to being a gas, and its molecules have moved into the air and mixed thoroughly with the other air molecules. It has evaporated.

Inside a body of liquid water the molecules are attracted to one another. They move constantly and completely randomly, but every molecule is attracted toward its neighbors on all sides. This attractive force pulls it equally from all sides, so although it moves freely within the liquid—being equal in all directions, the forces cancel—it cannot escape from its companions unless it is able to overcome the force holding it.

For a molecule at the surface, however, the situation is different. There are no molecules attracting it from above, so it is held less securely than are the molecules below. It is able to escape, and molecules are constantly leaping free from any exposed water surface. Escape requires energy, so the more energy the molecules have the faster they move into the air. That is why warm water evaporates faster than cold water—the warmth makes the molecules move faster, so they break from the surface more readily.

This is what conditions are like for molecules at a level surface, like that of the water in a bowl. If the surface is curved, like that of a drop, the forces are weaker. This is because there are no molecules exactly to either side of a surface molecule—because of the curvature they are slightly below it. Consequently, the lateral forces (pulling to the sides) are reduced, and the greater the curvature the greater the reduction. This explains the curvature effect, according to which small droplets evaporate faster than do big ones.

There are also water molecules in the air above the surface. They, too, are moving randomly, but when they are very close to the surface they feel the attraction of the liquid molecules and join them, condensing from gas into liquid. All the time, therefore, molecules are both leaving the liquid and entering it.

If more molecules leave the liquid than enter it, obviously the volume of liquid will decrease. It will evaporate. If there are so many molecules in the layer of air immediately above the surface that they are entering the liquid as fast as molecules are leaving it, the water will not evaporate, and the layer above the surface is saturated. The pressure it exerts on the surface is the saturation vapor pressure.

Latent heat

Heat is a form of energy. It is not the same thing as temperature. When atoms or molecules absorb heat energy they move faster, or, if they are locked together as a solid, they vibrate more vigorously. When moving or vibrating molecules strike another substance, they transfer some of their energy to it. The faster they are moving and the harder and more often they strike it, the greater the amount of energy they transfer to it. Sensors, such as certain of the nerves in our skin and the liquid in the bulb of a thermometer, can detect this bombardment. Our skin nerves send a message that our brain interprets as warmth; the liquid molecules in the thermometer move faster, so the liquid expands up the fine tube, where we can read it as temperature. Add heat to water, and its temperature increases.

In order to escape into the air from a liquid surface, water molecules need to gain a little energy. They need it to break the bonds holding them to the molecules around them. Similarly, when ice melts the water molecules locked to one another in the ice crystals need to gain enough energy to break the bonds holding them together. This energy does not make the molecules move faster, so a thermometer would not measure it and your hand would not feel it. It is hidden energy. Joseph Black (1728–99), the Scottish chemist who discovered it around 1760, called it latent heat, and this is the name by which it is still known.

For ice to melt at 32°F (0°C), it must absorb 334 joules of heat per gram (J g^{-1}; 334 J g^{-1} = 80 cal g^{-1}). For water to evaporate at 32°F, it must absorb 2,501 J g^{-1} (600 cal g^{-1}). In dry, cold air, ice will also change directly from solid to gas without melting into liquid first. This is called sublimation, and at 32°F it absorbs 2,835 J g^{-1} (680 cal g^{-1}) of heat—the sum of the latent heats of melting and vaporization. Latent heat varies slightly with temperature, which is why the temperature is mentioned.

When water vapor condenses into liquid or changes directly into ice (called deposition), and when water freezes, it releases its latent heat. Ice

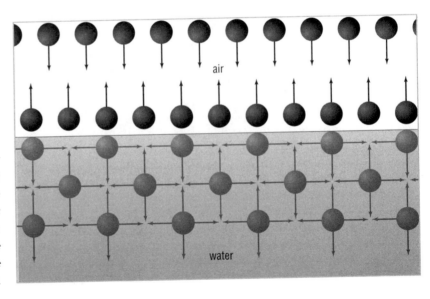

Forces acting on water molecules. Molecules inside the liquid are attracted by forces acting in all directions. Those at the surface are not held by a force acting from above.

contains less internal energy than water, and water contains less than water vapor. The amount of latent heat released during freezing is exactly the same as the amount absorbed in melting, the amount released in condensation is the same as that absorbed in vaporization, and the amount released in deposition is the same as that absorbed in sublimation.

Water and climate

Water molecules absorb latent heat from their surroundings, and when they release it they release it into their surroundings. The absorption of latent heat does not raise or lower the temperature of the water—it is used to break hydrogen bonds and is released when the bonds reform—but it does alter the temperature of the surroundings.

The absorption and release of latent heat is another way by which energy is transported through the air. In the tropics, where the weather is hot, water evaporates rapidly. This cools the surface by absorbing latent heat from it. The evaporation of sweat cools our skin for the same reason. The water vapor then rises in the warm air, but as the air rises it also cools (see sidebar, page 18), and it is carried along horizontally by the wind. When the air cools to the dewpoint temperature its water vapor starts to condense to form clouds. This releases latent heat, warming the air. In this way heat is carried from the warm region where water evaporates to somewhere cooler, where the vapor condenses. If Earth were completely dry, the Tropics would be much hotter than they are, and everywhere else would be colder.

Life on Earth would be impossible without water, but having made life possible for us, water goes on to make it more pleasant. It moderates climates, cooling those of the Tropics and warming those nearer the poles. Water also cleans the air, and it does so with remarkable efficiency. Without water to wash the dirt from it, the air would soon be too dusty and poisonous to be breathable.

Types of fog

Fog is cloud, but cloud that you meet at ground level. As you walk through it in daylight, objects a few yards away look faint and indistinct. Distant objects and landmarks are completely hidden. If the fog is very dense you may be able to see very little of anything. As the saying has it: "You can't see your hand in front of you."

If you are caught in fog in open country or on a mountain, the rule is to stay where you are until the fog clears unless you are absolutely certain you know where you are and can navigate by compass alone. Otherwise, proceeding can be hazardous. At best you may become totally lost, and at

Adiabatic cooling and warming

Air is compressed by the weight of air above it. Imagine a balloon partly inflated with air and made from some substance that totally insulates the air inside. No matter what the temperature outside the balloon, the temperature of the air inside remains the same.

Imagine the balloon is released into the atmosphere. The air inside is squeezed between the weight of air above it, all the way to the top of the atmosphere, and the denser air below it.

Suppose the air inside the balloon is less dense than the air above it. The balloon will rise. As it rises, the distance to the top of the atmosphere becomes smaller, so there is less air above to weight down on the air in the balloon. At the same time, as it moves through air that is less dense, it experiences less pressure from below. This causes the air in the balloon to expand.

When air (or any gas) expands, its molecules move farther apart. The amount of air remains the same, but it occupies a bigger volume. As they move apart, the molecules must "push" other molecules out of their way. This uses energy, so as the air expands its molecules lose energy. Because they have less energy they move more slowly.

When a moving molecule strikes something, some of its energy of motion (kinetic energy) is transferred to whatever it strikes, and part of that energy is converted into heat. This raises the temperature of the struck object by an amount related to the number of molecules striking it and their speed.

In expanding air the molecules are moving farther apart, so a smaller number of them strike an object each second. They are also traveling more slowly, so they strike with less force. This means the temperature of the air decreases. As it expands, air cools.

If the air in the balloon is denser than the air below, it will descend. The pressure on it will increase, its volume will decrease, and its molecules will acquire more energy. Its temperature will increase.

This warming and cooling has nothing to do with the temperature of the air surrounding the balloon. It is called *adiabatic* warming and cooling, from the Greek word *adiabatos*, meaning impassable.

Adiabatic cooling and warming—the effect of air pressure on rising and sinking air. A "parcel" or "bubble" of air is squeezed between the weight of air above and the denser air below. As it rises into a region of less dense air, it expands, which makes its temperature fall. As it sinks into dense air it is compressed, which makes it grow warmer.

worst you could head into a marsh or a bog or fall over a cliff. Aircraft pilots are taught never to descend through low cloud unless they are being guided by a ground controller. The reason is the same: many airplanes have crashed into mountainsides their pilots failed to see.

Driving through fog is much worse and much more dangerous. The driver faces what looks like a solid, featureless, white or gray wall that reflects car lights. Many driving accidents happen in and because of fog. Fog at sea is even worse. At sea there are not even walls, trees, and road curbs to guide you. All the sailor can see is the fog all around and the sea below. If there are rocks or the shore nearby or another ship is on a collision course, until ships were equipped with radar their crews often knew nothing about it until it was too late.

Fog, then, is seriously bad news. Technically, a fog reduces horizontal visibility to less than 1,093 yards (one kilometer). If the visibility is reduced but is more than 1,093 yards, the condition is called mist. If visibility is reduced but is still more than 1.2 miles (2 km), it is haze. Haze is usually caused by solid particles, commonly dust consisting mainly of soil particles, but if the air is moist the particles can act as condensation nuclei and water vapor will condense onto them. The reason the air seems so clear after rain and you can see distant objects so sharply is that the rain has washed haze particles out of the air. Unless you are a landscape painter or photographer, prior to the rain you might not have been aware of the haze, but you see the difference when the air is clear.

Lapse rates

Mountaineers and hill walkers encounter fog more than most people. Gazing at the mountains from down in the valley you can see why. The mountaintops are often hidden by cloud. Anyone walking up the mountain has to walk through the cloud—and sometimes through it into clear air—and cloud at ground level is fog. But why is it there?

Air temperature decreases with distance from sea level, so when you go walking in the hills it is a good idea to take warm clothing. The air is colder up there. How much colder? Rising air cools adiabatically (see sidebar). Dry air cools at a fairly steady 5.5°F for every thousand feet (1°C per 100 m). The rate at which air cools with height (or, to put it another way, its temperature lapses) is called the lapse rate, and this version of it is the dry adiabatic lapse rate (DALR).

Warm air can hold more moisture than cold air. Consequently, as the air temperature falls the relative humidity (RH) rises, and when the RH reaches 100 percent water vapor starts to condense and cloud begins to form. The height at which this happens is called the lifting (or lifted) condensation level. If you know the air temperature and dewpoint temperature at ground level, it is possible to calculate the height of the lifting condensation level, but making an accurate calculation is complicated. It is easy to see, however, that if the air temperature at the foot of a mountain is 70°F (21°C) and the dewpoint temperature at the foot is 50°F (10°C), a climber will reach the 50°F level at about 3,600 feet (1,000 m). That is about the height at which cloud forms and at which the climber can expect to meet fog.

Once water vapor starts condensing it also starts releasing latent heat. This warms the surrounding air, reducing the lapse rate from the DALR to the saturated adiabatic lapse rate (SALR), which is the lapse rate for moist air. The SALR is always smaller than the DALR, but its precise value varies with the amount of condensation taking place, from about 2.7°F to 4.9°F per 1,000 feet (5–9°C per 1,000 m); an average value is 3°F per 1,000 feet (6°C per 1,000 m).

As their names imply, both adiabatic lapse rates apply to air that cools adiabatically, but not necessarily to the conditions in the real world. Measure the temperature at ground level, subtract it from the temperature at the tropopause, divide the result by the height of the tropopause in thousands of feet or meters, and you will have calculated the actual lapse rate. Suppose the air temperature at the foot of the mountain is still 70°F (21°C). In mid-latitudes the tropopause is at about 37,000 feet (11,000 m), and the temperature there averages –67°F (–55°C). The temperature difference is therefore 137°F (76°C). Divide this by the height, and the lapse rate is approximately 3.7°F per 1,000 feet (7°C per 1,000 m). This is known as the environmental lapse rate (ELR), and in this example it lies between the DALR and SALR. The relationship between the ELR, DALR, and SALR determines several important characteristics of the atmosphere. For example, it determines whether fog is likely to form at ground level away from the mountains.

Stability and instability

Fog forms in stable air. If stable air is forced to rise, it sinks again as soon as the lifting force is relaxed. This happens if the ELR is less than both the DALR and the SALR.

Suppose that on a particular day the temperature at ground level is 60°F (15.5°C) and the ELR is 2.5°F per 1,000 feet (4.5°C per 1,000 m). The ELR is less than the DALR (5.5°F per 1,000 feet; 10°C per 1,000 m). If air is forced to rise it will cool at the DALR, and at every height it will be cooler than the surrounding air. At 1,000 feet (300 m), for example, the temperature in the rising air will be 60 – 5.5 = 54.5°F (12.5°C), but the temperature in the surrounding air will be 60 – 2.5 = 57.5°F (14°C). The rising air is cooler than the surrounding air, and therefore it is denser, so as soon as it can the air will sink back to the level at which its density is equal to that of its surroundings.

In this example the ELR is also less than the SALR (3°F per 1,000 feet; 6°C per 1,000 m). Consequently, even if the rising air becomes saturated, it will nevertheless remain stable.

If the ELR is greater than both the DALR and SALR, the opposite will happen, and the air will be unstable. At any height above the surface, rising air will be warmer and therefore less dense than the surrounding air. It will continue to rise. The diagram shows the two situations as a graph.

These are known as absolute stability and instability. There is also a second type of instability, called conditional instability. It occurs when the ELR is less than the DALR but greater than the SALR and the rising air

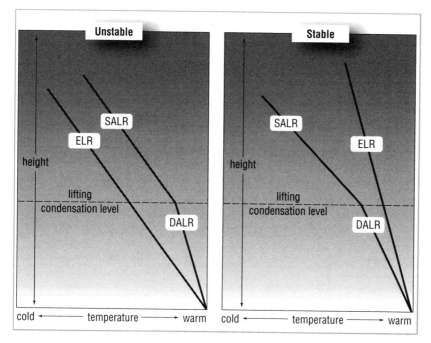

Stability and instability. Air is unstable if the environmental lapse rate (ELR) is greater than both the dry adiabatic lapse rate (DALR) and the saturated adiabatic lapse rate (SALR).

is moist. At first it cools at the DALR. This is greater than the ELR, and so the air is stable. Should it rise above its lifting condensation level, however, it will continue to cool at the SALR. This is less than the ELR, and so at any height above the lifting condensation level the rising air will be warmer and less dense than the surrounding air, so it will continue to rise.

Water vapor that condenses in unstable air forms clouds that grow upward. They are cumuliform—cumulus and cumulonimbus (see sidebar, page 22). Such clouds can shroud mountains, forming fog on mountainsides, but they do not form ground-level fog because they depend on air that is moving away from the ground. In stable air clouds form in horizontal sheets, such as stratus and nimbostratus, and these can hug the ground. Indeed, fog is often described as stratus with its base at surface level.

Fog that blankets hillsides is either cloud formed at that height and extending beyond the mountain or cloud formed in air that has been forced to rise in order to cross the high ground. In this case the air cools adiabatically as it rises, and the cloud starts developing when the air rises above its lifting condensation level. This type of fog is known as orographic, or upslope, fog. Orography is the branch of geography that specializes in the study of mountains; the Greek word *oros* means "mountain."

Cheyenne fog

Upslope fog can form on quite shallow gradients provided the air is lifted high enough. This type of fog is common on the western Great Plains of

Cloud types and cloud classification

Clouds are classified by their appearance into 10 basic types, or genera, with names based on the Latin names cirrus, cumulus, and stratus, meaning "hair," "pile," and "layer" (from *stratum*), respectively. The 10 cloud genera are cirrus, cirrocumulus, cirrostratus, altocumulus, altostratus, stratocumulus, stratus, nimbostratus, cumulus, and cumulonimbus. Several genera occur as different varieties, and there are also supplementary and accessory cloud features. Each of these has its own name.

Cirrus is thin and wispy, forming streaks that sometimes curl at the ends. Cirrostratus forms a thin, featureless sheet through which the Sun is clearly visible. Cirrocumulus consists of many small, puffy clouds. These three genera are made from ice crystals.

Altocumulus forms rolls or patches of cloud. Altostratus forms a featureless sheet through which the Sun and Moon appear as bright areas. *Alto-* means "high"; alto- clouds are made mainly from water droplets but sometimes are mixed with ice crystals.

Stratocumulus forms soft, gray rolls or patches that sometimes join together into a continuous layer. Stratus is a featureless sheet of gray cloud; drizzle sometimes falls from it. Nimbostratus resembles stratus but is darker in color; it often produces steady rain or snow. Strato- clouds are made from water droplets.

Cumulus forms bright, white, dense clouds, often with a flat base and "cauliflower" top; they may join together to make bigger clouds. Cumulonimbus is a storm cloud; dark, towering, and often with the top stretched to one side into an anvil shape. It produces heavy showers and thunderstorms. Tornadoes develop in cumulonimbus cloud. Cumulus consists of water droplets. Cumulonimbus consists of water droplets at lower levels and ice crystals near the tops.

Clouds are then classified by the height of their bases, as high, middle, and low.

Cloud level	Height of base					
	Polar regions		Temperate latitudes		Tropics	
	'ooo feet	'ooo meters	'ooo feet	'ooo meters	'ooo feet	'ooo meters
High cloud:	10–26	3–8	16–43	5–13	16–59	5–18
Types: cirrus, cirrostratus, cirrocumulus						
Middle cloud:	6.5–13	2–4	6.5–23	2–7	6.5–26	2–8
Types: altocumulus, altostratus, nimbostratus						
Low cloud:	0–6.5	0–2	0–6.5	0–2	0–6.5	0–2
Types: stratus, stratocumulus, cumulus, cumulonimbus						

the United States when maritime tropical air from the Gulf of Mexico moves westward, gradually rising toward the Rocky Mountains. As it rises the air cools adiabatically by up to 22°F (12°C).

An easterly wind sometimes intensifies this process by carrying moist air into the foothills of the Rockies. This produces Cheyenne fog, a dense fog that can extend all the way from Amarillo, Texas, to Cheyenne, Wyoming.

Why do clouds have tops?

You can see why cloud begins to form at the lifting condensation level and that this marks the base of clouds—and may be at ground level—but it tells you nothing about the upper limit of cloud or fog. When you fly above clouds you can see the tops clearly. One of the joys of hill walking is to climb through the fog, or cloud, until you are above it and can look down on it. Above you, if you are lucky, the sky is clear and blue. It often happens, though, that although the air at your level is clear, there is another layer of cloud above you.

Just as water vapor will condense when the RH approaches 100 percent, so droplets will evaporate when the RH falls. The RH reaches approximately 100 percent at the lifting condensation level, but outside the moist air where cloud is forming the RH is much lower, and no condensation occurs. The air is drier, either because it contains less moisture or because it is warmer.

Condensation removes water vapor from the air. Consequently, although the air may be filled with liquid cloud droplets, the amount of gaseous water vapor is reduced. As air rises and cloud forms, the rising air reaches a level at which the amount of water vapor it contains is sufficiently diminished to reduce the RH significantly below 100 percent. At that level condensation ceases, and above it the air is clear. The cloud top appears sharply defined from a distance, but in fact there is a topmost layer in which the cloud grows thinner until finally it ends.

Sometimes there is a layer of clear air between two layers of cloud. This situation develops when an advancing frontal system carries warm air above colder air. Convection in the unstable cold air below produces cumulus, which may form a layer. Above it, borne on a warm or occluded front, stable warm air produces a layer of altostratus or cirrostratus.

Cloud forms when moist air rises through denser air. The denser surrounding air is also drier. Consequently, liquid cloud droplets that drift sideways out of the cloud evaporate. The boundary between the saturated air inside the cloud and unsaturated air outside it defines the sides of the cloud.

Radiation fog

Early on a fine morning people living on hilltops often find themselves enjoying bright sunshine while folks down in the valley fumble around in fog. The hilltop is above the fog, and people there look down on it. It is a pale gray cloud hugging the ground with the tops of tall buildings projecting through it.

This is radiation fog. During the day the ground absorbs warmth from the Sun. It also loses warmth by radiation, because as soon as anything is heated to a higher temperature than its surroundings it begins radiating heat. This is called blackbody radiation. By day the ground absorbs heat faster than it radiates it away, so it warms up. Once the Sun has set, how-ever, there is no more warmth to be absorbed, but the blackbody radiation continues. The ground radiates away the heat it absorbed by day. If the sky is cloudy, the clouds reflect most of that radiation. This reduces the rate at which the ground cools and is why cloudy nights are warmer than clear nights.

On a clear night the ground cools rapidly by radiation, and air close to the ground is chilled by contact with it. A layer of cold air forms next to the ground. The air is then very stable, because the air above it is markedly warmer. Air near the ground remains near the ground. If the air is moist, the lower layer may be cooled to below its dewpoint temperature. Water vapor will condense, and the resulting cloud will form at ground level. It will be fog.

If the air is very still, this layer can be quite shallow. It is even possi-ble for a layer of radiation fog to be no more than knee-deep. You can walk through it with the fog swirling around your legs and a clear, blue sky above. A slight wind of no more than 2–2.5 MPH (3 to 4 km/h) creates eddies that mix the fog with the air above it. The fog layer can then be up to 100 feet (30 m) deep.

On hillsides air on the upper slopes is cooler than air below it. At night, as the entire hillside loses warmth by radiation, this difference remains. Fog is likely to form first on the higher slopes, but because the air is colder than the air below it is also denser, so it sinks down the hill-side, taking its fog with it. By morning the fog lies in the valley and the hilltops are above it.

Radiation fog soon clears in fine weather. As the Sun rises and begins to warm the ground, the temperature next to the ground rises above the dewpoint temperature, and the fog begins to evaporate. It evaporates from the ground upward because the sunshine passes through the air without warming it and is absorbed by the ground, so the only way air is warmed is by contact with the ground. Because it evaporates from the ground upward the fog appears to lift. It is not actually lifting—its top is still at the same height. Usually it clears altogether, but a trace may remain as a layer of low stratus cloud.

Advection fog

Fog will also form when moist, warm air moves over a cold surface. This is advection fog. Advection is the transport of heat by the horizontal movement of air or water (such as ocean currents). The air in contact with the surface is chilled, turbulent movements of the air mix it with the air above, lowering its temperature, and water vapor condenses.

Advection fogs are deeper than radiation fogs, extending up to 2,000 feet (600 m) above the surface. They are also more extensive and last longer. They are deep because they need a wind of 6–10 MPH (10–30 km/h) to produce enough turbulence to mix the air, and a wind of that strength both cools a thicker layer and also carries the fog higher. The wind also carries the fog farther over the surface, which is why it is more extensive than radiation fog. It is more persistent because, unlike radiation fog, it is not caused by a daily cycle of temperature change—warming by day and cooling by night. Advection fog lasts for as long as moist air continues to be chilled by a cold surface.

Sea fogs are of this type. They form over cold ocean currents and places where cold water is welling up to the surface, chilling the air passing over it. Winds can carry advection sea fog inland. San Francisco frequently experiences sea fog sweeping into and across the bay. The fog develops in warm, moist air that crosses the cold California Current, flowing in a southeasterly direction parallel to the coast.

San Francisco experiences an average of 18 days of thick fog every year. It seems more frequent because the bay is famous for its photographs of the Golden Gate Bridge with fog swirling beneath it. Farther north, Cape Disappointment, Washington, at the mouth of the Columbia River, is foggy for almost one-third of the year—a total of more than 2,500 hours, equivalent to 106 full days. On the East Coast, Moose Peak Lighthouse, Maine, has fog on 66 days in an average year, and St. John's, Newfoundland, has fog on 124 days a year. The foggiest place in the world is Argentina, Newfoundland, close to where the cold Labrador Current, flowing southward from the Arctic and often carrying icebergs, meets water warmed by the Gulf Stream. Argentina has more than 130 days of fog in an average year, and in 1936 it had fog on 230 days.

Steam fog

Fog will also form where cold air crosses warmer water. Water evaporating from the warm water saturates a layer in the colder air. The water vapor condenses but continues to rise in the air that has been warmed from below. As it rises farther into drier air, the fog evaporates. The result looks like steam rising from a bathtub, and it is called steam fog.

Steam fog is common over lakes and rivers in autumn. The ground cools faster than water, so for a time there is a sharp difference in temperature between them. The difference is most extreme in the Arctic, where air moving off ice sheets can be more than 35°F (20°C) colder than the sea. The resulting fog, known as arctic sea smoke, is often very dense.

Frontal fog

Sometimes in truly dismal weather, the low, drizzly cloud reaches all the way to the ground. This is frontal fog and is distinct from the cloud above it, although the two are attached.

It happens when a warm front lies above cold air that is almost saturated. Steady rain or drizzle from nimbostratus cloud on the warm front falls through the front into the colder air below. As it falls some of the rain evaporates. This raises the RH in the cold air to saturation, and the vapor condenses, producing fog that extends the cloud all the way to the surface. This is the wettest of all fogs because rain is falling through it.

Freezing fog

Perhaps the most unpleasant fog of all is the type that freezes onto surfaces, including car windshields, covering them with a layer of rime ice. This is freezing fog.

Water droplets do not always freeze when their temperature falls to 32°F (0°C). They need freezing nuclei, which are particles on which ice crystals can form. These are much rarer than cloud condensation nuclei, with the result that cloud and fog droplets often remain liquid despite being below freezing temperature. Under laboratory conditions water droplets can be cooled to –40°F (–40°C) before they freeze spontaneously. Such droplets are said to be supercooled.

Supercooled fog droplets are surrounded by air that is below freezing temperature (otherwise they would warm up). Consequently, solid objects nearby are also below freezing. When fog droplets make contact with a surface below freezing temperature they freeze instantly.

The droplets are so small that the whole of them freezes at once—with a bigger drop the part in contact with the surface freezes, and liquid water behind it spreads to the sides before it also freezes. One after another the droplets form ice crystals coating the surface and one another. The crystals trap air between them, making the ice white and opaque.

FIRES, CARS, SMOGS, AND FOGS

What happens when fuel burns?

Fog may be unpleasant, and traveling in fog can be hazardous, but breathing fog cannot harm you. The cloud condensation nuclei onto which fog droplets condense may be made from poisonous substances, but they are distributed far too thinly to damage the tissues of your respiratory passages and lungs. What you are breathing is basically nothing more dangerous than wet air.

Problems arise when substances that are not present naturally are added to the air. If these substances are added in amounts large enough to harm plants, animals, or people, then by definition the air is polluted.

The burning of fuel causes a great deal of the air pollution we suffer. This is not a new phenomenon. Fires have been polluting the air throughout history, sometimes very severely.

In the world as a whole the burning of fuel provides about 85 percent of all the energy used. Hydroelectric and nuclear power and, to a much smaller extent, wind and geothermal power supply the remainder. In the United States 70 percent of electrical power is generated by burning fuel (and more than half of that fuel is coal), 20 percent by nuclear reactors, and 10 percent by hydroelectric turbines (in dams). In Britain the corresponding figures are 71.2 percent (mainly natural gas), 27.4 percent, and 1.4 percent. The percentages are similar for most industrialized countries other than France, where 78.4 percent of power generation is from nuclear reactors, 13.8 percent is hydroelectric, and only 7.8 percent is generated by burning fuel. Most of the less-industrialized countries rely more heavily on burning fuel, although some, such as Bhutan (99.6 percent), Burundi (98.3 percent), and the Democratic Republic of the Congo (99.7 percent) use mainly hydroelectric power.

What is fuel?

Fires need fuel, and a fuel is anything that will burn. Combustion, which is the process of burning, is an extreme form of oxidation—the chemical reaction in which oxygen combines with another substance or a substance loses electrons. The substance losing oxygen or gaining electrons is said to be "reduced," so oxidation and reduction always occur together. The combined reactions are often called redox reactions.

In combustion, however, oxidation is concentrated in a local area, while reduction affects the much larger surrounding area, and its effects are quickly dissipated. Oxidation is the side of the redox reaction that matters.

Oxidation is an exothermic reaction—a reaction that releases energy in the form of electromagnetic radiation, of which the useful part is heat. That is what allows us to exploit oxidation as a source of power to heat our homes and perform useful work.

Energy cannot be created or destroyed. There is just so much of it in the universe, and the amount is fixed. What we can do is change one form of energy into another, although always with a significant loss. Combustion converts the chemical energy stored in the fuel to heat and light—electromagnetic radiation. (Nuclear power converts the kinetic energy [energy of motion] of particles into heat; hydropower converts the kinetic energy of falling water into electrical power.)

The fuels we burn in our homes, factories, power plants, and vehicles are hydrocarbons, compounds consisting of only hydrogen and carbon. Methane is the simplest hydrocarbon. Its molecule comprises one atom of carbon bonded to four of hydrogen (CH_4). Methane is the principal constituent of natural gas. Peat, wood, coal, and petroleum are also hydrocarbon fuels in that they contain hydrocarbons. There are many hydrocarbon compounds, and many contain very complicated mixtures of them.

Soot and smoke

Combustion is a chain reaction (see sidebar, page 31) in which the oxidation of one molecule triggers the oxidation of several more. The reaction spreads outward very rapidly and generates temperatures high enough to break the bonds holding hydrocarbon molecules together, so hydrogen and carbon are oxidized separately.

When hydrogen is oxidized the product is water:

$$2H_2 + O_2 \rightarrow 2H_2O + energy.$$

When carbon is oxidized the complete reaction produces carbon dioxide (CO_2):

$$C + O_2 \rightarrow CO_2 + energy.$$

If there is insufficient air for complete oxidation, however,

$$2C + O_2 \rightarrow 2CO.$$

CO is carbon monoxide, and it is poisonous. Carbon monoxide can reach dangerous concentrations where gas or oil fires are used in poorly ventilated rooms. Concentrations can also rise, although not to levels high enough to cause permanent harm, in congested city streets bounded by high buildings.

When hydrocarbons burn, after the hydrogen has been oxidized some of the carbon is left behind in the form of various gases. Molecules of the carbon-rich gases combine into large groups. The substance resulting from this process is soot. If combustion is efficient, the chain reaction continues and the soot is completely oxidized. The hydroxyl radical (OH) accounts for most of the oxidation of soot in and close to a flame. This reduces the concentration of OH, so less of it is available for the oxidation of other gases.

Combustion is not always efficient, however, and inefficient combustion allows the soot to escape among the hot gases. As the gases cool, the soot condenses into solid black particles consisting of carbon mixed with ash. Water vapor from the oxidation of hydrogen also condenses, and the mixture of water droplets and soot is what we see as smoke. Open domestic fires burning coal or wood are grossly inefficient and a major source of smoke. Industrial furnaces and incinerators burn a much higher percentage of their fuel, and consequently produce much less smoke. Nowadays, of course, factories are not permitted to release smoke into the air. Nevertheless, atmospheric scientists have estimated that each year over the world as a whole, the burning of fuels together with brush, grass, and forest wildfires, the use of fire to clear forest and crop wastes, and other burning of plant material releases nearly 13 million tons (12 million tonnes) of carbon into the air as soot.

Nitrogen and sulfur

Nitrogen, making up 78 percent of the air, does not react readily with other elements and compounds, but it will react with oxygen if enough energy is supplied to drive the oxidation reaction. High-temperature combustion, especially in car engines, causes the oxidation of some nitrogen. Oxidation produces nitrogen oxides, known as NO_x. There are seven oxides of nitrogen, but only two of them are produced by combustion and classed as pollutants: nitrogen oxide (NO) and nitrogen dioxide (NO_2). They are constantly changing from one to the other by the gain or loss of an oxygen atom ($NO_2 \leftrightarrow NO + O$), with ultraviolet radiation supplying the energy, so it makes sense to think of them as one.

They are serious atmospheric pollutants. At high concentrations they irritate the respiratory passages, although they rarely cause serious injury. Their real significance is that below about 15 miles (25 km) NO_x trigger the formation of ozone and contribute to the production of photochemical smog. Above that height they deplete ozone. NO_x also dissolve in cloud droplets to form nitrous acid (HNO_2), which is unstable and is quickly oxidized further to nitric acid (HNO_3). This makes the cloud as well as precipitation falling from it more acid.

The fuels we burn are not pure hydrocarbons. They contain a wide variety of other substances. One of these is sulfur. The amount varies, but sulfur is a common ingredient of most types of coal and, to a lesser extent, petroleum. When the fuel is burned its sulfur is oxidized to sulfur dioxide (SO_2). At high concentrations SO_2 is an irritant that makes people cough. Occasionally it accumulates in cities to levels high enough to cause serious lung damage. Like NO_x, however, the main significance of SO_2 is its ability to acidify clouds and precipitation. It oxidizes to sulfur trioxide (SO_3), which then dissolves in cloud droplets to become sulfuric acid (H_2SO_4). Some of the acid then reacts with other substances to form solid sulfate (SO_4) particles. These may settle to the surface or act as cloud condensation nuclei, once more becoming sulfuric acid. Soot readily absorbs SO_2, so soot is often acid.

The residues

Nowadays industrial users of fuel remove sulfur dioxide from the gases that result from burning the fuel. The desulfurization process by which this is done (see "Trapping Pollutants," page 150) leaves a residue. This is a dry or moist material consisting mainly of calcium and sulfur, with some fly ash and quicklime (calcium oxide, CaO) and slaked lime (calcium hydroxide, $Ca(OH)_2$). For every ton of coal burned and treated to remove the sulfur, about 350 pounds of this material remains (144 kg per tonne).

Fly ash is a powdery residue containing silicon, aluminum, iron, and calcium. Each ton of coal leaves around 160 pounds of it (66 kg per tonne). Industrial boilers also produce bottom ash and boiler slag. Bottom ash is similar in composition to fly ash but has a texture like sand. Burning a ton of coal leaves about 40 pounds of it (16 kg per tonne). At high temperatures fly ash particles stick together and eventually melt to form molten slag that solidifies into a hard, crystalline substance when it cools. It is called boiler slag and consists of irregularly shaped, glasslike particles similar chemically to fly and boiler ash. Combustion produces about 100 pounds of boiler slag per ton of coal (41 kg per tonne).

All of these substances are collected and have uses. Fly ash is used as an alternative to cement to stabilize waste heaps and soils, in mine reclamation, and in road building. Bottom ash is used in making concrete blocks. Boiler slag is used to filter water and as blasting grit for heavy industrial cleaning. The residue from the removal of sulfur is used as a soil conditioner, in making wallboards, and in road building.

What are fossil fuels?

Once upon a time a fossil was anything that was dug from out of the ground. Minerals, including gemstones, were fossils. So were pieces of coal and so, too, of course, were the remains and traces of long-dead animals and plants. These were not always recognized for what they were. Some people thought they were minerals that had formed below ground—they are made from rock, after all—and that their resemblance to seashells, bones, teeth, and leaves was purely coincidental. They were mistaken, but

What is a flame?

Strike a match and it bursts into flame. Blow it out and the flame disappears. What made the flame appear, what was it, and where did it go? These are questions people asked for thousands of years, but it was 1815 before anyone found the answer. The British chemist Sir Humphry Davy (1778–1829) had been commissioned to design a lamp for miners that would not cause explosions in coal mines by igniting inflammable gases. When he started work on the project in 1815 he found no one knew what happened inside a flame, so he had to find this out for himself.

The head of a modern match is made from red phosphorus (which may be dyed another color). Striking it against a rough surface or, in the case of safety matches against a compatible surface that contains some of the combustible material, causes friction. Friction raises the temperature of the head high enough for the phosphorus to ignite. It burns for just long enough to ignite the stick, made from wood, cardboard, or waxed cotton and partly impregnated with paraffin wax.

The stick starts burning when its temperature is high enough to vaporize hydrocarbons (compounds of hydrogen and carbon) in the paraffin wax and trigger the oxidation of the carbon and hydrogen. Oxidation releases energy. Neighboring molecules absorb some of this energy. It makes them move faster, and part of the material vaporizes as they escape into the air.

Collisions between molecules become more frequent and more violent. Some of the collisions are so violent they smash molecules into their constituent atoms or into free radicals—groups of atoms with unpaired electrons that are highly reactive. Single atoms and free radicals combine with gas molecules. This facilitates the oxidation of those molecules, thus increasing the number and violence of collisions and releasing more free atoms and radicals. This is a chain reaction in which the oxidation of one molecule triggers the oxidation of several more.

The absorption of energy also excites one or more of the electrons surrounding each atomic nucleus. The excited electrons jump to a higher energy level, but almost at once they fall back to their former level. When an electron drops from a higher energy level to a lower one it emits a photon, a quantum, or "particle," of radiation. If enough electrons are falling back to release a steady stream of photons, these will be visible as light, with a color that depends on the wavelength of the photons. That is how a flame becomes visible.

The heat from the oxidation chain reaction vaporizes more of the hydrocarbons in the stick, releasing hydrocarbon gases that mix with the air. The chain reaction expands very rapidly in all directions, like a wave sustained by the stream of gas. The heat of the reaction, which is also the heat of the flame, is enough to "crack" hydrocarbons into hydrogen and carbon, and these are oxidized separately. Match and candle flames burn at about 2,700°F (1,500°C); the energy of their electrons releases photons with the wavelength of yellow light, so the flame is yellow. Natural gas burns at about 3,600°F (2,000°C) with a blue flame.

Obviously, the hydrocarbon gases must mix with oxygen if the chain reaction is to be sustained. Near the center of the flame there is insufficient oxygen, so the gases do not burn. Outside this region the gas–air mixture supports combustion. Beyond that there is too little of the combustible gas. The chain reaction proceeds only in the region where the mixture supports it. This defines the extent of the flame.

Flames burn upward because hot air rises by convection. This is due to gravity. What really happens is that cooler, denser air sinks beneath the warm air, displacing it upward. Convection is a gravitational phenomenon, and so it cannot occur in the absence of gravity. Flames on spacecraft are spherical, and their heat radiates spherically.

A flame dies when it runs out of air or fuel. When you blow out a flame, your breath rapidly dilutes the gas-air mixture until there is too little gas to sustain the reaction. Electrons cease to be excited, so they cease to fall back to lower energy levels. No more photons are emitted, and the visible flame ceases to be.

their use of the word *fossil* was reasonable. It comes from the Latin word *fossilis*, which means "dug up."

Fossil fuels, then, are fuels that we dig up from below the ground. Nowadays, however, we use *fossil* in a more restricted sense. When we talk about fossils everyone knows that what we mean are the remains or signs of organisms that lived long ago (technically, more than 10,000 years ago; if an object is younger than that it is called a subfossil). Fossil fuels qualify on that ground, also, at least up to a point. They are the remains of what were once living organisms, even though those organisms are no longer recognizable as such. The fossil fuels are coal, natural gas, and petroleum. As well as being found below ground, these fuels are much more than 10,000 years old. Some people include peat as a fossil fuel, although it is much less than 10,000 years old (so perhaps we should call it a subfossil fuel). Uranium and thorium, which are used as fuel in nuclear reactors, are also obtained from the ground and are certainly old, but they are not counted as fossil fuels.

Peat

When plants die usually their leaves, stems, roots, and branches decompose fairly quickly. Broken down into their chemical constituents, they return to the soil, and the nutrients they contain nourish the living plants.

Material left lying on the ground is eaten by small animals such as ants, snails, and worms. Fungi and bacteria also feed on it. Between them, these organisms break down the plant (and animal) remains and waste products. Most of them need air, however, and cannot survive in airless conditions. They are unable to live below the surface of bogs. Bogs are waterlogged, and the water displaces all the air. Consequently, plant and animal material that falls into a bog is only partly decomposed. More material falls on top of it, and the overlying weight compresses the partly decomposed remains. Eventually these are made into a dark brown or black fibrous substance in which small pieces of roots and stems can still be seen. This is peat, and if the bog partly dries out it can be extracted and used.

Peat is the traditional domestic fuel for heating and cooking over large areas of northwestern Europe, especially parts of Scandinavia, Ireland, and the Highlands and islands of Scotland. In Ireland it is burned in some power plants, but in general its use is declining. To use it, first it must be cut. This involves digging it out with a special spade that cuts it into brick-shaped pieces (turfs). These are then stacked to allow some of the water to drain from them, after which they are built into walls, where they dry. The cutting, transporting, and stacking of peat is very hard, slow work that occupies every available hour during the summer. By winter the peat is dry enough to burn. Peat destined for industrial use is cut by machinery.

Peat burns slowly and gives out only a modest amount of heat. It would be highly polluting if it were used on a large scale in a city, but in the small, remote villages and farms where it is burned it causes no problems.

Coal

Peat is the first stage in the transformation of plant remains into coal. To become coal, the peat must be compressed until it is less than one-tenth its original thickness and then be heated under airless conditions. Coal forms only in tropical swamps. Most of the coal being mined today is made from plants that lived beside tropical rivers and coasts about 300 million years ago, during the Carboniferous period. Some dates from the Silurian period, around 400 million years ago. Since then, movements of the Earth's crust have carried the coal-bearing rocks to every part of the world, far away from the tropics. There are large reserves of coal in Antarctica.

When coal is heated some of its ingredients vaporize and are lost into the air. These are called "volatiles," and the smaller the percentage of volatiles it contains, the higher is the quality of the coal. Peat contains about 50 percent volatiles, lignite (soft brown coal) about 45 percent, bituminous coal 18 to 35 percent, and anthracite about 10 percent. Bituminous coal is the ordinary black coal used in domestic fires. Anthracite is the very best coal, so hard that it can be carved to make ornaments and handled without dirtying the hands but difficult to burn on a domestic open fire. Volatiles pollute the air, so the better the quality of coal the more cleanly it burns.

Coal mines also produce methane (CH_4). This is called "natural" gas to distinguish it from the "town" gas it replaced. Town gas used to be made by heating coal in airless conditions and consisted mainly of carbon monoxide. It was an important domestic and industrial fuel, but it was poisonous and is no longer made. Methane forms in association with coal and can be released when the coal is disturbed (see sidebar, pages 38–39). It is very dangerous and has been the cause of many explosions and fires. Between 1980 and 2001 more than 1,400 people were killed worldwide by methane explosions in mines. Methane from mines is now starting to be recovered and used. In 1999 U.S. mines fed almost 43 billion cubic feet (1.2 billion m³) of methane into the public and industrial gas supply.

Charcoal and coke

Coal will not burn at a temperature high enough to make steel, and wood will not burn hotly enough to separate iron from its ores. When iron and steel became important commodities, alternative fuels were needed. The first was charcoal, made by heating wood under airless conditions over several days. The final product consists mainly of carbon. It is light and highly porous, which means that although it burns at a high temperature, it is a very bulky fuel. Nowadays its main fuel use is for barbecues.

Charcoal is used mainly for absorbing gases and purifying liquids. Its capacity for absorption comes from its porosity and can be increased by heating it to about 1,650°F (900°C) in a vacuum or with carbon dioxide or steam. This produces activated charcoal, used in gas masks and other purification devices.

Coke is denser than charcoal and is used in blast furnaces and other processes in the metallurgical and chemical industries. It is made by heating bituminous coal in the absence of air, a process called destructive distillation. This drives off almost all the volatiles and some of the hydrogen to yield a substance with a much higher percentage of carbon. Smokeless fuels for domestic use are also varieties of coke, made at a lower temperature than those for industrial use.

Although cokes emit no visible smoke, they do release sulfur dioxide and other combustion by-products. Like all fuels based on carbon, they also emit carbon dioxide.

Oil and gas

Most natural gas is recovered from oil and gas fields, not coal mines. It forms along with petroleum and is held under great pressure in the rocks.

Like coal, petroleum is derived from what were once living organisms. Their remains are buried in sediment, usually in a river delta. Gradually, the sediment is compressed by the weight of overlying material. If a thick layer of compressed sediment becomes trapped between two layers of impermeable rock, the organic material that is mixed with the mineral grains may be converted to petroleum. For this to happen, the sediment must be compressed even more strongly and then heated. This "cooks" the organic material into thick, smelly, crude petroleum and gas.

Often petroleum is found beneath an anticline, which is a place where rocks have been folded upward. It also occurs above some salt domes. A salt dome is a mass of salt that forms deep below the surface. It is less dense than the surrounding rock, which gradually sinks beneath it, pushing the salt upward slowly but with great force. The rising salt dome then pushes the rock above it into an anticline.

In both cases, the petroleum and gas are held in a trap. They fill all the tiny spaces between the grains of a porous rock, such as sandstone—the original sediment—and slowly drift upward mixed with water so they accumulate beneath the upper layer of nonporous rock, called the cap, with the crude petroleum lying below the gas. Oil and gas traps sometimes lie one above another, like a sandwich. Once the upper reservoir is exhausted, further drilling through the lower layer of nonporous rock allows access to the deeper reservoir.

When a drill pierces the cap and releases the pressure, the gas and water rush to the surface. If the drill penetrates more deeply or if the well contains very little gas, oil rushes to the surface.

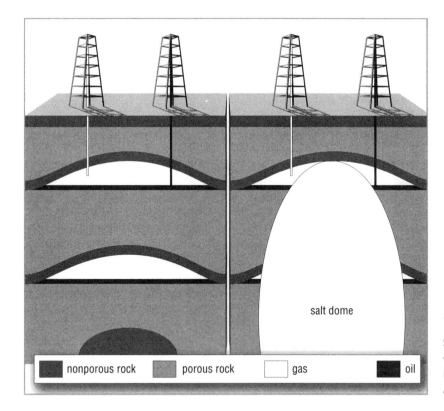

salt dome

nonporous rock   porous rock   gas   oil

The structure of oil and gas traps. Oil and gas are held in porous rock trapped between layers of nonporous rock.

Refining

Coal can be used directly: as soon as it leaves the mine it can be shipped to customers. Gas and oil cannot. Gas must be cleaned to remove water and impurities. Oil must be processed into usable products. The processing is called refining.

Crude petroleum is a mixture of many hydrocarbons, each of which boils at a different temperature. Consequently, they can be separated out by heating the crude petroleum and then cooling it in stages so that the vapors condense a few at a time. Purifying a substance by vaporizing it and condensing the vapor is called distillation—the way pure, or distilled, water is made. In the case of petroleum, a different group of hydrocarbons condenses at each stage. These groups are known as fractions, and the refining process is called fractional distillation.

Fractional distillation takes place in a tower divided into a number of levels by horizontal trays. On top of each tray except the lowest there is a hemispherical, perforated cap to facilitate condensation. The tower is heated strongly from below, and the temperature is lower at each successive level because each tray is farther from the source of heat than the one below it.

Crude petroleum is fed in at the bottom. It is heated to more than 750°F (400°C), and most of it evaporates. What remains consists of hydrocarbons that are removed and separated by a different process. The residue yields ingredients for lubricating oils, solid paraffin wax that is separated by dissolving it and then extracting it from the solvent, and finally a black tar containing asphalt and bitumen.

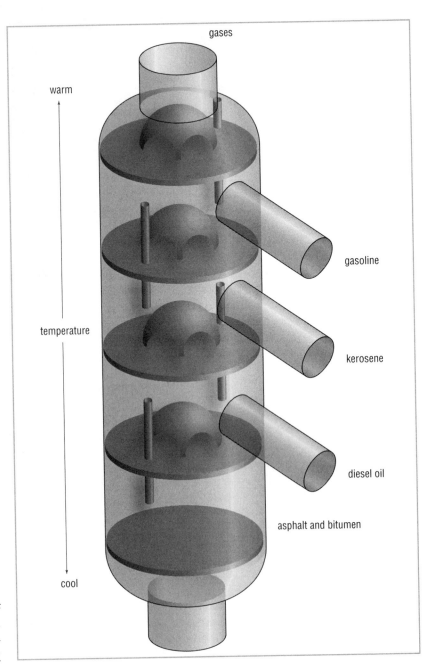

gases

warm

temperature

gasoline

kerosene

diesel oil

asphalt and bitumen

cool

Fractional distillation. As the temperature falls, different fractions condense and are removed.

The vapor rises to the next level, where the first fractions condense and are removed as a liquid. Further fractions condense at each succeeding level. The order in which the fractions condense is determined by the number of carbon atoms in their molecules. Asphalt, bitumen, and paraffin wax have large molecules with many carbon atoms. Diesel oil (or gas oil) is a mixture of hydrocarbons with 13–25 carbon atoms. It condenses at 425–630°F (220–350°C) and is the first to be removed. Kerosene (paraffin oil) molecules have 11 or 12 carbon atoms, and it condenses next at 320–480°F (160–250°C). Kerosene is used as fuel for jet aircraft and for domestic central heating boilers. It is also cracked further to produce lighter hydrocarbons used in gasoline. Gasoline condenses next at 74 to 355°F (40–180°C). Its molecules have five to eight carbon atoms, so it is a mixture of pentane, hexane, heptane, and octane. Pentane (C_5H_{12}) condenses at 97°F (36°C). Hexane (C_6H_{14}, although the molecule can be arranged in five ways, called isomers) condenses at 140 to 176°F (60–80°C). Heptane (C_7H_{16}, a group of nine isomers) condenses at 208°F (98°C). Octane (C_8H_{18}, a group of 18 isomers) condenses at 210–257°F (99–125°C). By the time it reaches the filling station, many other compounds have been added to make gasoline a much more complicated mixture.

Above this level the fractions are at room temperature and are still gases. They include methane (CH_4, which condenses at –258°F; –161°C), ethane (C_2H_6, which condenses at –128°F; –89°C), propane (C_3H_8, which condenses at –44°F; –42°C), and butane (C_4H_{10}, which condenses at 32°F; 0°C). These are known as refinery gases. They are used as fuels (bottled gas) and as raw materials for the chemical industry (see diagram, page 38).

At each level in the fractionating tower, the distilled fractions are mixtures of substances. Before they can be used they need further refining. Each group of fractions is fractionally distilled separately, and the products of those distillations are then subjected to further purification processes before they are ready to leave the refinery.

Pea soup: The original smog

To those who know the city, the early morning signs are not good. For several days there has been hardly a breath of wind. The air has hung stagnant over the city, growing progressively dustier and smellier, with a haze that blurs the outlines of distant factory chimneys and church spires.

Last night was clear. With no cloud to absorb the warmth, the ground soon radiated away such heat as it had absorbed by day and became very cold. Then, in the hours after midnight, cold, dense air sank down the hillsides into the valley. The sinking air moved beneath the cold air on the valley floor, lifting it a little and mixing the two. Now the air

Methane hydrates

In the 1930s, with the expansion of the motor industry and aviation and the conversion of coal-burning steamships to fuel oil, the petroleum industry was growing rapidly. It was then that engineers began to experience trouble with the blocking of pipelines carrying oil from fields in the far north. They found the pipes were being choked by what until then had been nothing more than a scientific curiosity: clathrate hydrates, a curious form of matter discovered in the early 19th century by the English chemist Sir Humphry Davy (1778–1829).

Crystalline solids form lattices, structures in which the individual atoms are arranged in a very regular pattern. A clathrate is a structure in which small molecules of one substance are held in the spaces inside the lattice of another substance. In the case of a clathrate hydrate, that other substance is ice. The pipelines were choking on ice that contained several substances derived from petroleum. The hydrates clung to the sides of the pipes, forming a layer that quickly thickened. No sooner had the engineers cleared a pipe than it began to fill once more.

The hydrates form when water freezes under high pressure. They are found below the surface in seabed sediments and permafrost—soil in which the water remains permanently frozen. Under these conditions ice can freeze into a 12-sided, three-dimensional shape called a dodecahedron. Each of its faces is a pentagon, and the companion gas is held inside the hollow "ball." The drawing shows what it may look like, greatly enlarged.

Clathrate hydrates were a nuisance and added to the cost of pumping oil, but more recently they have aroused a different interest. At first it was assumed that they occur only in the arctic and around its borders, but

as the oil industry continued to expand and offshore oil fields were opened all over the world, this proved to be wrong. Oil industry scientists found clathrate hydrates below the seabed almost everywhere they looked. Only a very small percentage of them are held in permafrost on land. The map shows the approximate location of known and suspected sources of them.

The most abundant gas associated with them is methane, so they are now known as methane hydrates. Methane is the principal constituent of natural gas, which is one of the most important fuels, so some people call them gas, or natural gas, hydrates. The discovery of their abundance has two implications, apart from the difficulties they cause for oil pipelines.

Methane hydrates. This shows what the hydrates may look like at the molecular level.

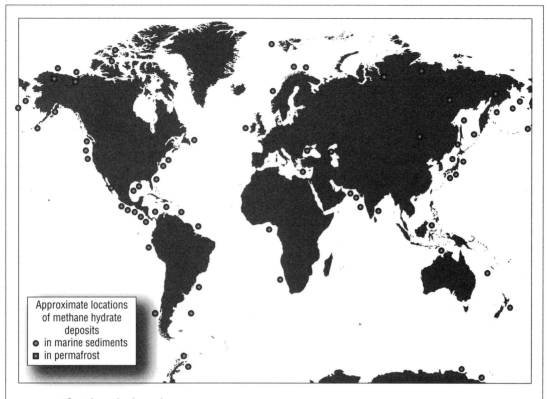

Location of methane hydrate deposits

The first relates to what might happen if the methane were to be released accidentally. Some scientists believe that sudden large methane releases can sink ships very quickly and with no warning. This is because a ship floats as a result of the air it contains and is less dense than seawater. When a huge amount of gas bubbles up from the seabed, however, what a moment ago was water becomes a mixture of water and gas, and its density decreases dramatically. This happens suddenly; the effect lasts no more than a moment or two, but that may be long enough to doom the ship by removing its support. While the effect lasts, the ship is much denser than the water, so it sinks vertically downward like a stone and fills with water.

The second possibility is that a massive release of methane might contribute to climate change. Methane is a greenhouse gas that is 21 times more effective than carbon dioxide at absorbing heat.

Beside the fears, though, there is an exciting possibility. Scientists estimate that in the world as a whole there are between one and 50 million billion ($1–50 \times 10^{15}$) cubic meters ($35–1,766 \times 10^{15}$ cubic feet) of methane held in hydrated form in sediments within 6,500 feet (2,000 meters) of the surface. That is more than double the total of all the other fossil fuel reserves in the world, and its location beneath relatively shallow coastal waters places it potentially within reach of the offshore oil industry.

At present it is uncertain whether the hydrates could be mined for their methane economically, but if ways are found to obtain the methane it will be by far the world's most important source of fuel. Methane is also the most benign of all the fossil fuels because it burns cleanly and releases less carbon dioxide than oil or coal for every unit of energy.

near the bottom of the valley was colder than the air higher up. An inversion had formed. As they mixed the sinking air lowered the temperature to below the dewpoint. By dawn there was a thin radiation fog trapped beneath the inversion.

In most places the rising sun would quickly warm the ground, and the fog would evaporate from the ground upward. However, this is not most places. It is the city, and it is winter.

Dawn is when people light their fires or add coal to fires they had damped down last night before going to bed. Stokers arrive at the factories for the day shift, and before long the furnaces and boilers are burning freshly added fuel. Smoke is soon billowing from every chimney. It, too, is trapped beneath the inversion. The illustration shows what has happened.

Smoke particles cling to the water droplets of the fog. Overhead the mixture is a greenish-yellowish color. Toward the end of the 19th century someone said the smoke and fog was the color of pea soup, and the name stuck. (Such fogs are called "pea-soupers" in Britain.) In 1909 a pea soup of this kind killed more than 1,000 people in Glasgow, Scotland. Dr. Harold Antoine Des Voeux, a member of the Coal Smoke Abatement Society that had been formed in 1899, prepared a report on the incident, which he presented to a meeting of the society held in Manchester in 1911. In his report he proposed *smog* as a name for this kind of mixture of smoke and fog.

The character of smog depends on the density of the fog. If the fog is thick, visibility will be reduced much more than in a thinner fog, and the smog will be very wet. Like ordinary fog, wet smog clings to surfaces, coating them with smoke particles. Dry smog is less unpleasant.

As well as smoke, the fires release warm air. This rises through the colder air, producing turbulence that mixes the air. Mixing brings the pea-souper down to ground level. The smog was established, and, as everyone knew, with calm weather and clear skies above the inversion it could last for several days.

By midday the smog is blocking out the sunlight. In the years before steps were taken to reduce this type of pollution, between November and March many British industrial cities lost 25 to 55 percent of their incoming sunlight—the light was reflected from the top of the smog layer, especially when the Sun was low in the sky.

The streetlights switch themselves on automatically when the light intensity falls below a certain level. Buses and cars turn on their lights, and the drivers try to see their way by leaning out their open side windows because their windshields are coated with a layer of greasy soot. At lunchtime it is like evening. People start leaving their offices to try to reach home before travel becomes any more difficult. Schools close, and students are sent home.

The air is filthy. Even without the fog, the smoke clings to windows and blackens laundry left hanging outdoors to dry. The smog is worse. As

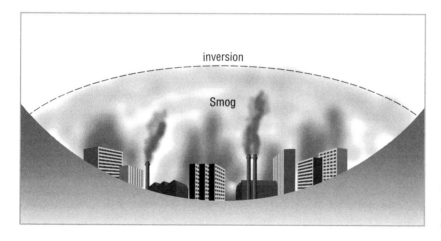

inversion

Smog

Valley smog. Fog forms in the valley and mixes with smoke trapped beneath an inversion to create smog.

they fumble and grope their way home, sometimes having to run one hand against the walls and shopfronts to avoid becoming hopelessly disoriented, people in the street grow steadily dirtier. Worst off are the cyclists, who arrive home hours late with their faces and clothes blackened.

An amateur theater group had arranged to perform *Everyman*, the medieval morality play, in a church about 10 miles away, and they had hired a bus. They reached the church safely and gave their performance. It was about 8 P.M. when they left and climbed back into the bus. By now the smog was so thick that one person had to walk ahead of the bus holding a white cloth and trying to follow the side of the road. A second person walked behind the first, also holding a white cloth. The first person guided the second and the second guided the bus driver. From time to time others took their turns as guides. They reached their starting point safely a little before midnight.

Smogs as bad as this happened at least once or twice every winter in most of the industrial cities of Europe. There was so much smoke in the air of Edinburgh, Scotland, that the city was nicknamed "Auld Reekie" ("Old Smokey"). It was estimated in 1945 that in the city of Leicester, in the English Midlands, sunlight was reduced by 30 percent in winter but by only 6 percent in summer.

Smoke from coal fires contains sulfur dioxide, so smog is acid. During a smog episode in Sheffield, Yorkshire, in December 1964, the sulfur dioxide concentration rose to three times the December average.

Between 1860 and 1880 there was fog in Prague, in the Czech Republic, on an average of 79 days a year. In the period from 1900 to 1920 Prague had fog on an average of 217 days. A particularly bad smog in London lasted a whole week from December 17, 1813, until January 2, 1814, and there were further severe smogs in 1873, 1882, 1891, and 1892. During the 1873 smog, 1,150 people died, and livestock became so ill that some animals had to be destroyed.

In 1904 the chairman of the Coal Smoke Abatement Society complained about the London house of the duke of Wellington (the grandson of the first duke, who fought Napoleon) to a royal commission studying the situation. "Upon my word," he wrote, "the Duke of Wellington's house is like a factory chimney in the morning, in fact, some of the factories do not emit so much smoke as the Duke of Wellington's house."

North America did not escape. People living in the industrial cities of the Northeast were also familiar with winter smog. The first American municipal laws aimed at reducing black smoke pollution were passed in the 1880s, and in 1912 the Bureau of Mines began the first study of ways to control smoke.

The Great London Smog

People accepted it because they thought the winter smog was natural and unavoidable. It was just one of the discomforts city dwellers learned to endure. They complained sometimes, but most working people were fairly cheerful about it and never imagined the fires that warmed their homes and cooked their food were the cause of it. Children enjoyed it because it meant time off school—and the excitement of the journey home from school.

That attitude changed in 1952, and the change was reinforced in 1962 as a result of two especially bad smogs. On both occasions very wet smog was trapped beneath an inversion. In the first episode the inversion lasted from December 5–9, 1952, and the fog cleared on December 10. Visibility was reduced to less than 33 feet (10 m) for 48 consecutive hours. Conditions became so bad that a performance of the opera *La Traviata* at Sadler's Wells Theatre had to be abandoned because the audience was unable to see the stage. Movie theaters also closed when audiences could not see the screen. Sulfur dioxide from coal fires meant the smog was also very acid, with a pH of about 1.6—more acid than pure lemon juice.

An interim report issued by the government the following spring stated that 12,000 people died in the Greater London area between December and the following February as a direct consequence of the weather. When the final report was issued toward the end of 1953, a cut-off date of December 20 had been imposed, reducing the number of deaths to about 4,000. Both figures were calculated as the difference between the number of deaths during that winter, later reduced to the period of the smog and for 10 days afterward, and the number during the same period in an average year. Most of the victims died from chest complaints: seven times more people died from bronchitis and pneumonia than in the same period in earlier years.

It is true that many of those who succumbed were already gravely ill and probably would not have survived the winter in any case, but nevertheless even the reduced figure of 4,000 excess deaths was shocking. What is more, the deaths happened in London, where lawmakers and members of high society had to breathe the lethal mixture. It led to the introduction of legislation to forbid the burning of coal and wood in London.

December is when the British livestock industry holds its annual cattle show at Smithfield Market, in London. That year smoke entered the area where the prize cattle were housed. Many became ill, and 13 had to be destroyed. Autopsies revealed that their respiratory passages were badly inflamed.

The second smog incident occurred in December 1962. About 700 people died as a direct result of that smog. The reduction compared with the 1952 death toll was attributed to the new law, which by then was starting to take effect.

Meuse Valley

The politicians had had plenty of warning of what could happen, because it had happened many times before, most notably in December 1930 in Belgium. That was the first modern air pollution catastrophe to be recorded.

To the southwest of the city of Liège and northeast of Namur, the towns of Seraing and Huy stand in the valley of the River Meuse (or Maas). Between Seraing and Huy there is a stretch about 15 miles (24 km) long where the hills rise to 330 feet (100 m) on either side of the valley. That is where the incident happened. The map shows the location.

It is an industrial region. In 1930 there were steel mills, power plants, lime kilns, glass works, and factories refining zinc and manufacturing fertilizer and sulfuric acid. All the factories used coal-burning furnaces, and most of the local citizens burned coal in their homes. Then, from December 1 to 5, a spell of cold weather combined with a cold wind blowing down the hillsides produced fog that was trapped beneath an inversion, a classic valley fog. The fog mixed with smoke from all the chimneys, and soon there was a smog that contained more than 30 pollutants, of which the most serious was sulfur.

People began complaining of chest pains, shortness of breath, and coughing. Elderly people and those already suffering from respiratory complaints were the most seriously affected. By the time the episode ended and the smog cleared, several hundred people had been made ill, and more than 60 had died. It was not only the human inhabitants of the valley who suffered. Many cattle also had to be destroyed.

Donora

America suffered its first major smog disaster in October 1948 in Pennsylvania. Donora is a small town (population 7,500) beside the Monongahela River, 28 miles (45 km) south of Pittsburgh. It was the same story: an inversion trapped fog beneath it, and smoke from coal fires mixed with the fog to produce smog.

The smoke and fumes came from the Donora Zinc Works and an iron works. The American Steel and Wire Company owned both factories. Fog over the entire Pittsburgh area had remained trapped beneath an inversion for a week. It was on Friday, October 28, that people began to realize

Meuse Valley, location of the world's first air pollution tragedy in 1930

something was wrong. Sulfur dioxide from the factories had dissolved in the fog droplets, forming a sulfuric acid mist, and by Saturday people started arriving at hospitals complaining of breathing difficulties, headaches, nausea, and abdominal pains. That was when the first deaths occurred. The basement of the community center was made into a temporary morgue.

On Sunday officials closed the town to traffic, including ambulances, partly because of poor visibility. Firefighters visited homes with oxygen to help people with respiratory problems. The zinc works had closed by 6 P.M. on Sunday evening, but rain was already washing the acid from the air, and the factory opened again on Monday. About 6,000 people—half the population at the time—were made ill, and 17 died. Two more people died later from the effects of the pollution. The U.S. Steel Group, the parent company, admitted liability and paid compensation. Both factories closed by 1970.

Vehicle exhausts

Almost all modern automobiles, trucks, and buses are powered by internal combustion engines. They are called internal combustion engines because

---

Fogs in literature

Fog hides some things we might prefer not to see. Novels and movies about dark deeds in Victorian London set them in streets shrouded in fog. London was not the only industrial city to suffer from dense winter fogs, but it probably had more than its share. The city itself featured in so many stories that authors could hardly avoid incorporating its seemingly permanent fog. It was Charles Dickens, in *Bleak House*, who called the fog "a London particular," forever fixing the association.

In "The Doom of London," a short story published in the English magazine *The Idler* in November 1892, Robert Barr (1850–1912) turned the fog into an apocalyptic device. Barr was a popular author of thrillers and detective stories known for their wit. In this story the fog suffocates almost the entire population of London.

London fogs continued long after the Victorian era, of course. The English travel writer E. V. Morton (1892–1979) mentioned them in his biography, *The Heart of London* (1925).

"Everywhere the fog grips the throat and sets the eyes watering," he wrote. "It puts out clammy fingers that touch the ears and give the hands a ghostly grip. . . . I go out into the fog and enter an incredible underworld. The fog has turned London into a place of ghosts."

Robert Browning (1812–89) also knew the feel of the fog in the throat. His poem *Prospice* (1864) begins:

"To fear death?—to feel the fog in my throat,
The mist in my face,

When the snows begin, and the blasts denote
I am nearing the place,
The power of the night, the press of the storm,
The post of the foe:"

Even indoors there was no escaping the fog. "The yellow fog that rubs its back upon the window-panes," is how T. S. Eliot (1888–1965) described it in *Love Song of J. Alfred Prufrock*.

The imagery of fogs sometimes applies to sinister events that actually happen. In 1941 Hitler issued an order called *Nacht und Nebel* ("Night and Fog"). The aim was to suppress resistance by arresting suspects in the middle of the night and removing them to a distant place from where they would never return while concealing their fate and whereabouts from everyone associated with them. They would simply vanish. The director Alain Resnais portrayed this dreadful episode in his 1955 documentary *Nuit et Brouillard* ("Night and Fog").

John Carpenter's horror film *The Fog* (1980) centers on vengeful ghosts returning a century after they were murdered. Woody Allen sets his 1991 *Shadows and Fog* in a European city in the 1920s, where a strangler is being hunted by hysterical mob. This, of course, is comedy.

Meanwhile, the mysterious possibility of unanticipated encounters and the privacy dense fog confers on those it enshrouds have inspired countless songwriters. Fog, even "a foggy day in London town," can be the stuff of romance as well as horror.

they burn fuel internally—inside a cylinder. When the fuel burns the rise in temperature causes the gases in the cylinder to expand, and their expansion pushes a piston linked to the wheels. A steam engine is an example of an external combustion engine. It burns its fuel outside the engine proper, using the heat of combustion to boil water. It is the expansion of the resulting water vapor that pushes the pistons in their cylinders.

The very first automobiles—literally, self-propelled vehicles—were steam driven (see sidebar), but by the early 19th century several inventors were trying to develop internal combustion engines. The first truly

Steam cars

We are so used to the idea that road vehicles are powered by internal combustion engines or electricity that we forget their predecessors. Long before anyone thought of filling a tank with gasoline, there were cars, trucks, and buses that burned coal and ran on steam.

The first steam-powered road vehicle was designed in 1769 by the French military engineer Nicolas-Joseph Cugnot (1725–1804). It drove a tricycle, and Cugnot intended it to be used to move artillery pieces—self-propelled guns. He built a sec-

ond tricycle in 1770 that still exists and can be seen in the Conservatoire Nationale des Arts et Métiers in Paris. It was big and heavy, but it proved the idea worked, although it was not a great success. The first tricycle ran off the road when trying to negotiate a bend at its top speed of 3 MPH (5 km/h); horses could move artillery more easily. Cugnot's second tricycle ran into a wall in 1771, thereby suffering the first motoring accident. A steam carriage for civil use was built in France in 1790, and by about 1800 there were steam buses on the streets of Paris.

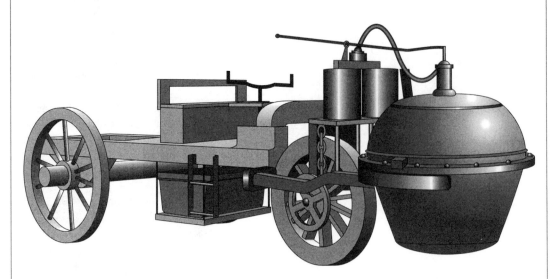

The Cugnot steam tricycle. The first self-propelled road vehicle, it was built in 1769.

successful one was a two-stroke engine built in 1859 by the Belgian-born French engineer and inventor Jean-Joseph-Étienne Lenoir (1822–1900). It burned domestic gas (in those days made from coal and consisting mainly of carbon monoxide). In 1860 he attached it to a small vehicle, which reached a speed of almost 2 MPH (3 km/h). He also built a boat driven by his engine. By the mid-1860s about 500 of Lenoir's engines were in use in Paris, but not to drive boats or "horseless carriages" at less than walking pace, with a heavy consumption of fuel and a great deal of noise. They were used to drive factory machines, such as printing presses.

About the same time, steam road vehicles were also running in Salem, Massachusetts, and Hartford, Connecticut. In 1805 one appeared in Philadelphia.

The first steam vehicle to be commercially successful was designed by Sir Goldsworthy Gurney (1793–1875) and built in 1829. Gurney was trained as a surgeon and practiced in Wadebridge, Cornwall, in southwestern England, and in London, but his fame was as an inventor. He was knighted in 1863 for designing improved lighting for the House of Commons. He drove his steam carriage the approximately 100 miles (160 km) from London to Bath and averaged 15 MPH (24 km/h) on the return journey, with a top speed of 17 MPH (27 km/h), although an average speed of about 9 MPH (14.5 km/h) was more usual. Gurney built more of his carriages and in 1831 opened a scheduled service with four round trips a day between Gloucester and Cheltenham, a journey of 9 miles (14.5 km) that sometimes took as little as 45 minutes—an average of 12 MPH (19 km/h). This inspired others to open new routes. More steam carriages were built, but the opposition to them was powerful. Heavy taxes forced Gurney's bus service to close after barely four months.

By the 1860s private steam cars were becoming popular. Some of these could carry two passengers at 20 MPH (32 km/h). Others carried more people, but more slowly. Antagonism to them led to the passing of the Red Flag Act of 1865, a law that required a person holding a red flag to walk ahead of a steam carriage and that restricted the speed to a maximum 4 MPH (6.4 km/h). The Red Flag Act killed private steam motoring in Britain, but it did not kill the use of steam trucks for carrying goods. They were still being made in the 1920s, and there were still a few on British roads in the 1940s. During the South African war (1899–1901) the British army used road trains—wagons towed by a steam engine—to transport soldiers.

Steam cars were much more popular in the United States, and one built in 1906 won the world speed record by covering a measured mile in 28.2 seconds—a speed of about 128 MPH (206 km/h). It was built by the Stanley brothers—Francis Edgar Stanley (1849–1918) and Freelan O. Stanley (1849–1940)—who had begun building steam cars in 1897. They competed in a number of races between 1902 and 1909, and their steam cars often won against cars powered by gasoline. The Stanley Motor Company, which they founded, was still building Stanley Steamers in the 1920s.

In the end, steam cars lost in the competition with gasoline-powered cars. Reducing a steam engine to a size suitable for a road vehicle was possible, but the result was very complicated and the car was heavy. Gurney's cars weighed 1.5–2 tons (1.36–1.82 tonnes). Their weight damaged roads (and Gurney's first carriage had spikes around the rims of its wheels because he did not believe a smooth wheel would grip the surface). They were noisy and smoky. Private steam cars were also dangerous. High pressure steam was carried in pipes through the superheater inside the boiler and then cooled in the pipes of a condenser that ran around the body of the car. Not surprisingly, steam cars acquired a reputation for exploding.

Engine efficiency

The French physicist Nicolas-Léonard-Sadi Carnot (1796–1832) had described the principle behind all engines of this type in 1824. In his day steam engines were notoriously inefficient, wasting as much as 95 percent of their fuel, and Carnot wanted to find out whether they could be improved. He found that the efficiency of any engine that works by heat depends on the difference in temperature between the incoming fluid and the temperature it reaches inside the engine. Sadly, Carnot died in an outbreak of cholera when he was only 36. Had he lived longer he might have developed his discovery further—25 years later it formed the basis for the second law of thermodynamics.

One way to increase the efficiency of an engine was to use the combustion of fuel more directly by using the fire to drive a piston rather than using the fire to raise steam to drive the piston. This meant containing the fire inside the cylinder and hence gave rise to the idea of the internal combustion engine. Containing the fire in this way also made it possible to achieve higher combustion temperatures than were possible in a fire box that had to be open to allow for stoking.

There was also a final advantage that may have clinched the matter. It took a long time to light a fire, get it burning brightly, boil the water, and raise a sufficient head of steam for a steam-driven vehicle to start work. A spark would ignite the fuel inside a cylinder virtually instantaneously, and the vehicle could move away almost at once.

The four-stroke cycle

The Lenoir engine was not very efficient, and within a few years scientists and engineers suggested a way to improve it—by substituting a four-stroke cycle for Lenoir's two-stroke action. The first four-stroke engine was built in 1876 by the German inventor Nikolaus August Otto (1832–91). He formed a company to build and market his engines, and within a few years 35,000 of them had been sold. By the end of the 19th century they led the field. The first diesel engines had already been built, but the Otto design was too firmly established to be challenged easily. When the first internal combustion automobiles were built, and later the first airplanes, they were powered by four-stroke engines. The first commercially successful motorcar equipped with a four-stroke engine appeared in 1885. Built by the German engineer Carl Benz (1844–1929), its engine developed 1.5 horsepower, and the car had a cruising speed of 10 MPH (16 km/h).

The principle of a four-stroke engine is quite simple. The cycle begins with the intake of fuel. As the piston moves down the cylinder in the first stroke, a carefully adjusted mixture of fuel and air is drawn into the cylinder behind it through an inlet valve, which closes when the

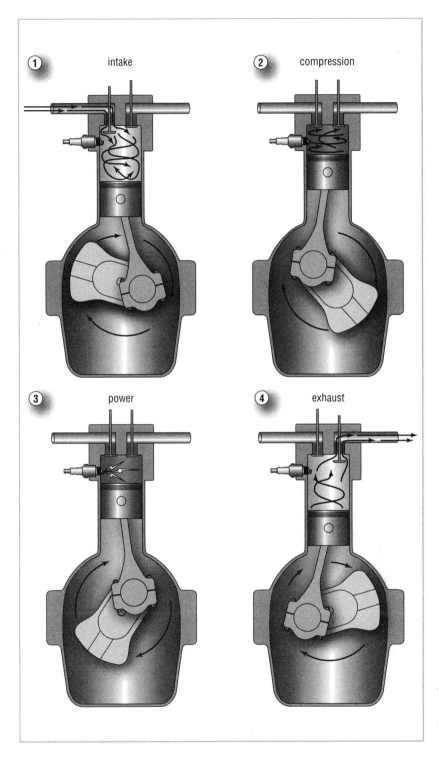

① intake

② compression

③ power

④ exhaust

An internal combustion engine, showing the sequence in the four-stroke engine

piston reaches the bottom of its stroke. The piston rises up the cylinder in the second stroke. This compresses the fuel-air mixture. At the top of the second stroke a spark ignites the fuel, which explodes. The explosion causes the air and gases to expand, driving the piston down the cylinder for the third, or power, stroke. As the cylinder rises again for the fourth stroke, an outlet valve opens at the top of the cylinder and the exhaust gases are expelled.

The piston is linked by connecting rods to a crankshaft, so that the reciprocating movement of the piston is converted into a rotary motion. Modern cars have four, six, or eight cylinders.

Diesel

Most trucks and buses, as well as most ships and some locomotives and cars, run on diesel oil. This is less highly refined than gasoline (see "What Are Fossil Fuels?" page 30), so it is cheaper to produce.

The engine that burns this fuel was invented by the German engineer Rudolf Diesel (1858–1913). He patented it in 1892 and 1893 and built his first commercially successful engine in 1897.

Diesel believed he could improve the efficiency of the internal combustion engine until it came close to the theoretical ideal engine described by Carnot. The way to do this, he calculated, was to greatly increase the compression in the cylinder. When a gas is compressed its temperature rises (see sidebar, page 18). Air is compressed to about 500 pounds per square inch (3,447 kPa) in the diesel engine, raising its temperature to

Diesel engine. There is no spark plug: instead, the fuel is ignited by compression.

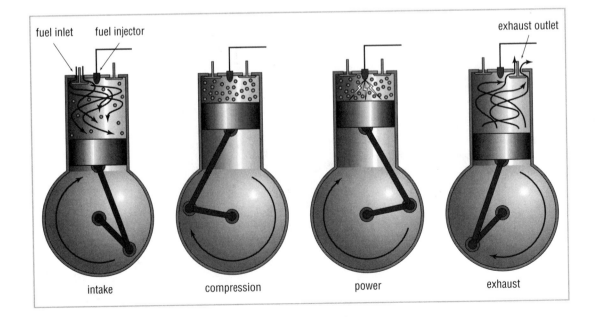

fuel inlet   fuel injector   exhaust outlet

intake   compression   power   exhaust

about 1,000°F (538°C), which is higher than the ignition temperature for the fuel. Consequently, a diesel engine needs no ignition system.

There are two-stroke diesel engines, but those in road vehicles are four-stroke engines. During the first, intake, stroke the piston descends and air is drawn into the cylinder. The air is compressed during the compression stroke and heated by compression. Fuel is sprayed into the cylinder at the end of the compression stroke. It ignites spontaneously, pushing the piston down by the expansion of gases. The exhaust gases are expelled in the fourth, exhaust stroke. The diagram shows the sequence.

The great advantage of the diesel engine proved to be its fuel economy, but for a long time it suffered serious disadvantages. The early engines were big, heavy, and ran at low speeds, so they were used in stationary installations. They were more expensive than gasoline engines and ran less smoothly. As they improved, diesel engines were introduced in ships, first in 1910, and then into heavy trucks, farm tractors, and in 1934 the first diesel trains ran in America.

Wankel engine

In 1929 Felix Wankel (1902–88), a German engineer and inventor, took out a patent for a rotary internal combustion engine. He continued developing his design through the 1930s and 1940s, finally completing it in 1954. The first Wankel engine was tested in 1957. The first car to be fitted with one was the Prinz, made by the German company NSU, which was launched in 1960, and in 1967 the Japanese manufacturer Mazda began producing the Cosmo Sport 110S. By the mid-1970s almost all the Mazda cars sold in the United States had Wankel engines, Citroën was marketing two models, and both Mercedes and General Motors were planning to start producing them.

The Wankel design was very advanced. It has fewer moving parts than the Otto-cycle engine, and it is lighter, more compact, and therefore its power output is greater in relation to its weight. It is also cheaper to manufacture and runs smoothly and quietly. Its greater efficiency and smooth running are due to the fact that its rotary motion is transmitted directly to the drive shaft that turns the wheels, without the need for a crankshaft to convert reciprocating into rotary motion.

The heart of the engine is a triangular rotor that rotates inside an oval housing. Its axis of rotation is offset from the center of the rotor, so the rotation is eccentric. All three points of the triangle remain permanently in contact with the sides of the housing. Because it rotates eccentrically, the space between each side of the rotor and the housing changes during the cycle. The diagram shows the arrangement. The engine is cooled by water that circulates through jackets in the casing. It is lubricated by oil that circulates through the inside of the rotor and by adding a small amount (about 0.5 percent) of oil to the fuel.

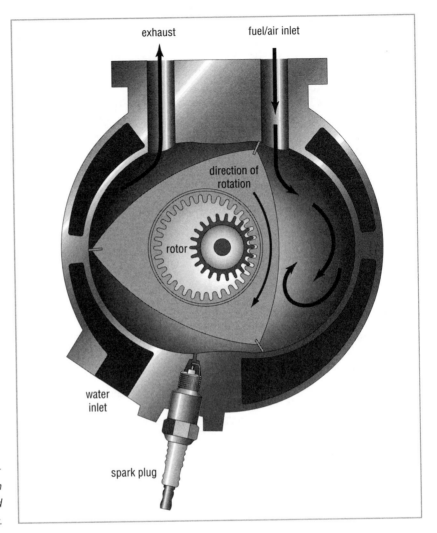

exhaust   fuel/air inlet

direction of
rotation

rotor

water
inlet

spark plug

Wankel engine. The rotation of the rotor draws in fuel, compresses it, and expels the exhaust gases.

There are four stages in the rotary cycle. As one tip of the triangle passes the fuel inlet port, the fuel-air mixture is drawn into the housing. The inlet port closes when the next tip passes it. At this point the chamber containing the mixture is at its maximum volume. As the rotor continues turning the volume of the chamber decreases, compressing the mixture. When it reaches maximum compression the fuel is ignited by one or two spark plugs. The expanding gases drive the rotation. With the next stage of its turn the chamber expands, and the exhaust gases are expelled.

Jet engine

Until the 1940s all aircraft were powered by internal combustion engines using high-octane gasoline. That changed with the introduction of the jet turbine, or turbojet, engine. Frank Whittle (1907–87), later Air Commodore Sir Frank Whittle, invented the jet engine in 1937, but on August 27, 1939, the German Heinkel He 178 was the first jet aircraft to fly, with an engine designed by Hans Joachim Pabst von Ohain (1911–98). Von Ohain knew nothing of Whittle's work. The aircraft powered by Whittle's engine made its first flight on May 15, 1941, and the first British jet fighter, the Gloster Meteor, flew for the first time on March 5, 1943. It was powered by two Rolls Royce Derwent engines, each developing 3,500 pounds (15.57 kN) of thrust.

The principle of the turbojet is very simple. At the front of the engine is a large fan called the compressor or impeller. As it spins at several thousand revolutions per minute, the compressor draws air into the engine and compresses it. The compressed air is pushed toward the rear, passing through and around a set of combustion chambers arranged around the central shaft. A steady stream of fuel is injected into each combustion chamber. The fuel is ignited when the engine is started and thereafter burns constantly. The gases expand toward the rear of the engine, and it is this expansion that exerts a forward thrust on the whole engine (by Newton's third law of motion: to every action there is a reaction equal in force and opposite in direction). As they leave the exhaust gases spin a turbine. The turbine is connected to the compressor by a shaft, and so it is the spinning of the turbine that drives the compressor. The diagram shows the general arrangement.

Jet engines run on kerosene, which is less highly refined than gasoline, and they deliver a large amount of power in relation to their weight. This makes them ideal for use in aircraft. They have disadvantages, however. The throttle increases the amount of fuel flowing into the combustion chambers, but the inertia of the compressor-turbine assembly means it can accelerate only slowly. This is not serious in an aircraft, where the engine is run at a constant setting most of the time, but it makes the

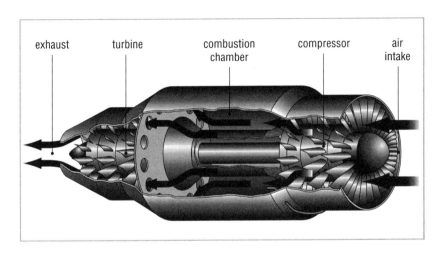

exhaust   turbine   combustion   compressor   air
                          chamber   intake

Turbojet engine. The compressor and turbine. with the shaft linking them. are the only moving parts.

engine too sluggish for use in road vehicles (although it was tried experimentally; the jet-propelled Rover car can still be seen in the Science Museum in London). More seriously, a jet engine uses a great deal of fuel. The Meteor fighter carried about 430 gallons (1,628 liters) of fuel in its two main wing tanks. This was sufficient for a mission lasting about 45 minutes.

Emissions

Despite its advanced design, the Wankel engine experienced problems. The most serious of these arose from the difficulty in achieving a tight seal between the rotor and the wall of its housing. Leaks in the seals reduced the efficiency of the engine, so it consumed more fuel than an Otto-cycle engine of similar power. It also emitted more pollutants. When gasoline prices rose in the 1970s, Wankel engines became less popular, and when emission controls were introduced, the Wankel had difficulty meeting them. These problems have now been solved, and Wankel engines are likely to reappear in years to come. However, they lost a great deal of ground and may be staging their comeback at a time when the entire concept of the internal combustion engine is being challenged on environmental grounds.

A completely efficient internal combustion engine would burn all of its fuel and release only the by-products of hydrocarbon combustion—carbon dioxide and water. No engine is totally efficient, however, and not all of the carbon is oxidized fully. Consequently, the carbon dioxide is mixed with carbon monoxide, which is a pollutant.

A portion of the fuel is not oxidized even to carbon monoxide. It is emitted as unburned hydrocarbons. These include benzene (C_6H_6), formaldehyde (HCHO), and other aldehydes (–RCHO–). In most modern automobiles fuel is injected into the cylinders. This is a much more efficient way to introduce a controlled mixture of fuel and air than was possible with the old-fashioned carburetor. Older cars sometimes dripped gasoline from their tailpipes.

Engines may also emit visible black smoke. If the engine is of the Otto-cycle or Wankel type, a smoking tailpipe means an overhaul is due. Lubricating oil may be leaking into the cylinders, air filters may be blocked, or the carburetor or choke mechanism may be faulty, resulting in an incorrect fuel-air mixture. Also, the ignition system may be faulty, so the fuel is not being ignited correctly. Smoke is unburned fuel, which is fuel wasted. Consequently, remedying the problem improves the performance of the engine and reduces fuel consumption.

Diesel engines are more prone than are gasoline engines to emit smoke. The smoke is due to worn or poorly maintained fuel injectors or pumps, dirty air filters, or an incorrectly adjusted fuel pump. Again, the smoke is unburned fuel.

Older vehicles using reciprocating engines (not Wankel engines) could also emit hydrocarbon gases from the crankcase. The crankcase is the housing containing the crankshaft, and it contains oil for lubrication. When the oil is hot, a portion of it vaporizes. The gases can dilute the oil, reducing its effectiveness and damaging the engine, so they were released into the air. In modern engines the gases are fed into the engine air intake and from there into the upper part of a cylinder, where they are burned along with the fuel.

The high temperature and pressure of combustion in an internal combustion engine provide sufficient energy for the oxidation of nitrogen. Consequently, engines emit nitrogen oxides (NO_x; see "What Happens When Fuel Burns?" page 27).

Ignition causes the compressed fuel–air mixture to explode. An explosion is simply a fire that burns extremely rapidly. If the engine is working properly, the fire starts at the spark plug and advances smoothly across the whole combustion chamber—the part of the cylinder above the piston. Manufacturers have improved engine efficiency partly by increasing the amount by which the mixture is compressed prior to ignition, and under high compression it is possible for fuel to ignite ahead of the advancing flame front. It then burns in an uncontrolled fashion, producing powerful, high-frequency pressure waves that can make the whole engine vibrate with a distinct knocking sound. This is called knocking, and it is best prevented by using more highly refined fuel with a higher octane number. The octane number is the percentage by volume of iso-octane (2,2,4-trimethylpentane, which is $(CH_3)_3CCH_2CH(CH_3)_2$) contained in the fuel. The same improvement can be achieved more cheaply by adding tetraethyl lead ($Pb(C_2H_5)_4$) to the fuel rather than refining the petroleum further. Fuel containing tetraethyl lead—leaded gasoline—functions well, but the lead is released with the exhaust gases. Airborne lead is a pollutant, and most countries have either banned the use of leaded gasoline or are in the process of phasing it out. Jet engines emit nitrogen oxides, and during take-off and climb some engines emit unburned fuel.

Photochemical smog

In 1542 three ships sailed from the Mexican port of Navidad (now called Acapulco) carrying a party of explorers. The expedition was led by Juan Rodríguez Cabrillo (also known by his Portuguese name, João Rodrigues Cabrilho), sailing on board the flagship, the *San Salvador*. They sailed north to Baja California and then continued to what Cabrillo described as "a closed and very good harbor." He called it San Miguel, a name that was changed 60 years later to San Diego. Continuing northward, the expedition may have reached Point Reyes, at 38°N, to the north of San Francisco, before bad weather forced them to return south. They wintered on San Miguel Island in the Santa Barbara Channel, where Cabrillo suffered a broken leg in a skirmish with the local people. He died of complications from the fracture on January 3, 1543. His date of birth is not known.

Cabrillo apparently failed to discover either Monterey Bay or San Francisco Bay, but he did record a "large bay" that was probably Los Angeles. He reported that "many smokes" were hanging over the bay. His fame therefore rests on two important discoveries: California and Los Angeles smog. The smog aroused no further interest until September 1943, when there was serious air pollution, and Angelinos learned for the first time of the downside to their much vaunted sunshine and fondness for big cars.

The smog Cabrillo observed was quite unlike the pea-soup smog of the industrial north. It was a brownish haze that reduced visibility, but by much less than a fog. From a distance it must have resembled smoke. Cabrillo did not approach closely enough to be directly exposed to it. The fact that he saw and described it in the 16th century proves that it is an entirely natural phenomenon. Human activities make it worse, but to a lesser extent it would occur anyway.

Smog everywhere

This type of smog—photochemical smog—was first identified in Los Angeles, but it is not confined to that city. Mexico City suffers from it very badly, and the authorities are doing what they can to combat it. In November 1999 they suggested planting roof gardens to reduce the problem by capturing smog particles. A little earlier, on October 15, pollution levels had risen to three times the acceptable limits. Already the city authorities had issued regulations requiring vapor traps to be fitted to gasoline pumps to prevent pollution from gasoline vapor, increased car and industrial inspections, and improved fire-fighting, and they had promoted reforestation programs. Their efforts were rewarded by improved air quality. In 1999 there were only three smog emergencies covering five days, compared with the previous best year, 1996, when there were 10 covering 34 days. Ozone levels were considered acceptable on only 65 days, however, compared with 37 days in 1990.

Teheran, Iran, is another city with a smog problem. In December 1998 pollution levels rose to six times higher than the levels deemed acceptable by the World Health Organization of the United Nations. The elderly and people with respiratory problems were advised to remain indoors, schools were closed, and cars were allowed to be driven only on alternate days depending on whether their license plates ended with odd or even numbers. The air was just as bad a year later, in December 1999.

Athens also suffers. So do most Australian cities, as well as Beijing and Guangzhou (Canton) in China. Vancouver experiences it, although less severely than the Lower Fraser Valley nearby, and so does Toronto. The most severely affected region of Canada is the urban belt extending from Windsor, Ontario, to Quebec City.

On July 30, 2000, temperatures over 86°F (30°C) combined with industrial fumes and vehicle exhausts caused pollution levels to exceed safety limits in Paris, France, and the surrounding Île de France. Speed limits were reduced by 12 MPH (20 km/h) for the rest of that day and all of July 31, and drivers were urged to leave their cars at home and use public transport. Pollution levels were also high in the cities of Rouen and Le Havre.

It began in Los Angeles—at least, that is where it was first recorded. Now it happens all over the world. So what is it, what causes it, and why has it spread?

The necessary geography

All of these cities share certain features. They are all big, of course, and industrialized. Also, all of them are low lying with higher ground on at least one side, and they are all in latitudes lower than 50°N or S, lying in regions that enjoy warm, dry summer weather with very bright sunshine. Smog is unusual in northern cities, although Rouen and Le Havre suffered because of unusually warm weather.

Urban basins are places where temperature inversions are common (see sidebar, page 8). Summer sunshine heats the ground, and the streets and buildings of a city heat up quickly. The warm surfaces heat the air in contact with them. The air rises by convection, but it cannot penetrate the inversion because it arrives at a level where the air above it is warmer and so less dense. It is trapped, but the continuing convection establishes a vertical circulation that thoroughly mixes the air.

Gases and particles that are released into the air from buildings and vehicle exhausts are also trapped beneath the inversion. They accumulate there, and convection mixes them throughout the trapped air.

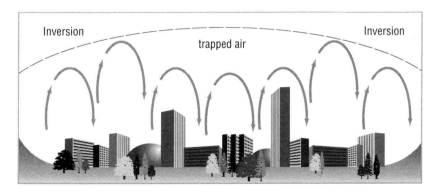

Convection beneath an inversion. Air trapped beneath the inversion is thoroughly mixed.

Once the pollutants reach a certain concentration, individual molecules have a good chance of colliding with one another, and molecules that meet are able to react chemically. Chemical reactions become possible, but energy is needed to drive them. That is where the bright sunlight comes in. It supplies the energy. The mixture of chemicals, trapped beneath the inversion and heated by the sun, are like the ingredients for a soup mixed together in a pot on top of the stove. Cooking can now commence.

The chemical ingredients

The ingredients needed to make smog are nitrogen dioxide (NO_2) and reactive hydrocarbons (H_C). Both are released by vehicle exhausts.

Cooking begins with the photolytic cycle (see sidebar). This comprises three reactions, the first of which produces atomic oxygen. It happens when NO_2 is exposed to ultraviolet radiation:

$$NO_2 + \text{ultraviolet radiation} \rightarrow NO + O.$$

Ordinarily, the photolytic cycle continues with the formation of ozone (O_3), which then oxidizes the NO to NO_2, the O_3 being reduced to O_2; the NO_2 then breaks down once more as the cycle repeats. In the presence of H_C, however, some of the extremely reactive atomic oxygen oxidizes H_C to H_CO^*. This is a free radical (it has unpaired outer electrons and is therefore highly reactive). It is oxidized further, then reacts with nitrogen oxides to produce NO_2 and the first ingredients of the smog. Further reactions between NO_2 and H_C radicals produce peroxyacetyl nitrates.

The sequence of reactions is:

$$H_C + O \rightarrow H_CO_3{}^*$$
$$H_CO_3{}^* + NO \rightarrow H_CO_2{}^* + NO_2$$
$$H_CO_3{}^* + H_C \rightarrow \text{aldehydes, ketones, etc.}$$
$$H_CO_3{}^* + O_2 \rightarrow O_3 + H_3O_2{}^*$$
$$H_CO_X{}^* + NO_2 \rightarrow \text{peroxyacetyl nitrate}$$

The asterisk (*) indicates a free radical group. Aldehydes are compounds containing the aldehyde group –CHO. They include formaldehyde (HCHO, also called methanal). Formaldehyde and other aldehydes are partly responsible for smog's distinctive smell. Aldehydes also cause throat irritation. Ketones are compounds such as acetone (also called propanone, CH_3COCH_3) that contain the carbonyl (–CO–) group. The reactions also produce ethene (also called ethylene, C_2H_4).

Peroxyacetyl nitrate (PAN) causes throat irritation. When this type of smog was first being investigated, chemists realized it contained a mysterious "ingredient x". This turned out to be PAN, $CH_3CO.O_2NO_2$.

PAN is fairly stable in the cold air of the upper troposphere, but in warm air it decomposes to release nitrogen dioxide (NO_2) and the highly reactive peroxyacetyl radical ($CH_3CO.O_2$). Depending on the air temperature, PAN decomposes and re-forms by a reversible reaction:

The photolytic cycle

Burning fossil fuels at high temperatures and pressures produces nitrogen oxides (NO_x). Vehicle exhausts are the principal source in urban areas and naturally occurring isoprenes and terpenes in rural areas (see the section Killer Trees?). In the presence of strong sunlight. ultraviolet radiation provides enough energy to drive a sequence of chemical reactions in which an oxygen atom (O) is removed from nitrogen dioxide (NO_2) and added to diatomic oxygen (O_2) to form ozone (O_3). The ozone then reacts with nitric oxide (NO) to produce NO_2 and O_2. This is known as the photolytic cycle (from the Greek words *photo-*. "light." and *-lysis*. "disintegration"). The reactions are:

$$NO_2 + \text{ultraviolet radiation} \rightarrow NO + O \quad (1)$$
$$O + O_2 \rightarrow O_3 \quad (2)$$
$$O_3 + NO \rightarrow NO_2 + O_2 \quad (3)$$

The ultraviolet radiation that breaks NO_2 into NO and atomic oxygen is at a longer wavelength than that which is absorbed in the stratosphere through reactions that form and then break down ozone. Ozone produced during the photolytic cycle is not affected by the ultraviolet radiation to which it is exposed in the lower atmosphere. The photolytic cycle produces ozone but quickly destroys it again. and it neither adds to nor reduces the concentration of NO_x. Consequently. it has very little polluting effect in itself. Pollution occurs only when the photolytic cycle is disrupted by hydrocarbon compounds.

NO_2 = nitrogen dioxide
NO = nitrogen oxide
O = oxygen atom
O_2 = oxygen molecule
O_3 = ozone

Photolytic cycle. These are the reactions that take place in strong sunlight.

$$CH_3CO.O_2NO_2 \leftrightarrow CH_3CO.O_2 + NO_2$$

PAN is constantly forming, decomposing, and re-forming, but in warm air the reaction favors the release of NO_2 and peroxyacetyl radical. Some of the PAN survives to be carried aloft by convection currents, however, and in colder air the same reaction favors the PAN. Consequently, PAN can be dispersed over a wide area.

NO_2 and the scattering of light by airborne particles produce the brownish color of smog. O_3 contributes to the throat and respiratory irritation people suffer.

Smog also damages plants. The culprits there are nitrogen oxides, ethylene, ozone, and PAN.

The need for bright sunlight

Photochemical smog requires the energy of brilliant sunlight. Without intense solar radiation at just the right ultraviolet wavelength, the necessary reactions will not take place. Consequently, this type of pollution occurs during daytime in summer and early fall.

It can also travel, however. In the 1960s scientists became intrigued by damage to the leaves of tobacco plants that were being grown near the shores of Lake Erie. They identified the damage as being caused by ozone but at first had no idea where the ozone could be coming from. Eventually the mystery was solved. The ozone was an ingredient of the photochemical smog that formed during the day over the lakeside cities—Cleveland, Toledo, Detroit, and Buffalo all border the lake. It was carried out over the lake, where it subsided and flowed back toward the shore as an afternoon lake breeze (see sidebar, opposite page).

Low-level ozone

Occasionally, a violent thunderstorm leaves the air with a quite distinct, acrid odor. It is the same smell as the one you notice around electric sparks, which is not surprising because lightning is simply a very big spark. The smell was noticed around electrical equipment as long ago as 1785 by the Dutch chemist Martinus van Marum (1750–1837). In 1840 the German-Swiss chemist Christian Friedrich Schönbein (1799–1868) realized that the smell must be due to a previously unknown gas. He called it *Ozon*, from *ozein*, the Greek verb meaning "to smell." Later, the Irish physical chemist Thomas Andrews (1813–85) showed that ozone is not an element, but one of the two possible forms, or allotropes, of oxygen.

Ordinary diatomic oxygen is O_2. Ozone is triatomic oxygen, O_3, and it is formed from diatomic oxygen: $3O_2 \rightarrow 2O_3$. This reaction requires an input of energy (it is endothermic) to break the bond between the atoms of diatomic oxygen. In the lower atmosphere strong electric sparks can supply this energy, and ozone is produced industrially by pass-ing an electric discharge through pure oxygen or dry air. Ozone also forms during the photolytic cycle (see the box). Ozone is a pale blue gas 1.658 times the density of air. It freezes at $-420°F$ ($-251.4°C$) and boils at $-170°F$ ($-112°C$).

Its smell is so strong some people can detect it at concentrations as low as one part of ozone in one billion parts of air. A concentration of 0.15 parts per million (ppm) makes some people cough, and asthma sufferers and persons with other respiratory complaints find 0.17 ppm distressing.

Ozone is a powerful oxidant. It will convert sulfur dioxide (SO_2) to sulfur trioxide (SO_3), which becomes sulfuric acid (H_2SO_4) when it dissolves in water droplets, and it plays a key role in the formation of photochemical smog. Low-level ozone (below an altitude of about 15.5 miles; 25 km) absorbs more outgoing long-wave radiation from below than incoming short-wave radiation from above. Consequently, it causes an increase in the surface air temperature.

Land and sea breezes

A sea or lake breeze blows from water to land during the day. A land breeze blows from land to sea or lake by night.

During the day the land warms faster than the water. Warm air rises over the land, and cool air is drawn in from over the water to replace it. As it rises the air over land cools. It then moves over the water surface, where it subsides and flows back toward the land.

At night the opposite happens. The land loses heat faster than the water. Consequently, air subsides over the land and flows out over the water as a land breeze. There, it pushes beneath the air next to the water surface, which has not yet cooled. This air rises and flows back toward the land. The diagram shows these processes.

sea breeze, day

land breeze, night

Land and sea breezes. By day, air rises over land, and cool air from the sea or lake flows toward the shore. By night, air flows from land toward the sea or lake.

Fogs and smogs of the past

When you see people on TV complaining about air pollution or urging us to do more to reduce it, it is easy to suppose that this is a new problem. The news stories make it sound as though pollution began with the invention of the automobile about a century ago, or perhaps a little earlier than that, during the Industrial Revolution. Before that, you may think, the air was clean and pure.

This is wrong. Air pollution has been troubling people for a very long time, indeed—for thousands of years, in fact. What is more, it is getting better, not worse. True, our air is not as clean as we might wish it to be.

We could make further improvements. Nevertheless, the air was much worse in the past.

Working with metals

The trouble began when our ancestors started working with iron and steel. The ancient Greeks were using steel 3,000 years ago. We know this because the poet Homer refers to it. Steel is made by adding carbon to molten iron, so people must have been working with iron for much longer.

Iron (chemical symbol Fe) oxidizes readily, so it rarely occurs naturally as the pure metal. Usually it is found as an oxide ore. Hematite (Fe_2O_3) is the most widespread ore and probably the one the first ironworkers used. Magnetite (or lodestone, Fe_3O_4), limonite ($FeO(OH)_nH_2O$), ilmenite ($FeTiO_3$), which contains titanium (Ti) as well as iron, and siderite ($FeCO_3$), or iron carbonate, are also common. So is iron sulfide (FeS_2), or pyrite.

In order to separate the iron from the oxygen or sulfur, the ore has to be heated strongly enough to melt the metal. Iron melts at 2,795°F (1,535°C). This presents a difficulty, because in ancient times wood was the principal fuel, and a wood fire is not hot enough to melt iron. This is because wood is not very dense. There is an alternative, however. Charcoal is a denser, more concentrated fuel. It can melt iron.

People used to be scared of charcoal burners, the folk who converted wood into charcoal. They lived most of the time in huts in the forest. Their clothes and faces were filthy, they were extremely poor, and no doubt they spoke roughly. The work was dirty, it meant they had to live in the forest where they had little contact with villagers living near the forest edge, and it did not pay particularly well.

First the charcoal burners collected sticks and branches, preferably of oak. They stripped away the bark (which they could sell to the tanners, who prepared leather from hides) and piled the wood in a shallow, circular pit with a tall pole in the center. They built up the pile of wood around the pole until it was about six feet (1.8 m) high, with the end of the pole protruding from it. Then they covered the pile with leaves, bracken, and turf, all packed down tightly, and sealed it with a layer of mud made from earth and ash. Once the outer layer had dried, they removed the pole, dropped a small amount of charcoal down the hole, then dropped some burning charcoal after it. This ignited the charcoal at the bottom. As soon as they saw flames, they sealed the top of the hole. After a time smoke started emerging from the heap, white at first and turning blue after several days. When blue smoke appeared the operation was completed. While the wood was "cooking" the workers had to check the pile regularly, sealing any cracks in the coating and looking down the hole for any sign of flames, which they extinguished with water. Once the process was completed they left the pile to cool slowly, then opened it and bagged up the charcoal inside. As soon as one pile had been lit the burners began building another, so they produced a fairly continuous supply of charcoal.

The effect of this process was to drive off the water held in the wood and then to drive off the oxygen. Dry wood is more than 40 percent oxygen. Removing some of it reduces the volume of the wood and increases the percentage of carbon it contains, producing a denser fuel that burns at a higher temperature. Burning charcoal produces at least half as much heat again as burning the same volume of wood. Charcoal could be used to smelt iron from its ores and then to work the metal in a forge. Dirty, smelly, impoverished, and uncouth they may have been, but the charcoal burners were the backbone of the metal industries. People also used charcoal to warm their homes and cook their foods.

Egypt, Greece, and Rome

Silver is easier to work with than iron. It melts at 1,764°F (962°C), a temperature low enough to be attainable with a wood fire. Articles made from silver have been found in Egyptian tombs dated around 4000 B.C.E., and Menes, the king who is believed to have ruled Egypt around 3100 B.C.E., decreed that one part of gold was equal to two-and-a-half parts of silver. Hence, silver could be used as a currency, and by 800 B.C.E. both silver and gold were probably being used for this purpose everywhere between the Rivers Nile (in Egypt) and Indus (in Pakistan). In addition, there was always—and still is, of course—a ready market for objects made from this beautiful metal.

The chemical symbol for silver is Ag, which is from the Roman name for the metal, *argentum*. That is not its original name, however. Before that it was known as *luna*, "moon," and it was often represented by the symbol of a crescent moon. Silver is found in very small amounts in the sulfide ores of copper and zinc, but most commonly in galena or lead glance (lead sulfide, PbS).

In *Historia Naturalis* the Roman author Pliny the Elder (Gaius Plintus Secundus, 23 or 24–79 C.E.) described how silver was obtained in his day. He said the ore was washed and sieved five times, melted with lead, and then cupelled. Cupellation is a process in which the solidified mixture of silver and lead is placed in a shallow dish (called a cupel) and melted with a blast of very hot air. The air oxidizes the lead (and any other base metals present), and the oxides are either absorbed into the sides of the cupel or blown away, leaving the silver behind. Cupellation was invented around 5,000 years ago, so metalworkers had been using it for thousands of years by the time Pliny observed and described it.

In 1994 a team of scientists led by geologist Claude Boutron of the Domaine University at Grenoble, France, reported what they had found in ice cores taken from the Greenland ice sheet. Ice sheets in Greenland and Antarctica are made from the accumulation of each year's fall of snow. The weight of the overlying snow compresses the lower layers into ice, but the sheet remains layered, with one layer for each year, and the layers are visible. This allows scientists to remove a core—a long cylinder of ice—

and date each part of it by counting the layers. They can then take samples of the ice and of microscopic air bubbles trapped in it and analyze their composition. The results of their analyses tell them a great deal about conditions at the time the ice formed.

In this case Boutron and his colleagues found that from about 500 B.C.E. to 300 C.E. the amount of lead in the snow falling onto the ice was four times the natural level. During the 800 years of the Roman Empire, about 400 tons (363 tonnes) of lead fell over Greenland. The lead came from cupellation to extract silver. The scientists calculated that around the time of the birth of Christ, Roman and Greek silver mines were producing about 80,000 tons (73,000 tonnes) of lead slag a year, and about one percent of the lead in the slag entered the air. This level of pollution from airborne lead was not reached again until the early years of the Industrial Revolution.

Coal and smoke

Charcoal was practical, and it remained in use for centuries. However, by medieval times people had found an alternative to it: coal. Marco Polo (1254–1324) thought this a very peculiar substance when he came across it in about 1275, during his travels through Asia with his father and uncle.

> Let me tell you next of stones that burn like logs. It is a fact that throughout the province of Cathay there is a sort of black stone, which is dug out of veins in the hillsides and burns like logs. These stones keep a fire going better than wood. I assure you that, if you put them on the fire in the evening and see that they are well alight, they will continue to burn all night, so that you will find them still glowing in the morning.

China is not the only country with substantial coal reserves, of course. It is abundant in many places, including Britain, and it was being used there locally long before Marco set off on his adventures. Archaeological investigation of an Iron Age settlement at Port Seton, near Edinburgh, Scotland, has revealed many fragments of coal, many of them partly burned. The settlement was occupied during the last few centuries B.C.E., so coal was certainly being used by then. There are coal deposits nearby, and the archaeologists suggested it was removed by people digging wells and ditches. They realized it could be burned, although in general people preferred to use wood, which was cleaner and easier to obtain and use.

By the late 13th century coal was being used in many parts of Britain. The smoke was so bad in Nottingham in 1257 that during a visit by Eleanor of Provence (1223–91), the wife of King Henry III, the queen fled from Nottingham Castle fearing for her life and moved to Tutbury

Castle some miles away. Interestingly, in 1157 Eleanor of Aquitaine (c. 1122–1204), the wife of Henry II, had been driven from Tutbury Castle because of the wood smoke.

Coal was also being carried to London from the northeast of England. It was transported by sea, so it came to be known as "sea-coal." It quickly became popular, but the amount of smoke it produced also gave rise to a health scare. The rumor spread that if you ate food cooked over a coal fire it would make you ill and might even kill you, so in 1273 King Edward I passed a law aiming to reduce the nuisance caused by smoke. A few years later, in 1306, the problem was getting much worse, and there was great public anxiety about it. The king then passed another law forbidding the burning of coal in London while Parliament was in session. The law was not very effective, although at least one prosecution was brought under it. A manufacturer who broke the law was tried, convicted, and beheaded.

Bad to worse

There was no stopping the use of coal, and the air over European cities continued to deteriorate. In 1578 Queen Elizabeth I refused to enter London because the air smelled so bad, and in about 1590 she complained about the coal smoke inside Westminster Palace. Cities were made visible from afar by the pall of smoke hanging over them, and visitors could expect to be set coughing and spluttering by it.

Timothy Nourse, who held an official position at the University of Oxford but lost it when he converted to Roman Catholicism, had a great interest in farming and gardening. He died in 1699 (his date of birth is not known), but his book on these subjects, *Campania Foelix: or Discourse of the Benefits and Improvements of Husbandry*, was published in 1700. In it Nourse bemoaned the city air:

> Twere endless to reckon up all the mischiefs which houses suffer hereby, in their furniture, their plate, their brass and pewter, their glass. . . . A bed of fourscore or one hundred pounds price, after a dozen years or so, must be laid aside as sullied by the smoke. . . .

John Evelyn (1620–1706) also hated the smoke. A keen observer and famous author and diarist, Evelyn devoted considerable attention to air quality. In *A Character of England* (1659) he said that London was:

> cloaked in such a cloud of sea-coal, as if there be a resemblance of hell upon earth, it is in this volcano in a foggy day: this pestilential smoke which corrodes the very iron, and spoils all the moveables, leaving a soot on all things that it lights; and so fatally seizing on the lungs of the inhabitants, that cough and consumption spare no man.

Consumption was the name for tuberculosis.

In 1662 he published *Fumifugium, or the Inconvenience of the Aer and Smoake of London Dissipated*, in which he said:

> The immoderate use of, and indulgence to, sea-coale in the city of London exposes it to one of the fowlest inconveniences and reproaches that can possible befall so noble and otherwise incomparable City. . . . Whilst they are belching it forth their sooty jaws, the City of London resembles the face rather of Mount Aetna, the Court of Vulcan . . . or the suburbs of Hell than an assembly of rational creatures. . . .

Evelyn records the smoke and fog in his diary several times, as well as mentioning the attempts being made to control it. On January 11, 1662, for example: "I received of Sir Peter Hall, the Queen's Attorney, a draught of an Act against the nuisance of the smoke of London, to be reformed by removing several trades which are the cause of it, and endanger the health of the King and his people". Clearly, the act was of little avail, for on December 15, 1671, Evelyn wrote: "It was the thickest and darkest fog on the Thames that was ever known in the memory of man, and I happened to be in the very midst of it." Again, on January 24, 1684: "London, by reason of the excessive coldness of the air hindering the ascent of the smoke, was so filled with the fuliginous steam of the sea-coal, that hardly could one see across the streets, and this filling the lungs with its gross particles, exceedingly obstructed the breast, so as one could scarcely breathe." (*Fuliginous* means "sooty.") And on November 15, 1699:

> There happened this week so thick a mist and fog, that people lost their way in the streets, it being so intense that no light of candles, or torches, yielded any (or but very little) direction. I was in it, and in danger. Robberies were committed between the very lights which were fixed between London and Kensington on both sides, and whilst coaches and travelers were passing. . . . On the Thames, they beat drums to direct the watermen to make the shore.

Industrial cities

Once industrialization began, the situation deteriorated rapidly. During the mainly preindustrial 18th century London had smog on an average of 20 days a year. By the end of the 19th century the city was smoggy on 60 days a year.

Luke Howard (1772–1864), the meteorologist who devised the system for cloud classification that formed the basis of the system we use to this day, also wrote the first account of an urban climate. In the three-volume second edition of *The Climate of London Deduced from Meteorological Observations Made in the Metropolis and at Various Places around It*, published in 1833, he described the fog he experienced on January 10, 1812.

> London was this day involved, for several hours, in palpable darkness. The shops, offices, &c. were necessarily lighted up; but the streets not being lighted as at night, it required no small care in the passenger to find his way, and avoid accidents. The sky, where any light pervaded it, showed the aspect of bronze. Such is, occasionally, the effect of the accumulation of smoke between two opposite gentle currents, or by means of a misty calm. I am informed that the fuliginous cloud was visible, in this instance, for a distance of forty miles. Were it not for the extreme mobility of our atmosphere, this volcano of a thousand mouths would, in winter be scarcely habitable.

Howard recorded another London fog on January 16, 1826. On that occasion: "Lamps and candles were lighted in all shops and offices, and the carriages in the streets dared not exceed a foot pace." He also noted that five miles (eight km) from London the sky was clear and the sun shining brightly from a cloudless sky. This shows that the fog was trapped beneath a local inversion covering the city. The fog on November 28, 1828, was one of the densest known. ". . . [T]he effect was most distressing, making the eyes smart, and almost suffocating those who were in the street, particularly asthmatic persons."

The American author Francis Parkman (1823–93), who wrote *The Oregon Trail*, visited London one May early in the 19th century. He declared that from St. Paul's Cathedral all he could see were tiled roofs and church steeples half hidden in mist and smoke. By May the winter fogs were usually past and the weather was often fine.

Soon after Parkman's visit and Howard's observations, city air began to improve. The coal that was being burned from medieval times until the middle of the 19th century contained much more sulfur than coal burned since then. Consequently, the smoke and fog were much more acid than are the smogs of the 20th century. Starting in the late 16th century, by about 1850 the average concentration of sulfur dioxide in London air had increased from about 50 μg m^{-3} to a little over 900 μg m^{-3} (1 μg [microgram] is one-millionth of a gram; 1 m^3 = 35.31 ft^3). The amount of smoke in the air increased from about 50 μg m^{-3} to about 450 μg m^{-3} by around 1875. These were the peak years, however, and by the end of the 19th century London air was already improving rapidly. The levels of both sulfur dioxide and smoke particles are lower now than they have been at any time since about 1585. The precise concentrations vary somewhat, but the other industrial cities of Europe and North America have also experienced increasing air pollution that peaked and has since declined sharply.

The improvement appears to result from increased affluence. Starting in the second half of the 19th century, people in what are now the industrialized countries were becoming more prosperous. As communities, their increasing prosperity meant they could afford to pay for the equipment needed to remove pollutants before they entered the air. At the same time, instead of coal they began to burn oil and then natural gas as these fuels became available. These are much cleaner fuels. They also began asking whether it was necessary for the air to be so filthy. As they became more aware of the poor quality of their environment, they became less tolerant of it. They demanded improvement, improvement was possible and had already begun with the change in fuels, and so improvement was achieved.

This is not the case in most of the large cities in the less-industrialized nations. Even the worst of them are not quite so bad as London was at its worst, but their air is often seriously polluted. It should be improved, and there is reason to suppose that in years to come, as people in those countries become more prosperous, their air quality will also improve.

Factory and power plant chimneys and the gases they emit

Potatoes originated in South America. They were introduced into Europe some time during the second half of the 16th century, probably by a ship's cook who loaded a store of them in Cartagena, Colombia, for use on the voyage home to Spain. Some were still on board when the ship reached its destination, and the cook may have sold or given them away.

The new food was believed to possess various medicinal properties, and its use spread, although its main attraction was economic. Potatoes yield a heavier crop than any cereal, they can be grown in climates that are too wet for cereals to ripen reliably, and consequently they produce more food than any other staple crop for a given area of land. Finally, they can be stored simply by leaving them in the ground, a useful attribute at a time when war often drove people from their homes and destroyed crops growing aboveground. They were especially favored in Ireland, and before long the population became dependent on them. By the early 19th century an Irish peasant family was eating about eight pounds (3.6 kg) of potatoes a day.

Then, in 1845, a second species entered Europe from America—this time uninvited and by accident. Scientists believe it came from Mexico, although recent research has questioned this. It was a water mold, *Phytophthora infestans*, that, given the right conditions, lived inside potato plants. It destroyed the plants and reduced the tubers to a black, inedible, smelly, slimy mess. The disease was called late blight of potato, and it had devastated the North American crop in 1843. It reached Ireland late in the year, and its spores passed the winter in the soil. It was not until the following year, 1846, that it attacked the crop. There was a warm, wet summer that year, providing it with the conditions it needed. The blight spread widely across western Europe, destroying the potato crop wherever it went, its spread southward and eastward limited by the fact that it could not tolerate dry air and soil. The infestation was especially severe in the British Isles and worst of all in Ireland, because there the potato was a much more important crop than it was anywhere else. The destruction of the crop caused the Irish potato famine that lasted until 1850.

Potatoes everywhere died and rotted in the ground—except, that is, for just a few places. In those places the potatoes grew normally. No one knew what was causing the late blight. Because the weather was so wet, many people thought the blight was a type of wet rot. What some noticed, however, was that the unaffected potatoes were invariably growing downwind from factories where copper was being smelted. Then, in 1882, a French scientist, P. M. A. Millardet, noticed that grapes that had been sprayed with a mixture of copper sulfate and lime to deter thieves had escaped infestation with a very similar disease, downy mildew. In 1885 Millardet published a scientific paper in which he showed that copper sulfate also protected potatoes from late blight.

Copper compounds were being emitted from factories. These pollutants were being carried through the air and deposited on plants growing downwind. In this case the pollutants protected the plants, and the discovery of their effect led to the development of copper-based fungicides that are only now being phased out because they poison most fungi, including species that cause no harm.

Nonferrous metals

It is extremely rare for an industrial pollutant to have a beneficial effect. Indeed, the word *pollutant* clearly implies a substance that is harmful. Copper compounds are poisonous to many organisms except in quite small doses. They poison fish, in large doses they harm most plants, and in still higher doses they are poisonous to mammals, including humans. Those emanating from 19th-century copper smelters poisoned fungi. The fact that certain funguslike organisms severely damaged important crops was a fortunate coincidence, no more.

Smelting is a process in which heat is used to separate a metal from its ore. This is one of the main methods by which copper is obtained.

The ore is a mineral that contains the metal in the form of a chemical compound, and the ore mineral is often (but not in all cases) embedded inside rock. It is concentrated by separating it from the rock, mixed with a flux, which is a substance that makes the metal melt more readily, and heated to a temperature high enough for the metal to melt. Limestone is often used as the flux in smelting copper. Pure copper melts at 1,982.12°F (1,083.4°C), so the ore must be raised to a temperature higher than this.

The elements with which the metal was combined in the ore react with one another to form compounds that float as slag above the molten metal. Matte, a mixture of molten copper, iron, sulfur, and slag, is drawn off from the bottom of the furnace. The matte is then heated for a second time to separate the copper.

Any furnace that achieves high temperatures will release hot gases and particles that rise rapidly. It is not difficult to see how the gas emitted from copper smelting might carry dust containing particles of metallic copper, copper sulfate, and copper oxides.

In addition, although it would have no effect on fungi, the gas would contain the products of fuel combustion. Coke, made by heating coal to 1,600–2,300°F (871–1,260°C) in the absence of air to drive off the more volatile ingredients, was the fuel used. It burns at a high temperature, releasing carbon dioxide, nitrogen oxides, and a small amount of sulfur dioxide. Sulfur is an impurity that reduces the quality of the metal, so coke used for smelting should not contain more than 1 percent of it.

Copper is also obtained by electrolysis. An electric current is passed through a solution of copper sulfate from a positive electrode (the anode) made from copper ore to a negative electrode (cathode) made from pure copper. Copper ions from the solution move to the cathode, and sulfate ions move to the anode.

Fluorine

Almost all the aluminum we use is obtained by electrolysis. This is because the metal has such a strong affinity for oxygen that it is difficult and expensive to separate the metal from aluminum oxide by heating the ore. When pure aluminum is exposed to the air a thin layer of oxide forms immediately, completely covering the surface. Other metals are often added to prevent this from happening.

Aluminum oxide, known as alumina (Al_2O_3), is fed into rows of pots, called potlines, containing molten aluminum, a sodium compound, and cryolite, which is a mineral consisting of sodium, aluminum, and fluorine (Na_3AlF_6). The alumina is heated to about 1,750°F (950°C), which drives off any water it may contain, and an electric current is passed through the pots from carbon anodes to carbon cathodes on the base of the pots. The alumina reacts with the carbon: $2Al_2O_3 + 3C \rightarrow 4Al + 3CO_2$. Molten aluminum is then poured off from the bottom. The process loses some fluorine, so this is replaced by adding aluminum fluoride (AlF_3). The lost fluorine is released as a gas consisting mainly of hydrogen fluoride (HF).

Airborne fluorine compounds are carried downwind and settle onto vegetation. They accumulate in plants, including grass, and can injure them. Cattle grazing on the grass can be poisoned by quite low fluorine concentrations. Excessive ingestion of fluorine causes a disease called fluorosis. Fluorine replaces calcium in bones. The bones thicken but at the same time become soft and brittle, and bony masses grow where there were none previously. Cattle grazing downwind of aluminum refineries have suffered from fluorosis in the past.

Trees can also be affected. Hydrogen fluoride from an aluminum ore reduction plant at Spokane, Washington, was seen to be damaging the needles of ponderosa pine *(Pinus ponderosa)* in 1943, and by 1952 trees were affected in an area of 50 square miles (129.5 km^2).

It is not only aluminum production that is to blame. Brick kilns also emit fluorine, because the clays used to make bricks contain fluorine. Phosphate rock often contains fluorine compounds. Consequently, the processing of phosphate rock to make superphosphate fertilizer, with gypsum (hydrated calcium sulfate, $CaSO_4.2H_2O$) as a by-product used in the building industry and in a number of manufacturing processes, also releases hydrogen fluoride.

Long before the discovery of aluminum (in 1825), alum was used as a mordant in dyeing. A mordant is a chemical substance that makes the dye pigment fast, so the dye will not wash out of the cloth. Alum is aluminum sulfate ($Al_2[SO_4]_3$) combined with the sulfate of another metal and with water. There are many alums, but the most important is potassium, or potash, alum, in which aluminum sulfate is combined with potassium sulfate ($KAl[SO_4]_2.12H_2O$). This occurs naturally and is known as alumstone or alunite, but it can also be manufactured. Alum production began in England around 1600, and by 1627 the residents of one part of London were complaining that they were being poisoned by the fumes from a nearby alum factory. It is not clear what was harming them.

Mercury

The Mad Hatter in Lewis Carroll's *Alice in Wonderland* suffered from a disease of the nervous system. His symptoms included loss of appetite—the tea party went on for a long time, but he seemed to eat nothing—gum disease, and anemia. He had contracted this illness through his occupation. Hatmakers (hatters) used to coat hatbands with mercury. This helped keep the bands in place on the hats, but it exposed the hatters to very small amounts of mercury. If, like the Mad Hatter, they remained for long enough in this occupation, the mercury they absorbed through their skin would make them ill. The Mad Hatter suffered from a form of mercury poisoning known as mad hatter's disease.

It is very unusual to be poisoned by mercury in this way—and hatbands are not fixed in this fashion nowadays—but mercury still causes pollution. It is present in very small amounts in many substances, especially in coal. When these are burned the mercury is released into the air and then settles out. Some settles onto rivers and lakes, where it sinks into sediments on the bed, and bacteria alter it to methylmercury, which is one of its most poisonous compounds. Fish then absorb methylmercury in the food they eat, and it lodges in their bodies. People who frequently eat contaminated fish can be harmed by it. Coal-burning power plants are the principal source of airborne mercury.

In parts of tropical South America fish have been contaminated by mercury from a different source. Gold and silver miners were (and are) using mercury to separate the precious metals from their ores. This is an ancient and fairly simple method. The ore is ground to a powder and then mixed with mercury. When the mixture is stirred vigorously it forms a liquid or paste called an amalgam. This is left to stand while the amalgam separates from the powdered rock, which is then removed. The final step is to separate the gold and silver from the amalgam. Mercury boils at 673.84°F (356.58°C), gold at 5,085°F (2,807°C), and silver at 4,014°F (2,212°C). Heating the amalgam boils off the mercury, leaving the precious metal behind. The mercury vapor is then cooled to make it condense, so that the mercury can be recovered. Mercury is expensive, and large processing plants recover it efficiently, so very little escapes into the air. Small-scale mining operations in remote regions are less efficient, however, and in South America the mercury they release has raised concerns for the health of people who depend on fish they catch in the rivers.

Iron and steel

The iron and steel industry is a major source of air pollution in countries where its emissions are not strictly controlled. Pittsburgh, Pennsylvania, used to be known as Iron City or Steel City, but also as Smoky City. Anshan, a city in northeastern China, was called "The invisible city for satellites" because it was permanently blanketed in such a dense pall of smoke it could not be seen from above.

Iron is obtained by smelting ore with added limestone and using coke as fuel. Carbon monoxide (CO) from the hot coke reacts with the iron ore, reducing it to iron ($2C + O_2 \rightarrow 2CO$; $Fe_2O_3 + 3CO \rightarrow 2Fe + 3CO_2$; Fe is iron, and Fe_2O_3 is hematite, a common iron ore mineral). Molten iron is removed from one part of the furnace and molten slag, made by reactions between the limestone (mainly calcium carbonate, $CaCO_3$) and other ingredients of the ore, from another. Molten iron is then mixed with small amounts of other metals to make steel.

Coke ovens, producing coke from coal, release fine particles of coke consisting mainly of carbon. Iron smelting releases sulfur dioxide or hydrogen sulfide, fine particles, and carbon monoxide. Hydrogen sulfide (H_2S) causes damage to certain crop plants if they are continuously exposed to concentrations of 0.3–3.0 parts per million (ppm), and some species fail to grow properly if the air contains more than 0.03 ppm. Steelmaking also releases nitrogen oxides and ozone. Fluorite is also used as a flux (to facilitate melting of the metal). It is a mineral made from calcium fluoride (CaF), and dust escaping from the furnace often contains fluorine. An analysis made many years ago of the dust from a steel mill (processing steel into sheets, rods, and tubes rather than manufacturing it) in Hamilton, Ontario, found the dust contained arsenic, cadmium, lead, mercury, and zinc as well as fluorine. The dust was implicated in the high incidence of lung cancer among people living close to the mills or working in them.

Chemicals and petrochemicals

The manufacture of chemicals for industrial use produces many poisonous waste substances that cause serious pollution if they are released into the air. They include certain widely used compounds, such as benzene and toluene.

Benzene (C_6H_6) is obtained as a by-product from coke ovens and from petroleum, of which it is a natural constituent. The drawing shows its structural formula. It is used in the manufacture of ethyl benzene, phenol, and maleic anhydride, which are used to make plastics. It is also used in making aniline for dyes, dodecylbenzene for detergents, and chlorobenzenes for

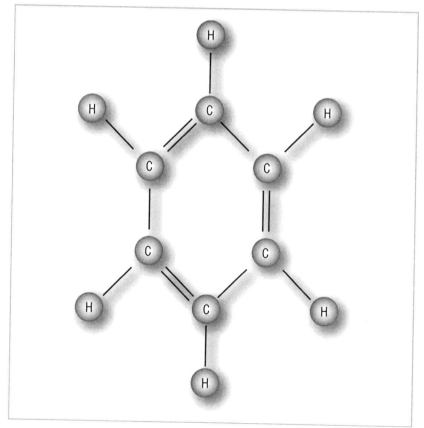

The structural formula of benzene

insecticides. Benzene is also an excellent solvent for rubber, gums, fats, and a number of resins.

Toluene is used in the manufacture of the explosive trinitrotoluene (TNT), benzoic acid used as a food preservative, and also saccharin sweetener, dyes, photographic chemicals, and pharmaceuticals. It is also used as a solvent and an antiknock additive for aviation gasoline.

Both benzene and toluene are involved in the reactions that produce photochemical smog. In addition, and more seriously, benzene is directly poisonous and causes nonlymphocytic leukemia, a type of cancer, at doses above about 500 parts per billion (ppb). The main source is tobacco smoke, however. Industry releases very little in the industrial countries of North America, Europe, and Australasia, although there may be more in the air of cities in some newly industrializing countries. In December 1994 an analysis of air over London, England, found it contained 2.47 ppb of toluene and 1.92 ppb of benzene. These are minute amounts, and more than one-third of the total came from gasoline and diesel vehicle engines—partly released into the air during refuelling.

Computers and other electronic devices cause no pollution whatever while they are being used, but substances employed in their manufacture can cause pollution. These include, for example, cadmium, nickel, lead, mercury, selenium, and tin, all of which form poisonous compounds.

Power plants

Most power plants generate electrical power by converting water to steam and using the steam to spin turbines. The process requires heat to raise steam, and the heat is supplied either by a nuclear reactor or by burning a carbon-based fuel. The fuels most widely used are coal, natural gas, and oil. Oil use has declined greatly owing to concerns about the security of supply and price instability. Peat is used in some countries.

Oxidation is an exothermic chemical reaction. This means that the reaction releases energy in the form of heat. It is the reaction that takes place when any fuel containing carbon is burned in air. If the reaction is completed, the carbon is oxidized fully to carbon dioxide: $C + O_2 \rightarrow CO_2$ Carbon dioxide is not ordinarily thought of as a pollutant because it is a natural constituent of air, and it is harmless except in very high doses—indeed, it is beneficial to plants. It is a source of concern nowadays because although it causes no injury, it traps heat. It is a greenhouse gas, and governments are anxious to reduce the amount of this gas that their factories and power plants produce in order to minimize its global warming effect.

Furnaces are not completely efficient, of course, and some of the carbon they use is not fully oxidized. It is released as carbon monoxide (CO). In high doses this is poisonous, although it is doubtful that it causes any injury except in very confined spaces where vehicle exhausts are the main source (see "Pollution and Health," page 143). When mixed with air, its further oxidation to CO_2 takes place very quickly.

Some of the carbon is not oxidized at all. It is combined with hydrogen, forming hydrocarbons. This is a huge class of compounds, most of which contain other elements in addition to hydrogen and carbon. As the temperature of the fuel rises inside the furnace some of the hydrocarbons vaporize and are carried upward in the hot gas stream before they have a chance to ignite. These are known as volatile organic compounds, or VOCs. VOCs condense to form black smoke (see "What Happens When Fuel Burns?" page 27). Some are directly harmful to health.

Fuel-burning power plants also release nitrogen oxides, usually symbolized as NO_X. NO_X and VOCs take part in the reactions that produce photochemical smog (see "Photochemical Smog," page 55), and NO_X is implicated in acid precipitation (see "Acid Rain, Snow, Mist, and Dry Deposition," page 90).

Natural gas consists mainly of methane (CH_4), but coal, oil, and peat contain many substances in addition to carbon and hydrogen. When the fuel is burned some of these are oxidized, and others are reduced to fine powder. These enter the air as particulate matter, or PM, which is categorized by the size of its particles. If the particles are less than 25 μm across the material is PM25; if they are less than 10μm across it is PM10. Both are injurious to the health of people who inhale them.

The gases and dust also contain the other elements present in the fuel. The most serious of these is sulfur dioxide (SO_2), which is also implicated in acid precipitation, but they also include mercury. Surprisingly perhaps, coal-burning furnaces also emit more radiation than nuclear power plants. This is because all natural substances contain some radioactive material. When coal is burned its radioactive content is released into the air, but nuclear plants are not permitted to release more than the tiniest amounts of radioactive gases or dust.

Nuisances

Not all the gases produced industrially are harmful to health. Some are simply bad smells. Factories that make industrial chemicals, oil refineries, and textile factories all produce odors, some of which are highly unpleasant.

Breweries use hops to flavor beer. They give it the slightly bitter taste without which it would be unpleasantly sweet. Hops are the female flowers of the cultivated hop vine *(Humulus lupulus)*, and when added to the hot brew they emit a very strong smell that spreads over a wide area around the brewery. Many people dislike it.

Tanneries, where animal hides are processed into leather, have always been sources of appalling smells. In the past they were often sited as far out of town as possible, at the insistence of the citizens, but they could not be too far away because the tannery workers had to be able to walk to them. Processing begins with the removal of bits of flesh and fat that cling to the insides of the skins. This is the first source of bad smells because the material quickly begins to putrefy. The skins are then treated chemically, traditionally using such ingredients as chicken manure and dog feces, followed in the next stage of the preparation by immersion in urine to supply ammonia. More wholesome chemicals are used nowadays, but tanning is still smelly.

Adhesives made from raw materials supplied by the chemical industry have largely replaced old-fashioned glue, but life near a glue factory used to be unpleasant. Some glues were made from animal hides along with sheep and cattle bones. The product is in the form of flakes or granules that are dissolved in hot water and applied while hot. Glues that could be used cold were made from fish bones, and there were other glues made from casein, obtained from milk. Processing milk to separate casein and bones and animal skins to release and concentrate the gelatin in them produced strongly offensive smells that at one time were simply released into the outside air.

Textile manufacture released fibers. These were harmless—they were much too large to find their way deep into the lungs—but they coated plants and entered houses. The fibers were a nuisance because they made the area look dirty and untidy.

Factories are no longer permitted to pollute the air with dangerous or offensive substances. Some of the pollutants are trapped before they reach the outside air (see "Trapping Pollutants," page 150). Others are no longer produced because advances in manufacturing technology have led to the introduction of processes that use resources more efficiently.

Chimney stacks and plumes

When people first began to heat rocks in order to obtain the metals they contained, the work was done outdoors. The ore was heated in a kiln by burning wood and later charcoal around and beneath the kiln, and the smoke and fumes rose into the air and dispersed. Copper was the first metal to be smelted. Its melting temperature of 1,982.12°F (1,083.4°C) is low enough to be attained by a wood fire, so the method worked. Iron, which melts at 2,795°F (1,535°C) was more difficult to smelt, but once metalworkers discovered the way to make charcoal that temperature also became attainable.

They worked outdoors because it was more convenient, and while they did so they had no need of tall chimneys. The smoke and fumes rose into the air and were carried away on the wind. If the wind blew the smoke into your face, you simply moved around to the other side of the fire, the way you might move around a bonfire.

This reflected the way the smoke from domestic fires moved. The Romans developed hot-air central heating, with chimneys to carry away the smoke, but peoples of the northern lands used wood fires for warmth and cooking. The hearth was in the center of the communal living room, and the smoke rose and left through a hole in the roof. Sometimes there would be a rudimentary chimney in the form of a barrel with both ends removed, set at the highest point in the thatched roof.

Chimneys shaped like those of today first appeared in medieval times, when builders began using stone for large buildings. For some time after that, however, some domestic chimneys had a lower part rising from the hearth that was built from stone and an upper part, outside the house, that was made from branches sealed with clay. Factory chimneys developed from the chimneys that were built to carry away the smoke and gases from domestic fires used for heating and cooking.

Where does the smoke go?

Ecologists, who study the cycles through which elements and energy move, often point out that everything has to go somewhere. If a substance is released into the environment, it does not instantly disappear. It goes somewhere.

Chimneys carry away hot gases and particles. The purpose is to remove them from the proximity of the people sitting around the fire, cooking the meal, or working at some industrial operation that requires a source of heat. The chimney deposits the offensive substances into the outside air, where it is assumed they will quickly disperse by mixing thoroughly into the immensely greater mass of the atmosphere. The emissions will be undetectable a short distance from the building.

How short is a short distance? That depends on several factors, the first of which is the height of the chimney or, more precisely, the effective stack height. A stack or chimney stack is a chimney that is built as a separate structure, rather than being a simple hole in the roof. *Stack* is from the Old Norse word *stakkr*, which means "haystack," suggesting the idea of making a chimney by piling stones or bricks one above another. A chimney, even a domestic chimney that projects only a short distance above the roof, is heavy. It has to be built independently of the building in which it is situated so that it does not support any part of the weight of the building, and it must have substantial foundations so it does not sink or tilt under its own weight. It is not too fanciful to picture it as a stack of stones or bricks.

Hot gases rise up the chimney because they are buoyant (see sidebar, page 78). When they leave the top of the chimney they are cooler than they were at the bottom, but they still retain some positive buoyancy and are being propelled upward by the gases rising from below. Consequently, they continue rising upward for some distance beyond the top of the chimney.

You can see the effect of this very clearly above the cooling towers of power plants and certain types of factories. As its name indicates, a cooling tower cools hot water. Air enters the tower through vents near the base and

Buoyancy

When a body is immersed in a fluid it displaces an amount of that fluid equal to its own volume. This was discovered by the Greek mathematician and physicist Archimedes (ca. 287–12 B.C.E.) and is known as Archimedes' principle. It reduces the weight of the body by an amount equal to the weight of the displaced fluid. The amount by which the weight of the body is reduced acts as an upward force on the body. This upward force is called buoyancy.

If a body weighs more than the amount of the fluid it displaces, it will sink through the fluid. It is then said to possess negative buoyancy or to be negatively buoyant. If the body weighs less than its own volume of the fluid it will rise to the top of the fluid and is said to possess positive buoyancy or to be positively buoyant. If the weight of the body is equal to that of the fluid it displaces it will neither sink nor rise. It then possesses neutral buoyancy or is neutrally buoyant.

A hot gas, or parcel of air, is buoyant if its density differs from that of the fluid surrounding it. A bubble of gas rises through water because the gas is less dense than the water and is therefore positively buoyant.

Hot air is less dense than cooler air, and so it is positively buoyant and rises. That is why hot air rises up a chimney into the cooler air above the roof, carrying with it other gases, solid particles, and liquid droplets derived from combustion or from a process in which materials are heated.

The force exerted by buoyancy can be calculated from the mass of the body or parcel of air or gas affected by it, its density, the density of the surrounding fluid, and the gravitational acceleration.

is expelled from the top by fans. Near the top of the tower hot water is sprayed into the rising cool air. As it falls, the water lands on and trickles through a series of racks extending across its path. These slow the descent of the water and increase the area of water surface that is exposed to the air. Liquid water collects in a basin at the bottom of the tower. The water is cooled partly by exposure to the cooler air and partly because a portion of the water evaporates, taking the latent heat of vaporization from the adjacent water and air.

Some of the evaporated water condenses once more, but the remainder is carried upward out of the top of the tower in the stream of rising air. Once in the air above the tower, it cools rapidly and condenses into a mass of droplets resembling cloud. On a still day the cloud above the tower can extend to a considerable height. It rises because it consists of air and water that possess positive buoyancy. The top of the cloud marks the height at which the density of the cloud is the same as the density of the surrounding air. The cloud has become neutrally buoyant. Despite its resemblance to white smoke, the cloud above a cooling tower consists of nothing more alarming than water droplets.

Except on those rare days when there is no wind at all in the lowest few hundred feet of the atmosphere, there will be a height above the top of the stack at which the gases become neutrally buoyant and begin to move downwind. This is the height at which the gas plume effectively enters the atmosphere: the effective stack height. It is measured as the height of the stack plus the plume rise, which is the additional height to which the gases rise before their movement becomes mainly horizontal. The drawing illustrates this.

The plume disperses

What happens to the plume next depends entirely on atmospheric conditions. The downwind movement of the plume is described as looping, coning, fanning, lofting, fumigating, or trapping. The set of diagrams illustrates each of these.

On a fine summer day when the ground is being heated strongly by the Sun, some surfaces will warm more quickly than others. This differential heating will cause local convection cells to form, so there are places where air is rising and other places where it is sinking. This will be reflected in the movement of the plume. It will rise and fall, sometimes coming quite low or even touching the ground and at other times rising quite high. This is looping. The loops increase in size with distance from their source. In this kind of weather a chimney plume may cause patches of pollution at ground level some distance from the chimney stack, but only during daytime (because at night there is no differential heating of the surface).

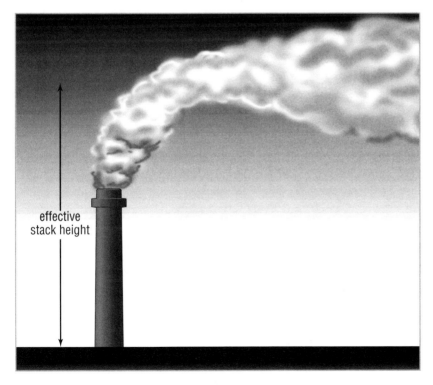

Effective stack height

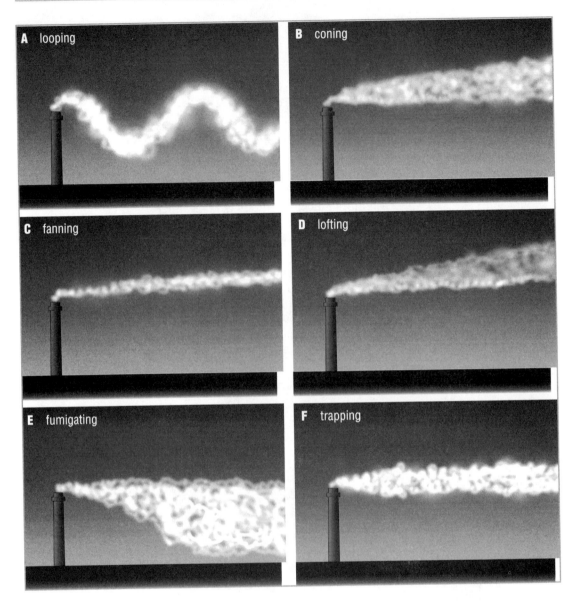

Types of stack plumes

When the air is stable, so there is almost no vertical movement, and a wind is blowing, the plume will spread as it moves downwind. It disperses more or less equally in all directions around a center line, so that it forms a conical shape. This is coning, and it can occur by day or by night. If the plume descends low enough to cause pollution near ground level, this will be at a considerable distance from the chimney stack.

Fanning occurs when the air is very stable. It is most usual beneath a temperature inversion (see sidebar, page 8), and it happens more often at night than during the day because the air is generally more stable at night.

There is almost no vertical movement of the air, and so the plume moves downwind horizontally, remaining at the effective stack height. Although there is no vertical air movement, in these conditions there is often some erratic horizontal movement. This will spread the plume to the sides, so that it looks fan-shaped when seen from directly below or above. A fanning plume can travel up to 60 miles (100 km) before it disperses into the surrounding air.

Temperature inversions often develop at night, and the inversion layer starts at ground level and spreads upward. The process begins early in the evening, soon after sunset, as the balance shifts between incoming solar radiation and outgoing heat radiation. As the ground radiates away its heat and cools, the layer of air in contact with the ground is chilled, so there is a layer of cold air lying beneath warmer air. This is a temperature inversion, and the top of it moves steadily upward as the layer of cold, stable air deepens. A plume discharging above the inversion is unable to sink into the cooler air of the inversion layer, but above the inversion layer it enters warm, relatively unstable air. Vertical air currents carry the plume upward, dispersing it well above the ground. This is lofting, and it is the ideal situation, because a lofting plume causes no ground-level pollution at all.

As the night progresses, however, the inversion layer continues to deepen until it is deeper than the effective stack height. The plume is then entering the inversion layer and lofting often gives way to fanning.

Around dawn the situation begins to change. The ground temperature starts to rise, causing air above it to start rising by convection. This forms a layer near the ground in which the air is well mixed. As the morning advances, the mixed layer deepens until it reaches the height of a fanning plume. There is still a temperature inversion above the plume preventing it from rising, but vertical air movements carry the gases and particles downward to the surface. The plume is then fumigating and causing severe pollution. Fortunately, the pollution is often short lived. After less than an hour the inversion dissipates, and the plume is able to rise rather than subside. If the fanning plume is carried along a valley and beneath a valley inversion, however, pollution caused by fumigation can affect people and wildlife many miles from the source.

Fumigation can also be caused by eddies of air around tall buildings. Buildings interrupt the flow of the wind. Walk between buildings on a windy day and it is impossible to tell which direction the wind is blowing because the direction keeps changing. Watch small scraps of paper as they are blown about, and you will see that not only do they keep twisting and turning but also keep rising and falling. The air moves vertically as well as horizontally because of all the eddies that form as the wind blows over and around the many obstructions. If a chimney is emitting a plume into the swirling air, the plume will be carried by the eddies and, as the drawing shows, the pollution will reach ground level. A somewhat similar effect sometimes occurs with chimney stacks that are sited on steep hillsides.

When the wind blows across the top of the hill, eddies develop in the air flowing downhill on the lee side, and these can bring the plume down to ground level.

Finally, a plume can be trapped. Trapping occurs when a weak inversion extends to above the effective stack height and the wind is light.

How the air cleanses itself

Air cleanses itself very quickly by a number of processes that together are known either as scavenging or dry deposition. Both of these remove pollutants from the air and deposit them on the surface.

The moment the gases and particles leave the top of the stack they start mixing with the outside air. Gas molecules and individual particles collide and ricochet, so that although the plume as a whole is rising upward, at the smallest level its constituents are moving in all directions. They move away from one another, air molecules move between them, and the visible effect is to widen the plume. It also dilutes the contents of the plume.

The process, called diffusion, continues for as long as the material from the stack remains airborne, and it is due entirely to the random movement of molecules and extremely small particles. You can see it for yourself. Light a candle in very still air, then extinguish it and watch how the smoke quickly dissipates and vanishes—by diffusion. Alternatively, drop a single drop of food dye into a basin of clear water and watch how the color spreads until finally it is dispersed evenly throughout the water. The color may be barely detectable in the water because of the extent to which diffusion has diluted the pigment. As the drawing shows, mixing begins at once.

Dry deposition

Pollutants trapped by buildings

Once the plume reaches the effective stack height it starts to drift downwind, still growing wider and more dilute. As the plume drifts it also slows. It has less energy than it possessed when it was rising by vigorous convection, and,

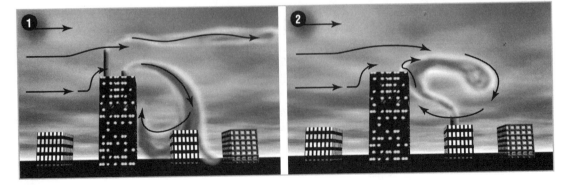

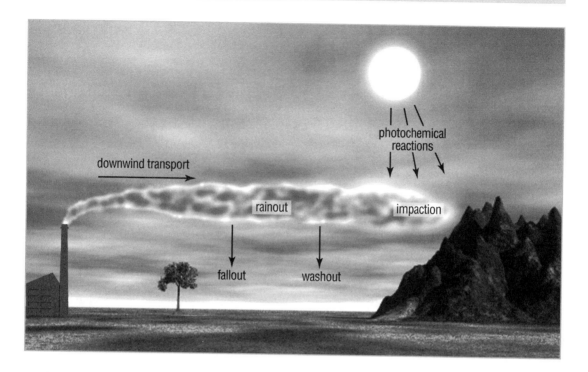

having less energy, it is less able to keep solid particles aloft. The largest and heaviest particles begin to fall by gravity. This is called fallout. You may have heard the word *fallout* used in connection with radioactive particles falling to the ground following a nuclear explosion or accident at a nuclear power plant, but in fact the term describes the process by which any particles are removed from the air by falling to the ground.

Fallout is one form of dry deposition. The other is known as impaction. This occurs when gases or particles from the plume strike a surface and adhere to it.

Scavenging

Some of the smaller particles may act as cloud condensation nuclei, or CCN. If the air is almost saturated with water vapor, some of the vapor will condense readily onto small particles. Solid particles are then enclosed inside cloud droplets, and soluble particles dissolve into the cloud droplets that condense onto them. The resulting cloud may dissipate if it drifts into drier air and its droplets evaporate. Its stock of CCN are then returned to the air—still dispersing by diffusion, of course—where they may trigger further condensation when they enter moister air. Eventually, the cloud droplets holding them grow into raindrops (or snowflakes or hailstones) and fall to the ground. This is called rainout.

Falling raindrops collide with other plume particles. These are swept into the rain or snow and carried to the ground in a process called washout.

The fate of pollutants. As smoke and gases emerge from the stack, they start to mix with the air. As they move downwind, they are diluted by diffusion and leave the air by fallout, washout in rain, and impact with surfaces. Some engage in chemical reactions driven by sunlight.

Fallout, rainout, and washout are highly efficient processes that cleanse the air rapidly. Large particles seldom remain airborne for as long as an hour, and smoke particles, which are smaller and lighter, remain airborne for less than a day.

Gas molecules do not leave the air by fallout or rainout, but they are removed by washout. Soluble gases dissolve in raindrops, and insoluble gases are converted into soluble compounds by reactions that take place in the air in the presence of unreactive molecules that assist in the reactions but remain unchanged by them. Most of these reactions involve free radicals, the most important of which is the hydroxyl radical (OH^-). Hydroxyl is ionized, which means the positive charge on the hydrogen atom (H^+) is insufficient to neutralize all the negative charge on the oxygen atom (O^-), leaving the ion with a net negative charge (OH^-).

Hydroxyl ions are produced mainly by the action of ultraviolet (UV) light with a wavelength of less than 315 nanometers. The UV splits ozone (O_3) molecules into molecular (O_2) and atomic (O) oxygen, and the atomic oxygen combines with water (H_2O) to produce hydroxyl: $O + H_2O \rightarrow 2OH$. Other reactions driven by light energy at longer wavelengths produce hydrogen peroxide (H_2O_2) and hydrogen dioxide (HO_2) radicals.

All free radicals are extremely reactive because of the charge they carry. Hydroxyl reacts with carbon monoxide (CO), for example, to produce carbon dioxide and hydrogen dioxide ($CO + OH \rightarrow CO_2 + H$; $H + O_2 + M \rightarrow HO_2 + M$ (M is an unreactive molecule) and to convert sulfur dioxide (SO_2) into sulfuric acid (H_2SO_4) and nitrogen dioxide (NO_2) into nitric acid (HNO_3). Both of these acids are soluble and are quickly carried to the ground. Because they are produced by reactions among the original pollutants released into the air—known as primary pollutants—these are called secondary pollutants, and they contribute to the form of pollution known as acid rain.

The effectiveness of scavenging is measured as the scavenging ratio. This is calculated as the concentration of the pollutant in rainwater divided by the concentration in the air. The higher the figure for this ratio, the greater is the efficiency of scavenging. Gases remain in the air longer than do solid or liquid particles. A sulfur dioxide molecule may remain airborne for up to about 10 days, for example, but a methane molecule remains in the air for an average of 11 years. Eventually, it is oxidized to carbon dioxide and water by reactions with hydroxyl.

ACID IN THE AIR

Acid rain and Manchester air

Manchester is a large industrial city in the northwest of England. The modern city has grown from what was once a small settlement called Mancenion. The Romans knew it as Mancunium, the Latin version of its name, and to this day the inhabitants are proud to call themselves Mancunians.

It is one of the places where the industrial revolution began. Following the discovery and application of steam power in the 18th century, the first canal in England was opened in 1761 to bring coal to Manchester to power the steam engines. In 1785 the power loom was invented, and the first steam-powered spinning mill opened in the same year—in this case in Papplewick, Nottingham, but within a few years steam engines were driving the Manchester textile mills. In the space of one generation Manchester grew from a small market town to a major city, its prosperity based mainly on the textile industries. It achieved the formal status of a city in 1853, and since 1893 the leader of the city government has held the grand-sounding title of lord mayor. The population in 1750 was 17,000. It had grown to 70,400 by 1800 and to 300,000 by 1835. Today the population of Greater Manchester is approximately 2.58 million.

Mills and factories sprang up everywhere in the burgeoning city, and, because the whole industry was powered by steam that was raised by burning coal, all the mills and factories had tall chimney stacks that poured forth smoke, steam, waste gases, textile fibers, and dust. The mill owners and their managers lived in the semirural suburbs, but the factory workers drawn into the city in search of paid employment as a preferable alternative to the harsh and uncertain conditions they knew as agricultural laborers lived crowded together in unimaginable squalor.

Friedrich Engels (1820–95), the friend and colleague of Karl Marx (1818–83), visited the city in 1840 and described it in *The Condition of the Working Class in England* (published in 1844). Of the district where the mill workers lived he wrote: "Right and left a multitude of covered passages lead from the main street into numerous courts which lead down to the [river] Irk, and which contain unqualifiedly the most horrible dwellings which I have yet beheld. . . . The first court . . . was in such a state at the time of the cholera that the sanitary police ordered it evacuated, swept, and disinfected with chloride of lime. . . . Below the bridge you look upon the piles of *débris*, the refuse, filth, and offal from the courts on the steep left bank; here each house is packed close behind its neighbour and a piece of each is visible, all black, smoky, crumbling, ancient, with broken panes and window-frames. The background is furnished by old barrack-like factory buildings."

Manchester in the 19th century was not a clean town, but neither were its leaders oblivious to the dangers of industrial pollution. By the middle of the century the city government was adapting its administrative procedures to address the situation and creating bodies to examine the environmental effects of industry.

Manchester was not alone, of course. There were more than 50,000 coal-fired steam engines driving British industry by 1870. One iron works in Wales consumed 280,000 tons (254,240 tonnes) of coal a year, and another had 63 separate steam engines, each driving a particular part of the factory. Together, the factories, not to mention the coal-fired railroad locomotives and coal-burning domestic fires and cooking stoves, emitted a prodigious quantity of smoke.

Progress and the discovery of acid rain

Rapid industrialization caused much pollution, but there was another side to it. Industrialization was based on new technologies, and equally rapid scientific advances accompanied the technological development. Scientists sought to elucidate the principles on which the technologies worked and the underlying natural laws governing the behavior of the world around them. Feeding this, there was a universal popular thirst for knowledge and self-improvement through education. Public lending libraries flourished alongside working men's institutes where evening classes were held. Eminent scientists regularly delivered public lectures to capacity audiences. Some of them were so good at it they acquired star status, but they were motivated to perform in this way by their firm conviction that it was the duty of a scientist to share his (very rarely her in those days) discoveries with the general public. It was a time when people believed fervently in progress based on the application of scientific discoveries to the welfare of society as a whole.

As part of this spontaneous movement all over Europe and North America—but especially, perhaps, in the industrial cities of Britain—groups of enthusiasts formed societies devoted to studying and discussing the latest ideas. Individuals also conducted their own experiments and observations, and most societies published their own journals. Members delivered papers at the regular meetings for later publication in the journal, and visiting lecturers were invited to share their knowledge with people who lacked formal education but were fervent in their desire to understand.

Manchester had its share of such societies, and in 1852 a Scottish chemist named Robert Angus Smith (1817–84) delivered a paper that was later published in the *Memoirs and Proceedings of the Manchester Literary and Philosophical Society. Philosophy*, or *natural philosophy*, was the name given to what we now call science. The paper was called "On the Air and Rain of Manchester." Smith had noticed that rain falling downwind from Manchester was more acid than rain elsewhere and that its acidity decreased with distance from the city. This was the first reference to acid rain.

The Alkali Inspectorate

A few years later the British government established a body called the Alkali Inspectorate to monitor and seek to control pollution from (according to the Alkali Act of 1863, which created it) "alkali and other works." R. A. Smith was appointed the first inspector and worked assiduously to bring environmental pollution under control. In 1872 Smith brought the problem of air pollution to the attention of a wider audience than the members of the Manchester Literary and Philosophical Society with the publication of his book *Air and Rain: The Beginnings of a Chemical Climatology* (published in London by Longmans, Green).

He was called the "Alkali Inspector" because at that time the worst polluter was the alkali industry, manufacturing washing soda (sodium carbonate, Na_2CO_3). This was a major industrial product. Some was for domestic use, but most was used in the glass, soap, dyestuffs, and paper industries.

In the late 19th century soda was made by the Leblanc process, devised in 1790 by the French chemist Nicolas Leblanc (1742–1806). This used common salt (NaCl) and sulfuric acid (H_2SO_4) as the raw materials. Salt was dissolved in the acid, giving the reaction: $2NaCl + H_2SO_4 \rightarrow Na_2SO_4 + 2HCl$. The sodium sulfate ($Na_2SO_4$) was then roasted with crushed coal and chalk or limestone (calcium carbonate, $CaCO_3$). This yielded sodium carbonate and calcium sulfide: $NaSO_4 + CaCO_3 + 2C \rightarrow Na_2CO_3 + CaS + 2CO_2$. Water was added to dissolve the sodium carbonate, and the solution was heated in order to recrystalize it.

The solid wastes from the Leblanc process included calcium sulfide (CaS) and lime. These formed an extremely alkaline sludge that was dumped in vast quantities on open land, where it poisoned all the plants and animals. If the land was adjacent to a river, it poisoned every living thing in the river, as well. Contaminated land remained bare for many years. The other waste was hydrochloric acid (HCl). This was released as a gas that simply left the factory through the chimney, again in huge amounts.

It was mainly this hydrochloric acid that made the rain acid downwind of Manchester. R. A. Smith did much to reduce the amount of hydrochloric acid being released by the simple expedient of explaining to the factory owners that hydrochloric acid had industrial uses. Instead of throwing it away they could recover it and sell it for profit. All they need do was to bubble the waste gas through water, and the acid would dissolve.

In 1919 the Leblanc process was replaced by a more efficient process invented by the Belgian chemist Ernest Solvay (1838–1922). The Solvay process, also called the ammonia soda process, begins by heating calcium carbonate to drive off the carbon dioxide, leaving calcium oxide (lime): $CaCO_3 \rightarrow CaO + CO_2$. The carbon dioxide rises up a tower, and a solution of ammonia (NH_3) dissolved in brine is trickled into it. This yields ammonium chloride (NH_4Cl) and sodium bicarbonate ($NaHCO_3$): $NH_3 + CO_2 + NaCl + H_2O \rightarrow NaHCO_3 + NH_4Cl$. The insoluble sodium bicarbonate is filtered from the solution and heated to drive off carbon dioxide, leaving sodium carbonate. The calcium oxide is mixed with the ammonium chloride to recover the ammonia, leaving calcium chloride ($CaCl_2$) as the only by-product. This is used for clearing ice from roads and as antifreeze in refrigeration plants and is mixed with concrete. No industrial process is totally efficient in using up all of its raw materials, however, and the Solvay process also generates alkaline waste. This causes less pollution than the older Leblanc process, but that is mainly because nowadays much greater care is taken with its disposal.

Monitoring the rain

Smith had identified acid rain as a problem, and scientists at the Rothamsted Experimental Station in Hertfordshire, to the north of London, began monitoring the acidity of rainfall over southern England in 1853. Monitoring was not extended to the whole of western Europe until the 1950s, however. The first scientific studies of the harmful effects of sulfur dioxide on plants in the United States were made in 1938. Scientists at Rutgers University, New Jersey, were the first to report plant damage by air pollution in the United States in 1944. They found two affected areas along the Delaware River.

These may have been the first instances to be reported, but they were far from the first to occur. In 1896 a copper smelter opened at the town of Trail, British Columbia, 11 miles (18 km) from the U.S. border in the gorge of the Columbia River. The smelter emitted sulfur dioxide at an increasing rate until by 1930 it was releasing nearly 10,000 tons (9,080 tonnes) of SO_2 every month into air that was funneled down the gorge. The damage it caused to trees was clearly visible for more than 50 miles (80 km) downwind.

There was also severe damage around Anaconda, in Deer Lodge County, Montana. A smelter was opened there in 1884 to extract copper from ore mined in Butte, and the town was built to accommodate workers at what soon became the biggest copper smelter in the world. The smelter was located on a hill 6,600 feet (2,013 m) above sea level at the southern end of a valley 35 miles (56 km) long. The effective stack height (see the section Chimney Stacks and Plumes) was 7,200 feet (2,196 m). Sulfur dioxide from the stack injured trees up to 19 miles (30 km) away. The smelter finally closed in 1980. The ground around the smelter was also seriously contaminated and became an EPA Superfund site that has now been restored.

Damage to stonework

In fact, there was no need to conduct detailed botanical studies in order to reveal the effects of acid rain. Ample evidence was there for all to see in every big industrial city. City buildings are often built of limestone or sandstone. Cities have long honored distinguished citizens by erecting statues to them, and the statues are often carved from limestone or sandstone. Limestone is mainly calcium carbonate ($CaCO_3$). Sandstone consists of sand grains that are embedded in clay or mud and bound together by a mineral that cements them. The mineral cement is often calcium carbonate. Calcium carbonate reacts with airborne acids, and the effect is highly visible. Limestone and sandstone buildings and statues are disfigured by it.

Calcium carbonate reacts with hydrochloric acid to yield calcium chloride and carbon dioxide: $CaCO_3 + 2HCl \rightarrow CaCl_2 + CO_2 + H_2O$. Indeed, geologists use this reaction in the field as a quick and simple way to identify limestone rocks. Pour a few drops of dilute hydrochloric acid onto the rock and if it fizzes, the rock is limestone—and the fizzing is due to the release of carbon dioxide. Calcium chloride is soluble, so it trickles away in the water and is washed away by rain. Before long the surface of the stone appears pitted, and fine detail begins to disappear from statues. Engravings become increasingly difficult to read on limestone grave-stones. Sandstone suffers even worse damage, because calcium carbonate is the cement holding the stone together. As it is eaten away by the acid, the sand grains fall away and the stone starts to crumble.

Hydrochloric acid was the first cause of damage, but sulfuric acid soon overtook it, producing a different type of damage. Sulfuric acid (H_2SO_4) also reacts with limestone: $H_2SO_4 + CaCO_3 \rightarrow CaSO_4 + CO_2 + H_2O$. It makes limestone fizz, just as hydrochloric acid does, but the reaction soon ceases. In this reaction the water does not run away. Instead, it combines with the calcium sulfate to form gypsum ($CaSO_4.2H_2O$). This is insoluble and remains as a coating on the surface. Stone surfaces are not perfectly smooth, however, especially if they have been outdoors for any length of time where they are exposed to the weather. There are minute cracks, depressions, and crevices in the surface layer, and gypsum forms inside them. Gypsum expands as it crystallizes. This widens cracks and causes small fragments of the rock to flake off, exposing a new surface and thus eroding the stone.

Damage of this kind began long before the start of the industrial rev-olution. Coal fires release acids, as do many manufacturing processes that were conducted in small workshops for centuries before they were con-centrated in factories. These acids steadily defaced buildings and eroded statues, although the damage accelerated rapidly during the 19th century. The Victorians were especially fond of erecting statues and must have noticed that the statues were quickly blackened by soot and eroded by something—they could not have known what—that was present in the air.

The problem R. A. Smith identified was relatively straightforward. Factories were emitting hydrochloric acid that was causing damage down-wind. This was a primary pollutant (see "Chimney Stacks and Plumes," page 76). He was able to identify it and trace it to its source. When the problem of acid rain emerged once again in the 1960s, it was more com-plex. This time it was being caused by secondary pollutants. These trav-eled much farther and were much more difficult to trace to their sources, and to complicate the picture still further, they were only partly responsi-ble for the damage that was being reported.

Acid rain, snow, mist, and dry deposition

Carbon dioxide is a natural ingredient of the air, present at a concentration of about 365 parts per million, or 0.0365 percent. It dissolves in water, including the water droplets that make up clouds, to form carbonic acid: $CO_2 + H_2O \rightarrow H_2CO_3$. Because carbon dioxide is distributed evenly throughout the lower atmosphere, every cloud encounters it and so every cloud contains dissolved carbon dioxide and is slightly acid. This means that water falling from the cloud as hail, snow, or rain is also acid, as are fog, dew, and frost. *Acid rain* is therefore a slightly misleading term. All rain (and snow, hail, fog, dew, and frost) is acid. That is its natural condition. What we really mean by *acid rain* is, of course, rain that is more acidic than "natural," or unpolluted, rain.

Even that qualification is not entirely satisfactory, however, because the acidity of natural rain varies. Volcanoes release sulfur dioxide (SO_2), for example, which forms sulfuric acid (H_2SO_4) when it reacts with water, and the energy of lightning oxidizes nitrogen to oxides that dissolve to form nitric acid (HNO_3). Volcanoes erupt in particular places at certain times, and lightning occurs during local storms. Consequently, the natural supply of sulfur dioxide and nitrogen oxides varies from place to place and from time to time and so, therefore, does the acidity of the rain. The acidity of rain varies naturally from about pH 4.8 to pH 5.6. Rain that has been made acid—the technical term is *acidified*—by pollutants has a pH of less than about 4.8. Conventionally, though, rain is considered to be polluted if its acidity is below pH 5.0.

What is an acid?

Scientists measure acidity on the pH scale, devised in 1909 by the Danish chemist Søren Peter Lauritz Sørensen (1868–1939). An acid is a compound that contains hydrogen (such as HX, where X is any element or group of elements) and that dissociates in water to release hydrogen ions (HX $\leftrightarrow$ H$^+$ + X). The double-headed arrow ($\leftrightarrow$) means the reaction is reversible, so H and X are constantly dissociating and recombining. The pH scale measures the concentration of hydrogen ions (H$^+$) in an aqueous solution, "pH" standing for "potential of hydrogen."

Water is important because one of its many remarkable properties is that in the liquid phase it can act as both an acid and a base (the opposite of an acid). A small percentage of water molecules, approximately one in every 10 million, separate: $H_2O + H_2O \rightarrow H_3O^+ + OH^- \cdot H_3O^+$ is known as the oxonium ion, hydroxonium ion, or hydronium ion, and OH$^-$ is the hydroxyl ion. In very pure water at 77°F (25°C), there are 10^{-7} moles per liter each of oxonium and hydroxyl ions. Because there is an equal concentration of oxonium and hydroxyl ions (which there must be, because they result from the dissociation of water molecules), their charges cancel, and water carries no net charge.

Pure water at 77°F (25°C) is therefore neutral and provides the standard against which the pH of solutions is measured. This can vary over a wide range, and to simplify it Sørensen used a negative logarithmic scale that produces positive values. The concentration of both ions in water is 10^{-7} moles per liter (mol 1^{-1}), and so that becomes $-\log_{10}(10^{-7})$. Working this through: $-\log_{10}(10^{-7}) = -(-7) = 7$. Water, which is neutral, has a pH of 7.0, and therefore pH 7.0 indicates neutrality.

If a solution is acid, it must contain a higher concentration of hydrogen ions than does water, but because the pH scale is based on the negative logarithm, its pH value will be less than 7.0. If the solution is basic, so it contains a lower concentration of hydrogen ions, it will have a pH value greater than 7.0. The scale is logarithmic to base 10, so each whole-number change in pH represents a 10-fold change in acidity. A solution with pH 3.0 is 10 times more acid than one with pH 4.0.

On the pH scale, oranges are about pH 3.5, lemons 2.0, blood 7.5, seawater 9.0, and oven cleaner 13.5. Strong acids, such as hydrochloric (HCl), sulfuric (H_2SO_4), and nitric (HNO_3), ionize completely in solution. Depending on the extent to which they are diluted, these acids can have pH values of 1.0 or even lower, and when concentrated the pH value may even be negative (less than 0). The highest pH value is 14.0. Sodium hydroxide (NaOH), also known as caustic soda, has a pH of about 14.0. In acidified clouds the pH often averages about 3.5, but the most strongly acid rain that falls on the United States is pH 4.3.

Acid in the air

Hydrochloric acid no longer pollutes the air. Controlling it proved fairly simple and was achieved long ago. Today the most important offenders are sulfur dioxide (SO_2) and nitrogen oxides (NO_X). Sulfur dioxide is produced mainly by burning coal (and to a much lesser extent oil) that contain sulfur as an impurity. Nitric oxide (NO) and nitrogen dioxide (NO_2) are produced wherever very high temperatures occur, such as certain industrial furnaces, but principally in high-compression gasoline engines. Nitrogen dioxide is also produced during the manufacture of nitrogen fertilizer. In parts of China where there are few cars to produce NO_X but where a great deal of coal with a relatively high sulfur content is burned, the sulfur content of rainwater is sometimes 6 times higher than that in New York City, but the nitrogen content is lower.

There are two sets of reactions that convert sulfur dioxide (SO_2) to sulfuric acid (H_2SO_4). One takes place with all the ingredients as gases, the other in liquid water droplets. As gases the sequence is:

$$SO_2 + OH \rightarrow HOSO_2$$
$$HOSO_2 + O_2 \rightarrow HO_2 + SO_3$$
$$SO_3 + H_2O \rightarrow H_2SO_4$$

The liquid reactions are more complex because there are several routes they can follow. The sulfur dioxide may be oxidized directly, or directly with the involvement of a metal catalyst, or by dissolved nitrogen oxides, or by ozone (O_3), or by hydrogen peroxide (H_2O_2) and other peroxides.

Nitric oxide is insoluble, but it reacts readily with ozone to produce nitrogen dioxide, which reacts with hydroxyl to form nitric acid (HNO_3).

$$NO + O_3 \rightarrow NO_2 + O_2$$
$$NO_2 + OH \rightarrow HNO_3$$

At night different reactions also take place involving nitrogen trioxide formed by the reaction between nitrogen dioxide and ozone ($NO_2 + O_3 \rightarrow NO_3 + O_2$) and either an organic molecule (RH) from which a hydrogen atom is extracted ($NO_3 + RH \rightarrow HNO_3 + R$) or a reaction between nitrogen trioxide and nitrogen dioxide. This produces dinitrogen pentoxide (N_2O_5), which dissolves in water ($N_2O_5 + H_2O \rightarrow 2HNO_3$). These reactions occur only at night because NO_3 and N_2O_5 break down rapidly in sunlight.

Rain, gas, fog, and snow

If *acid rain* is a misleading term because all rain is slightly acid, it is also misleading because it is not responsible for the most visible acid damage to plants. As the diagram shows in a very simplified form, factories, power plants, and vehicles emit a range of gases and particles. The gases are oxidized to sulfuric and nitric acids, and in this form, without having dissolved, they may collide with a solid surface and adhere to it. This is called dry deposition. Dissolved acids reach the surface by wet deposition, of which there are three varieties: mist or fog, snow, and rain.

Dry deposition is especially important in dry climates or during prolonged periods of dry weather. In the Los Angeles area, for example, 12 times more nitric acid is deposited dry than in liquid precipitation. Once deposited on leaves, the acid may be absorbed into the leaf cells through the stomata (pores through which gases are exchanged).

Mist and fog differ only in the density of droplets in them (see preface, page xi). Fog is stratus cloud with a base at ground level. Cloud that forms above ground level may nevertheless blanket the sides of mountains that rise into it. That is why you are much more likely to find fog on a mountainside than in a valley.

When you walk through fog it makes you very wet. It is "wetter" than rain. There is a reason for this. Rain falls because it consists of drops that are too heavy to remain airborne. Because it is falling, it strikes mainly those surfaces exposed to it. If it is falling vertically, undersurfaces are not exposed and so they remain dry; if it falls at an angle, driven by the wind, surfaces sheltered from the wind are also sheltered from the rain. Fog droplets are much smaller and remain in the air. Because the fog is not falling, it envelops objects exposed to it, allowing droplets to coat all surfaces, both above and below. The drawing illustrates this. It shows that the head, shoulders, and upper arms of the man standing in the rain will be soaked, but the lower part of his body will remain fairly dry. His brother standing in the fog will be much wetter because no part of his body is protected.

Fog is wetter than rain, and if the water has been acidified, it is also much more acid. Acid fog has an average pH of 3.4. Los Angeles fog sometimes has a pH value as low as 2.2 due to nitrogen oxides from rush-hour traffic. Fog on mountains can be 10 times more acid than rain falling on low ground and 100 times more acid than unpolluted rain.

Part of the reason for this is that small droplets have a combined surface area that is much greater than the surface area of big droplets with a similar total volume. Suppose a volume of 20 (the units are unimportant) is contained by one (spherical) droplet and the same volume is also contained by five droplets. The surface area of the single large droplet is 35.47. That of each of the five small droplets is 12.19, making a total surface area of 60.95 (5 × 12.19).

The small droplets offer a bigger surface for collecting gas molecules, and remain in the air for much longer, so pollutants have more opportunity

Transport of pollutants

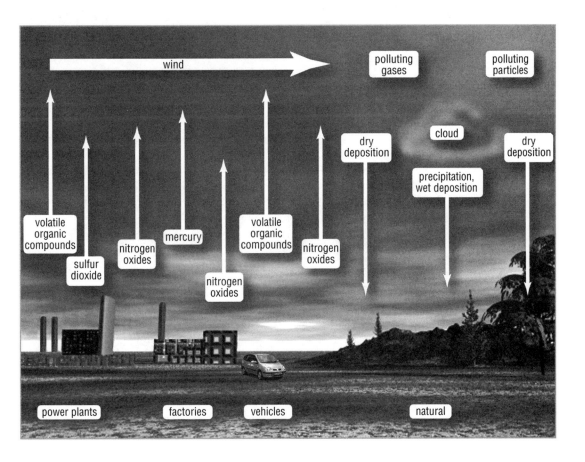

Why fog is wetter than rain. With rain, water falls only on the upper surface. In fog, water coats all surfaces.

to dissolve into them. In addition, acid particles may act as condensation nuclei, so that five small droplets contain five nuclei while a single large droplet contains only one.

Acid fog is therefore likely to have a lower pH than acid rain, and it also coats the surfaces of plants and other objects much more effectively. Consequently, acid fog is more damaging than acid rain.

In winter precipitation often falls as snow, which can also be acidified. The snow may lie on the ground until spring. When it melts the water flows into rivers and lakes, where it can produce a sudden flush of acid that is especially harmful to fish eggs and larvae.

Acid rain, in contrast, causes much less harm to vegetation. It runs off leaves and down plant stems. It does reach the soil, of course, so although it may cause less direct damage to vegetation, it causes indirect damage by altering soil chemistry.

Acidification of soils, forests, and lakes

In the late 1960s Swedish scientists became aware of accelerating acid damage to limestone and sandstone buildings and monuments. Soon afterward they reported effects on lakes in southern Sweden, where fish populations were declining and the water was becoming clearer as its pH fell. As the map shows, by 1970 the precipitation falling over southern Sweden and Norway was below the pH 5.0 that is taken to be the limit for unpolluted rain. Scandinavia was being polluted, but the affected region was not heavily industrial, so it seemed that the pollution must have been coming from elsewhere. When meteorologists plotted the prevailing winds they found the most likely culprits were Britain, Germany, Poland, and Russia.

At about the same time a similar problem was becoming evident in eastern North America and especially in eastern Canada. There the pollution was found to originate in the coal-burning power plants and factories of the U.S. Midwest. By 1980 acid precipitation was affecting a large part of the continent lying to the east of the Great Lakes.

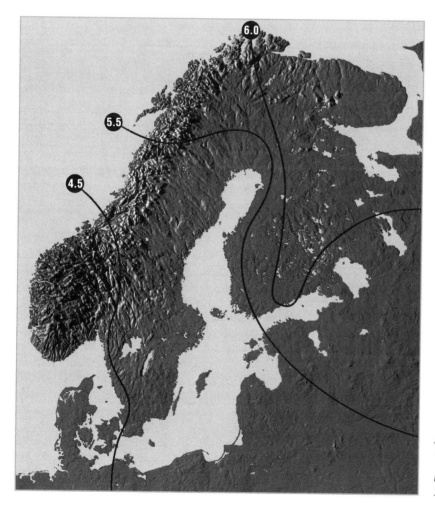

Acid rain in Scandinavia. This shows the average pH of precipitation over Scandinavia in 1970.

Then, in the late 1970s, attention turned to the effect on forests. German coniferous forests were reported to be suffering badly, and environmentalists coined a new term to describe the phenomenon, *neuartige Waldsterben* ("new form of forest death") with the implication that a significant percentage—some said as much as 10 percent—of the country's forests were threatened. Forests elsewhere in central Europe also appeared to be affected, as did some British forests.

Stack height

Clearly, pollutants were traveling a long way, and it became fashionable to dismiss earlier attempts to reduce pollution as having simply transferred it. This was not entirely fair.

Most pollution occurred close to its source, and the effects decreased with increasing distance—just as R. A. Smith had found a century earlier. It was also found that sulfur dioxide caused very little harm at concentrations lower than about 0.025 ounces per cubic foot of air (25 μg m^{-3}) and that as factory plumes spread away from the source, this dilution was reached fairly quickly. It was also found that over the course of a few days atmospheric sulfur dioxide, which is poisonous to plants, is oxidized to sulfate, which is much less toxic, and finally to sulfuric acid, which is toxic but present at such a high dilution as to be harmless.

This suggested that the best way to reduce pollution was to dilute the pollutant more efficiently. Chimney stacks were built taller, many of them to a height of 650 feet (200 m). The tallest stack in the world is 1,250 feet (381 m) tall at a nickel smelter at Sudbury, Ontario. The design of the stacks was also changed to accelerate the flow of gases. This meant the waste gases left the stack at a considerable speed, and the effective stack height (see "Chimney Stacks and Plumes," page 76) was very high. The gases mixed with the air quite quickly high above the chimney, and pollution at ground level was dramatically reduced.

This response usually worked, but it soon transpired that the situation was rather more complex than the engineers had supposed. There were places where the atmospheric conditions sometimes caused fumigation, bringing the plume to the ground and making the pollution worse despite the high chimney stack. In other places the gases were failing to mix with the air, and "slugs" of pollutants were traveling long distances before sinking to the ground. Gases from the Sudbury nickel smelter have been detected in Florida, more than 1,250 miles (2,000 km) away. Finally, it was found that altering the height of chimney stacks had very little effect on pollutant concentrations at a distance of more than 100 miles (160 km). This is because individual factories, where the stacks were built, were the source of only a fairly small percentage of the total pollution. Because they emitted large amounts of pollutant in a particular place, they caused severe local pollution, but farther away their emissions mixed with those from dozens or hundreds of other sources. In any case, despite

Acid rain in North America. The shaded area is the region where the average pH was 5.0 or less in 1980.

being diluted, the pollutants still entered the atmosphere and remained there for long enough to cause trouble. Then it was discovered that although the sulfuric acid in most rain was very dilute, it was often much more concentrated in fog and when deposited dry, and it was able to accumulate in soils.

A new solution had to be found, and it was emission reduction. Factories and power plants in many countries, including the United States, Canada, and the nations of the European Union, no longer emit significant amounts of sulfur dioxide. Between 1980 and 2000, emissions of sulfur dioxide from burning fossil fuels fell from 26.4 million tons (24 million tonnes) to 16.5 million tons (15 million tonnes) in the United States; they are predicted to fall to 15.4 million tons (14 million tonnes) by 2010. The equivalent figures for Europe are 65 million tons (59 million tonnes), 28.6 million tons (26 million tonnes), and 20 million tons (18 million tonnes), respectively. Asian emissions, on the other hand, are predicted to increase dramatically, from 16.5 million tons (15 million tonnes) in 1980 to 87 million tons (79 million tonnes) in 2010. At the time damage from acid rain was arousing most concern, sulfur emissions had already been falling for some time. Emissions of nitrogen oxides continue to increase, however. Although the rate of increase in emissions by the United States and the European Union has slowed greatly since about 1970, global emissions are still rising due mainly to the increasing use of farm fertilizer.

Damage to plants

It is important to remember that pollution is only one explanation for change. From time to time forests decline and recover quite naturally. Over the past two centuries there have been five major declines in different parts of Europe. During the 20th century there were 13 declines in North America, only six of which were linked to air pollution. Nevertheless, there is no doubt that pollution by sulfur and nitrogen have harmed some forests.

In moderate amounts sulfur is a fertilizer and stimulates plant growth, but in larger amounts sulfur dioxide is harmful. At one time it was impossible to grow trees in the Pennines, the range of hills running along a north–south line down the center of northern England, because of sulfur pollution from the industrial regions to both the east and west of the hills. Trees, especially coniferous species such as spruces and pines, were also damaged in parts of central Europe.

Sulfur dioxide was certainly responsible. Many lichen species are extremely intolerant of sulfur dioxide, and different species are killed at different concentrations. This makes it possible to use the distribution of lichens to map sulfur dioxide pollution. In many places where trees were suffering, the susceptible lichens were absent, so clearly sulfur dioxide levels were high. They were not absent everywhere, however. They were abundant in Germany and Scandinavia, proving that whatever was harming the trees in those countries was not sulfur dioxide.

Further research found that in many places the principal cause was nitrogen. This reached trees partly as nitrogen oxides, mainly from vehicle exhausts and power plants, and partly as ammonia (NH_3). Ozone may also have played a part, but this is less certain. Ammonia probably originated as urine excreted by farm livestock. The ammonia evaporates, dissolves in rain, and is then carried back to the ground as ammonia and ammonium (NH_4) compounds.

Nitrogen is a fertilizer, of course, and nitrogen that reaches the ground in the form of nitric acid and ammonia or ammonium stimulates plant growth. This ought to be beneficial, but many forests grow on poor land, and in these areas an excess of nitrogen can be harmful. Other essential mineral nutrients are often deficient on poor soils. Adding nitrogen stimulates tree growth, but the trees then suffer from nutrient deficiencies. The most important effect of this is to interfere with the processes by which plants prepare for winter, making them less able to cope with desiccation and cold. Desiccation occurs in winter because when water freezes plant roots are no longer able to absorb it. It is not only trees that are affected. Grasses, including wheat, also suffer more damage from cold and drought if they receive excessive amounts of nitrogen from air pollution.

Ozone is able to enter plant leaf cells through the pores (stomata) that open to allow carbon dioxide to enter the plant for photosynthesis and oxygen to leave. Once inside the cell, ozone damages the membranes that contain the chloroplasts—the structures in which photosynthesis takes place—and reduces the rate of photosynthesis. There have been experiments suggesting this is a serious cause of injury to plants, but there are doubts as to whether this is really the case in forests.

Acid soils

It is natural to suppose that acid precipitation injures plants directly by falling onto them and flowing across the surfaces of leaves and stems. In fact, however, the serious damage takes place below ground. Acidifying the water that moves through the soil alters the soil chemistry, and it is that alteration that causes harm.

Organic material decomposes more slowly in acid soils than in soils that are neutral. Peat bogs are very acid and are renowned for their ability to preserve organic remains. Decomposition is the mechanism by which plant nutrients are released into the soil water, from where they can be absorbed by roots. Slowing this recycling process can starve plants of nutrients, with adverse effects on their health and rate of growth. Increasing acidity also has other, subtler effects.

Magnesium and calcium are essential plant nutrients. Like other mineral nutrients, they are released by chemical reactions—chemical weathering—from the rocks that supply the mineral component of soils. Clay particles and particles of decomposed organic material carry a negative charge. Magnesium and calcium ions carry a positive charge (Mg^+ and Ca^+, respectively), and so they bind to exchange sites on the surfaces of these particles by the attraction of opposites.

Ions with a positive charge are called cations. When acids dissolve in water they dissociate, so that sulfuric acid, (H_2SO_4) can also be written as $H^+ + H^+ + SO_4^-$ and nitric acid (HNO_3) as $H^+ + NO_3^-$. Hydrogen cations compete with magnesium and calcium for exchange sites on soil particles, and if there are enough H^+ cations they will displace Mg^+, Ca^+, and other cations by a process called mass action.

Soils that have developed from sedimentary rocks are often rich in magnesium and calcium. This is because the commonest sedimentary rocks are made from calcium and magnesium carbonates derived from the remains of the shells of marine organisms that accumulated on the beds of ancient seas. An abundance of cations makes it more difficult for hydrogen to dominate. This type of protection from acidification is called buffering. Well-buffered soils are less likely to be affected by acid precipitation. Poorly buffered soils, developed from such rocks as granite—

igneous rocks that originated as molten rock deep below ground—are more vulnerable.

Mass action can also liberate aluminum cations. Aluminum is very abundant in all soils, but the element is so strongly reactive that it never occurs in the pure form. There are aluminum cations (Al^+) attached to exchange sites, however, and if the pH falls below about 5.5 and there are overwhelmingly large numbers of hydrogen cations, some of the aluminum cations are dislodged. They enter the water in the soil, where they form groups in which one aluminum cation is surrounded by six molecules of water. If the pH falls below 5.0, one of the water molecules dissociates into OH^- + H^+, and the H^+ leaves the group. The aluminum cation is then surrounded by five molecules of water and one hydroxyl (OH^-). This increases the soil acidity.

Free aluminum cations can also enter the root hairs of plants. They are absorbed in the same way as magnesium and calcium and take their place. This blocks the further absorption of magnesium and calcium, leading to a nutrient imbalance in the plant. At the same time, the aluminum interferes with the movement of water through the plant, reducing the plant's ability to withstand drought.

Acid lakes

Acid precipitation lowers the pH of the water in the soil, and eventually the acidified soil water finds its way into rivers and finally to lakes. Lake water may be buffered, just like soil water. It is buffered by the presence of bicarbonate ions (HCO_3^-). Bicarbonate neutralizes the acid: H^+ + HCO_3 → H_2O + CO_2. This reaction delays any harmful effect and maintains the pH at higher than 6.0, but if strong acid continues to enter the lake, the stock of bicarbonate is depleted faster than it can be replaced from rivers flowing into the lake. A point is reached at which the pH fluctuates widely, and if acidification continues the pH finally stabilizes, usually below 5.0. Metal ions, especially aluminum, start to accumulate.

The first effect is a reduction in the number of species of single-celled plants, the phytoplankton, as the pH falls, although the total mass of these plants remains constant. The number of species of invertebrate animals also falls. Studies in Sweden found that water with about 17 invertebrate species at pH 7.0 had about 15 at pH 6.0, but only about 3 at pH 5.0 and none at pH 4.5. Fish are also affected.

Norwegian fisheries inspectors first reported damage to fish from acidification in the early years of the 20th century. Brown trout *(Salmo trutta fario)* do not migrate, and their numbers were declining in Norwegian mountain lakes as long ago as the 1920s. In 1940 about 8 percent of Scandinavian lakes had no brown trout. By 1960 this had increased to about 18 percent, and by 1975 it reached 50 percent. By the 1970s many lakes in southern Norway and Sweden had no fish at all. Salmon numbers began falling sharply in southern Scandinavian rivers in the 1970s.

The fish may have been succumbing to a reduction in their food supply—salmon and trout feed on invertebrate animals—but this was only part of the problem. They were also being poisoned by aluminum.

Fish absorb the oxygen they need for respiration through their gills. These consist of large areas of membranes that are permeable to oxygen and carbon dioxide. The membranes are also permeable to sodium and chloride ions, however, and salt is also lost in urine. Salt (sodium chloride, $Na^+ + Cl^-$) must be replaced by absorbing sodium and chloride through the gills. Calcium ions in the water reduce the loss of sodium and chloride and help prevent hydrogen from entering through the gill membranes. Increasing acidity reduces the concentration of calcium in the water, and fish die through losing sodium faster than they can replace it.

The permeability of the membrane is regulated by calcium cations. If the pH falls below 5.5, calcium can be replaced by aluminum. This reduces the ability of the gills to absorb oxygen, but the presence of aluminum also stimulates the production of mucus that clogs the gills. The fish suffer a respiratory illness that weakens them.

Ordinarily, freshwater lakes are slightly alkaline (pH 6.5–9.0). Freshwater fish can tolerate water at pH 6.0–6.4 unless the buffering reaction has resulted in very high levels of dissolved carbon dioxide. Fish begin to be affected seriously when the pH falls below 5.0, although some species can survive at pH 4.0 provided acidification occurred very gradually. Few species can survive below pH 3.5.

How serious is the problem?

Freshwater acidification became widespread and caused considerable harm in many parts of Europe and North America. Rising concern from scientists, conservationists, and sport anglers led governments to seek ways of reducing acid emissions. A "30 percent club" formed, comprising nations that committed themselves to reducing sulfur emissions by that amount, and little by little this was achieved. Between 1970 and 1998, for example, U.S. emissions of sulfur dioxide fell by almost 37 percent, although emissions of nitrogen oxides increased by almost 17 percent during the same period.

Benefits from this reduction have been slow to appear. This is not surprising, because the harm from acidification was due to a major shift in the chemistry of surface waters that inevitably takes a long time to reverse. The Ecological Society of America (ESA) has found that water quality is improving in the Northeast and upper Midwest of the United States. There is less sulfate and less aluminum in the water. Sulfate concentrations have not been falling in parts of the Southeast and East, although sulfur deposition has decreased. In addition, rivers are not recovering in the White Mountains of New Hampshire. The ESA found no sign or recovery in the Adirondacks, but researchers at the Darrin Fresh Water Institute of the Rensselaer Polytechnic Institute at Troy, New York, detected an increase in pH in about half of the 30 Adirondack lakes they studied. They found nitrogen levels had fallen in 18 of the 30 lakes, and there was an overall reduction in sulfuric acid. Nitrogen, rather than sulfur, is the principal cause of freshwater acidification in the western United States Rivers and lakes there have not recovered.

Forests are less seriously affected. The early alarm arose partly from an error in measuring damage. The first victim of acid rain was Norway spruce (*Picea abies*, also known as common spruce). It was believed to be suffering if it had lost more than 10 percent of its needles. Approximately one-third of trees had lost this many needles, and so the effect seemed to be extensive. Foresters then pointed out that many perfectly healthy trees lose more than 10 percent of their needles. There is now an internationally recognized system for classifying damage based on the percentage of needles lost. This is set out in the table.

Tree species vary in their susceptibility to acid damage. When German forests were assessed in 1986 by the federal authorities using the new classification, it was found that the total damage amounted to 17.3 percent of all species in class 2 and 1.6 percent in classes 3 and 4. A survey in 1999 found that about 25 percent of forest trees in Europe were suffering at least moderate damage (class 2 or higher). This suggests little change over the preceding decade. In Norway, however, there are clear signs of improvement.

The reasons for the damage also vary from species to species and from place to place. In the western United States, for example, ponderosa and Jeffrey pines (*Pinus ponderosa* and *P. jeffreyi*), white fir (*Abies concolor*), Californian black oak (*Quercus kellogii*), incense cedar (*Libocedrus decurrens*), and sugar pine (*P. lambertiana*) are suffering damage from ozone that began in the 1950s. Spruce (*Picea* sp.) and fir (*Abies* sp.) have suffered along the Appalachian Mountain chain, where in some places there was a rapid deterioration during the 1980s. Not all the damage can be attributed to acid rain, however. Insect and fungal infestations and drought have also contributed.

There are some fears that reducing air pollution by dust particles may actually increase the damage caused by acid precipitation. This is because

CLASSES OF ACID RAIN DAMAGE

Class	Percentage needle loss	Damage
0	less than 10	none
1	11–25	slight
2	26–60	moderate
3	61–98	severe
4	more than 99	tree is dead

some dust particles act as cations, buffering the water in clouds and thereby reducing the acidity of precipitation before it falls. A reduction in atmospheric cations has been measured since the 1960s over most of Europe and North America. Provided this reduction does not offset the benefits from reducing acid emissions, eventually forests, lakes, and rivers will recover from the effects of acidification.

OZONE AND ULTRAVIOLET RADIATION

Spray cans and the ozone layer

In 1985 the scientific journal *Nature* published a paper by three British scientists working for the British Antarctic Survey. The scientists were J. C. Farman, B. G. Gardiner, and J. D. Shanklin, and the title of their paper was "Large Losses of Total Ozone Reveal Seasonal ClO$_x$/NO$_x$ Interactions". This was the paper that reported the existence of what was quickly nicknamed "the ozone hole."

Publication of the paper marked a major development in a scientific story that began in the early 1970s and that culminated with two very important events. One was the signing in 1987 of the Montreal Protocol on Substances That Deplete the Ozone Layer, an international agreement reached under the auspices of the United Nations Environment Program. The other momentous event was the award of the 1995 Nobel Prize in chemistry to Paul Crutzen, Mario Molina, and F. Sherwood Rowland for having identified chlorofluorocarbon compounds (CFCs, also known as Freons; see sidebar, page 111) as being the substances principally responsible for the destruction of stratospheric ozone.

What is the ozone layer?

Ozone is a version of oxygen in which the molecule contains three oxygen atoms (O_3) rather than the two (O_2) of ordinary oxygen—often called diatomic oxygen to distinguish it. The gas was discovered in 1840 by the German–Swiss chemist Christian Friedrich Schönbein (1799–1868). Ozone has a very distinctive, acrid smell—it is the smell generated by electric sparks—and Schönbein called it *ozon* from the Greek word for "smell." In 1881 a British chemist, W. N. Hartley, found that ozone is a normal constituent of the upper atmosphere, where there is more of it than there is near the surface. In fact, about 90 percent of all the atmospheric ozone is found in the stratosphere (see sidebar, pages 105–106).

Amounts of atmospheric gases are sometimes reported in Dobson units (DU), and these units are always used to describe the amount of ozone. The unit is named for the British meteorologist G. M. B. Dobson (1889–1976), who spent much of his life studying atmospheric ozone. The Dobsun unit refers to the thickness, measured in millimeters multiplied by 100, that the gas would have if it were extracted from the air and then subjected to sea-level pressure. The layer of atmospheric ozone would then be about 3 millimeters (0.12 inch) thick, so the atmosphere contains about 300 DU. Ozone is produced mainly in the middle and upper stratosphere over equatorial regions. Air movements then transport much of it to the lower stratosphere over the poles. The average atmospheric content therefore varies from about 260 DU over the equator to 400 DU inside the Arctic and Antarctic Circles. The polar ozone is most concentrated between about 66,000 feet and 98,000 feet (20–30 km). This is the 'ozone layer.'

How ozone forms and is destroyed naturally

Sunlight consists of a wide spectrum of electromagnetic radiation. Violet has the shortest wavelength of visible light (and red the longest). Just beyond violet there lies ultraviolet (UV). For convenience the full waveband of UV radiation, ranging from about 4 nanometers (nm) to 400 nm, is divided into three sections, known as UV-A (315–380 nm), UV-B

Structure of the atmosphere

The atmosphere extends from the surface to a height of more than 600 miles (965 km), where it merges imperceptibly with the Sun's atmosphere. Our atmosphere has no precise upper boundary. About half of the total mass of the atmosphere is compressed by gravity into the lowest 3.5 miles (5.5 km), and only 10 percent lies more than 10 miles (16 km) above the surface.

Temperature changes with height throughout most of the atmosphere. Whether it increases or decreases divides the atmosphere into clearly defined layers. Counting upward from the surface, these are the troposphere, stratosphere, mesosphere, thermosphere, and exosphere. The layers are shown in the diagram with their heights.

The troposphere extends from the surface to a boundary called the tropopause. Its height averages 10 miles (16 km) above the equator, seven miles (11 km) over middle latitudes, and five miles (8 km) over the poles. Temperature decreases with height throughout the troposphere. This is the layer in which air rises by convection, causing it to be well mixed. It is the layer in which all weather phenom-

ena occur, although these are influenced by conditions in the lower stratosphere.

Temperature remains constant with height in the lower stratosphere. From about 12 miles (20 km) the temperature begins to increase with height, and it increases more rapidly above about 20 miles (32 km). The upper boundary of the stratosphere is called the stratopause. It is at about 29 miles (47 km), and above it lies the mesosphere.

Temperature remains constant with height in the lower mesosphere, but above 35 miles (56 km) it falls rapidly all the way to the mesopause, at a height of about 50 miles (80 km).

Again, the temperature remains constant with height in the lower thermosphere, but it begins to increase rapidly above about 55 miles (88 km). The thermosphere extends to the thermopause, some 310–620 miles (500–1,000 km) above the surface.

The exosphere lies above the thermopause. It has no upper boundary, and within it atoms and molecules are so widely scattered that they may never collide with one another.

(continues)

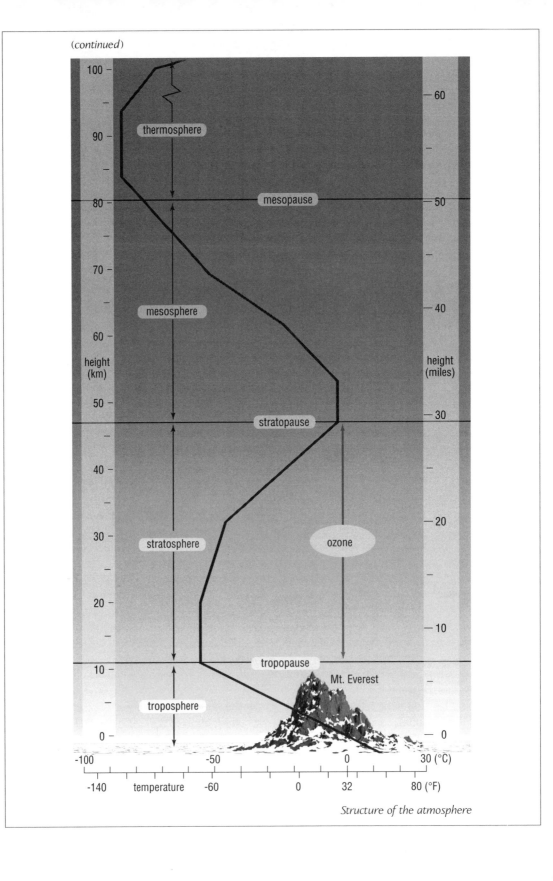

Structure of the atmosphere

(280–315 nm), and UV-C (shorter than 280 nm). UV-B is also called soft UV and UV-C is called hard UV. UV at 400 to 300 nm is called near UV, at 300 to 200 far UV. At wavelengths below 200 nm it is known as extreme UV or vacuum UV. A nanometer (nm) is one-billionth (10^{-9}) of a meter, or one-thousandth (10^{-3}) of a millimeter (1 nm = 0.0000394 inch).

UV radiation is able to break the bonds that link oxygen atoms. Ozone then forms in two steps:

$$O_2 + UV \text{ (less than 243 nm)} \rightarrow O + O$$
$$O_2 + O + M \rightarrow O_3 + M$$

M is a molecule of another element, usually nitrogen. It absorbs momentum from the oxygen molecule and atom, allowing them to bond together. The second reaction becomes slower with increasing altitude. This is because the air becomes rarer, reducing the likelihood that the O_2 and O will encounter the other molecule *(M)*. The first reaction accelerates with increasing altitude because the intensity of UV increases.

UV at a longer wavelength also destroys ozone:

$$O_3 + UV \rightarrow O_2 + O$$

This reaction also accelerates with increasing altitude, again because the intensity of UV increases. The changes in the rates of the reactions favor the production of O at high altitude and O_3 at lower altitude. This is partly offset by the fact that reactions involving UV cease at night and during the polar winter.

Some ozone is destroyed by reacting with single oxygen atoms:

$$O_3 + O \rightarrow 2O_2$$

but this reaction is very slow. In the lower stratosphere, where there is less O, ozone is destroyed by reacting with the hydroxyl radical (OH) and the short-lived hydrogen dioxide (HO_2):

$$O_3 + OH \rightarrow HO_2 + O_2$$
$$HO_2 + O_3 \rightarrow OH + 2O_2$$

Much more ozone is destroyed by reactions involving a catalyst, a substance that is necessary for a reaction to occur but that is not altered by that reaction.

Ozone, atmospheric structure, and climate

Stand outside in bright sunlight and before long you will start to feel warmer. Your clothes and exposed skin absorb solar energy and in doing so convert it to heat. Atmospheric molecules are no different. When they absorb a unit—called a photon—of solar radiation, its energy causes them to move faster, and so their collisions become more frequent and more violent. Those collisions are what we feel and our instruments measure as the temperature. When the air absorbs sunlight, its temperature rises.

The air is almost completely transparent to sunlight except for UV radiation at the wavelengths involved in the production and destruction of ozone. All of the UV-C and most of the UV-B are absorbed in the upper atmosphere, and the UV radiation that reaches the surface is almost entirely UV-A. The absorption of UV raises the temperature of the region of the atmosphere in which it takes place. That is why the air temperature increases with height through most of the stratosphere (see sidebar, pages 105–106).

When a layer of warm air lies above cooler air it acts as a lid, sealing the lower air. Air that rises from below reaches a level at which the air above it is less dense, so it can rise no further. This situation is called a temperature inversion (see sidebar, page 8). The stratosphere constitutes a huge worldwide temperature inversion. It explains why the atmosphere below the stratopause exists as two distinct layers—the stratosphere and troposphere—and why weather phenomena are held in the lower layer. Were it not for ozone, convection would carry air all the way to the top of the stratosphere, and the climates of the world would be very different. We would not be aware of this, of course, because an atmosphere without ozone would contain no oxygen, either, so there could be no air-breathing forms of life.

Stratospheric ozone also absorbs energy that would otherwise penetrate to the surface, where it would be absorbed and converted to heat. Without ozone to absorb energy at high altitude, the world climates would be warmer than they are, although the difference would be quite small.

The ozone hole

In winter air in the stratosphere over the North and South Poles becomes very still. The winds blow around the core of calm air, forming a polar vortex, or polar night vortex, because it is present only during the polar night. At a height of about 9 miles (15 km) the temperature in the air inside the antarctic polar vortex is usually just above –109°F (–78°C), which is the freezing temperature for water vapor at this altitude. Thin clouds of liquid droplets or ice crystals form there, and clouds of minutely small ice crystals form at about 15.5 miles (25 km), where the temperature is about –121°F (–85°C). These are called polar stratospheric clouds (PSCs). Air inside the arctic polar vortex is usually too warm for the second type of PSCs to form. About half of the water vapor for the formation of PSCs is supplied by the oxidation of methane (CH_4) to carbon dioxide (CO_2) and water (H_2O) by reactions with the hydroxyl radical. The other half is supplied by very small ice crystals that cross into the stratosphere over the equator. The amount of water that enters the stratosphere by this means has increased in recent years. Scientists believe the increase may be due to forest fires in equatorial regions, because these produce very small particles of ash that rise to a great height, where water vapor freezes onto them, then continue rising through the tropopause.

The cloud droplets and ice crystals also contain nitric acid (HNO_3), formed mainly from nitrogen dioxide (NO_2) and hydroxyl in the presence of a catalyst (M):

$$NO_2 + OH + M \rightarrow HNO_3 + M$$

Various reactions remove ozone from the stratosphere, but the most important begin on the surface of ice crystals in the PSCs and involve chlorine (Cl) that is released into the air to react with ozone. The significance of these reactions arises from the fact that the last reaction in the series returns the chlorine to the air, thus allowing the sequence to be repeated and therefore allowing one chlorine atom to destroy several thousand ozone molecules. Eventually the chlorine is trapped by a reaction that forms hydrochloric acid (HCl), which then dissolves in a water droplet that is large enough to fall back into the troposphere. This is a slow and uncertain process because hydrochloric acid tends to break down, releasing free chlorine and producing nitric acid in reactions with chlorine nitrate ($ClONO_2$).

$$HCl + ClONO_2 \rightarrow HNO_3 + Cl_2$$
$$and\ ClONO_2 + H_2O \rightarrow HNO_3 + HOCl$$
$$then\ HOCl + UV \rightarrow OH + Cl$$

Chlorine is also released from hydrochloric acid by reacting with hydroxyl.

$$HCl + OH \rightarrow H_2O + Cl$$

The chlorine then reacts with ozone.

$$2(Cl + O_3 \rightarrow ClO + O_2)$$
$$ClO + ClO + M \rightarrow Cl_2O_2 + M$$
$$Cl_2O_2 + UV \rightarrow Cl + ClO_2$$
$$ClO_2 + M \rightarrow Cl + O_2 + M$$

UV is ultraviolet radiation and M is any other molecule. Nitrogen dioxide interrupts these reactions by converting ClO back into $ClONO_2$, but other reactions on the surfaces of ice crystals remove nitrogen oxides (NO_x) by a process called denoxification.

The PSCs form in winter, during the polar night. At this time the reactions involving UV cease, and consequently ozone is not being formed. However, chlorine is being released, and denoxification is taking place. Ozone levels fall gradually, but in spring the returning sunlight allows the UV-driven reactions to resume. By summer—the beginning of November in Antarctica—the polar vortex breaks down and the ozone layer is replenished by ozone carried from lower latitudes. The recovery is incomplete, however, so that the average amount of ozone in the antarctic stratosphere decreased each year during the 1980s and 1990s.

Ozone depletion was less marked over the northern polar region. Stratospheric winter temperatures are higher over the arctic than over the antarctic because Antarctica is a large continent and colder than the Arctic Ocean. Consequently, the polar vortex is smaller over the arctic and breaks down earlier in the year.

The CFCs

These are reactions that take place among substances present naturally in the stratosphere in variable amounts. Volcanic eruptions can inject large amounts of chlorine into the stratosphere, for example, and this causes ozone levels to plummet. Solar storms intensify the stream of charged particles known as the solar wind, which can break interatomic bonds to produce dramatic falls in the amount of ozone. These events are short-lived, however, and once they are over the ozone level soon recovers.

The problem Crutzen, Molina, and Rowland identified arose when additional chlorine was added to the stratosphere in a steady and increasing stream. Scientists had been aware of the risk for some time. Certain types of rockets used to launch satellites and space vehicles release chlorine in their engine exhausts. Each space shuttle launch releases about 75 tons (68 tonnes) of chlorine, for example, and the Titan IV releases about 35 tons (32 tonnes). This destroys ozone, but only locally and temporarily. As the chlorine is removed from the air by natural processes, the ozone concentration rises to its previous level.

The new source of chlorine was a class of chemical compounds known as chlorofluorocarbons (CFCs) or by their trade name of Freons (see sidebar). These had many uses, all of which exploited their two most significant properties: stability and low boiling point. The low boiling point made CFCs eminently suitable for use in refrigeration and air conditioning equipment and as propellants in aerosol cans. Their stability made them completely nontoxic and also meant they could be used in fire extinguishers and as foaming agents in foam plastics. Their final virtue was that they were simple and cheap to manufacture on an industrial scale. They were invented in 1930, but global production of them accelerated rapidly from less than 200,000 tons (182,000 tonnes) in 1960 to more than 1.2 million tons (1.1 million tonnes) in 1988.

Several of their uses—in aerosol cans and fire extinguishers, for example—involved injecting them into the air directly. Other uses, such as in foam plastics and refrigerators, released them eventually, usually when the articles containing them reached the end of their lives and were destroyed. They also entered the air by leaking during their own manufacture and the assembly of the goods in which they were used. Because they were highly stable, CFCs did not react with other atmospheric constituents. They remained in the air completely unaltered until, little by little, they were carried across the tropopause and into the stratosphere. The most widely used CFCs, CFC-11 and CFC-12 (Freon-11 and Freon-12) survive in the atmosphere for approximately 45 years and 100 years, respectively.

CFCs and Freons

Freon is the trade name for a class of chemical compounds invented in 1930 by scientists working for the DuPont Company. They contain chlorine, fluorine, and/or bromine. Chemically, they are derived from alkanes (also called paraffins), which are hydrocarbons with the general formula C_nH_{2n+2}, by substituting fluorine for chlorine in an inexpensive compound. Chlorine and fluorine belong to the class of elements known as halogens, and CFCs are therefore classed as haloalkanes.

The effect of substituting fluorine for chlorine is to lower the boiling temperature of the resulting compound by about 90°F (50°C) for each atom substituted. Carbon tetrachloride (CCl_4) boils at 168.8°F (76°C), for example. Substituting fluorine for one chlorine gives CCl_3F, which is CFC-11 and boils at 77°F (25°C).

Before being phased out, the most widely used compound was CFC-12 (CCl_2F_2), which boils at −21.64°F (−29.8°C). Other CFCs that had fewer uses include the compounds CFC-22 ($CHClF_2$), CFC-113 (CCl_2FCClF_2), and CFC-114 ($CClF_2.CClF_2$).

The low boiling temperatures means CFCs change between liquid and gas at around room temperature. This property made them useful as refrigerants.

Also, the addition of fluorine tightens the molecular structure. As the diagram of CFC-12 shows, the molecule is shaped like a tetrahedron—a pyramid with a triangle at its base. A carbon atom is located at the center of the pyramid. It is able to bond with four atoms, and these are located at each of the four corners of the tetrahedron. Each halogen atom is pulling at an electron in the carbon atom, the carbon atom refuses to part with them, and consequently the bonds are very strong. This strength makes CFC-12, and all CFCs, chemically inert. CFCs do not react with other substances and are completely harmless if ingested or inhaled at concentrations as high as 20 percent continuously for several hours. This made them safe to use as propellants in aerosol cans and medical inhalers and as a gas to be blown into foam plastics.

Their chemical stability also means they will not react with oxygen, and therefore they will neither burn nor explode. Consequently, they could be used in fire extinguishers because they would smother flames and separate the burning material from its oxygen supply.

Production of them increased during the 1930s. During the 1940s they were introduced as dispersants for insecticides, such as DDT and pyrethrum, used to control disease-carrying insects such as mosquitoes.

In the stratosphere they are exposed to UV radiation. This is able to break one of the strong bonds holding the molecules together, in each case releasing chlorine.

$$CCl_3F \text{ (Freon-11)} + UV \rightarrow CF_2CL + Cl$$
$$CCl_2F_2 \text{ (Freon-12)} + UV \rightarrow CClF_2 + Cl$$

Recognition of the way CFCs were releasing free chlorine into the stratosphere led to the agreement in 1987 of the Montreal Protocol on Substances That Deplete the Ozone Layer. This is the international scheme by which the manufacture and use of CFCs and other substances that deplete stratospheric ozone is being phased out. Although CFCs are

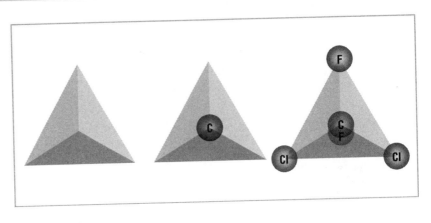

CFC-12. A carbon atom (C) is located in the center of the "pyramid." Carbon can bond with four other atoms. In this molecule these are two fluorine (F) and two chlorine (Cl) atoms arranged so that the molecule is shaped like a tetrahedron.

no longer used, their long atmospheric lifetimes mean it will be some time before stratospheric ozone increases to its former concentration and the "hole" disappears. The 2001 annual report of the Montreal protocol showed that by 1999 global use of ozone-depleting substances had fallen to 18 percent of its peak level, reached during the late 1980s. In the early southern spring of 2001 the hole was about the same size as it had been the previous winter, covering an area of about 10 million square miles (26 million km^2), but the depletion was less severe. The amount of ozone was 100 DU in 2001, compared with 98 DU in 2000 and 88 DU in 1993, the year when the depletion was worst. The hole is defined as the region where the total ozone is less than 200 DU.

Ozone depletion, UV exposure, and health

Depletion of stratospheric ozone allows more UV-B radiation to penetrate to the surface. This is serious, because exposure to too much UV-B damages living cells. In humans it causes eye cataracts and skin cancer, although mainly of a type that is easily cured, as well as causing aging symptoms, such as wrinkles.

The ozone hole depletion is centered over the uninhabited continent of Antarctica, but the hole expanded in the years following its discovery until at times it covered New Zealand. There was also some thinning of the ozone layer in the middle latitudes of both hemispheres, in 1998 amounting to about 3 to 6 percent below 1976 levels. Had the depletion continued the health effects might have become serious, but the depletion that actually occurred was sufficient to produce only a small effect.

The amount of UV-B radiation reaching the surface depends on the latitude and is greatest at the equator. The amount of UV-B that reaches the surface in New Orleans (latitude about 30°N), for example, is almost 50 percent greater than the amount to which people are exposed in New York City (about 40°N). The amount of additional UV-B penetrating to the surface because of depletion of the ozone layer is equal to the increase to which a person living in middle latitudes would be exposed by moving approximately 125 miles (201 km) closer to the equator.

It is true that in recent years there has been an increase in the incidence of skin cancer, but this increase is due mainly to the popularity of sunbathing and taking summer holidays in lower, warmer climates. It is likely that ozone depletion will cause an increase in skin cancers. This is expected to reach a maximum in 2060 of about 3 percent of the U.S. total number of cases and about 5 percent of all deaths from skin cancer.

NATURAL POLLUTERS

Volcanoes

On June 15, 1991, a mountain in the Philippines exploded. The explosion ejected ash into the lower atmosphere. Carried by the tropical easterly winds, this ash settled to the surface all the way from the Philippines to India. The explosion also hurled 15 to 20 million tons (14 to 18 million tonnes) of sulfur dioxide into the stratosphere. The plume spread quickly, and within three weeks it had formed a broad belt that extended right around the Earth. It altered the weather perceptibly. The winters of 1991–92 and 1992–93 were up to 5.4°F (3°C) warmer than average over North America, northern Europe, and northern Asia, but cooler over the Middle East and the southern part of the Southern Hemisphere. The summer of 1992 was up to 3.6°F (2°C) cooler than usual, and the effects could still be felt the following summer.

The mountain, called Pinatubo, is located on the island of Luzon. It is a volcano, of course, and its 1991 eruption was the second most violent volcanic eruption of the 20th century. (The most violent was that of Mount Katmai-Novarupta in 1912.) Pinatubo had been silent for 500 years but was aroused by a major earthquake that occurred 60 miles (100 km) to the northeast. It erupted a few hours after the earthquake. The gases it released included water vapor, hydrochloric acid, hydrogen, nitrogen, hydrogen fluoride, hydrogen sulfide, methane, ammonia, carbon dioxide, and sulfur dioxide. As well as these, the explosion ejected about 1.2 cubic miles (5 km^3) of molten rock and ash that formed a mushroom-shaped cloud 22 to 25 miles (35 to 40 km) high and 310 miles (500 km) across.

What is a volcano?

Beneath the solid rock of the Earth's crust—the ground on which we stand—lies a region called the mantle. It comprises rock that is much denser than the rocks of the crust, but it is so hot and compressed under such immense pressure that it behaves like a very thick liquid. The mantle is approximately 1,800 miles (2,900 km) thick, very much thicker than the crust, and it extends all the way to the Earth's core. The diagram shows the structure of the Earth, though not to scale.

The hot, plastic rock at the top of the mantle and the base of the crust is called magma. It is held under great pressure, and if there are cracks and fissures in the crustal rocks it will rise upward through them. That is how a volcano starts.

Rising magma accumulates deep below ground in a hollow space in the crust known as a magma chamber. Hawaiian volcanoes arise from primary magma chambers about 35 miles (56 km) below sea level. As more and more magma enters the chamber the pressure inside increases until it overcomes the strength of the rocks above. Then the magma rises through the overlying rocks, following the path of least resistance—which is often the path taken during previous eruptions—to fill a secondary magma chamber closer to the surface. As pressure inside the secondary chamber increases its roof may expand upward, making the overlying rocks bulge. The bulge is visible at the surface. It is called a lava dome, and its appearance indicates that the magma chamber is filling and an eruption is imminent.

Eventually, magma starts to rise through the overlying rocks. The route it follows is called a chimney. Many volcanoes have additional secondary magma chambers to either side of the primary chamber, each with its own chimney.

Lava rising from the magma chamber has to shatter the rocks above it, pushing them out of the way. This produces many small earthquakes. Volcanologists, scientists who study volcanoes, install instruments called seismometers around volcanoes they suspect of becoming active. When they detect these earthquakes they know the magma is rising.

When magma approaches the surface it is called lava. As the pressure on it eases, the lava expands and becomes more fluid. Just how fluid it becomes depends on its composition and temperature. The temperature of lava at the point where it leaves the top of the lava chimney ranges from about 1,340 to 2,175°F (727–1,190°C), depending on the mineral composition. Generally, the hotter it is, the more volatile substances are dissolved in it, and the less silica it contains, the more liquid the lava is and the faster it flows. Silica (silicon dioxide, SiO_2) is the commonest mineral in rocks of all kinds.

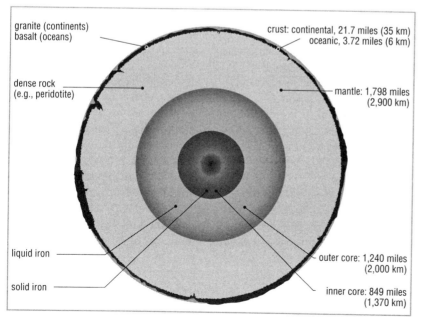

granite (continents)
basalt (oceans)

crust: continental, 21.7 miles (35 km)
oceanic, 3.72 miles (6 km)

dense rock
(e.g., peridotite)

mantle: 1,798 miles
(2,900 km)

liquid iron

outer core: 1,240 miles
(2,000 km)

solid iron

inner core: 849 miles
(1,370 km)

Structure of the Earth

Stages in a volcanic eruption. 1) Lava rises from the magma chamber, and the volcano erupts. 2) The eruption partly empties the magma chamber. 3) With the pressure relaxed inside the magma chamber, the top of the volcano collapses into it, leaving a crater, or caldera.

The eruption partly empties the magma chamber closest to the surface. This reduces the pressure inside the chamber until it is no longer able to support the weight of the rocks above it. These collapse into the chamber, forming a crater, or caldera, at the surface. This is the familiar volcanic crater. The diagram shows the sequence of events.

What remains of the magma chamber then consists of a layer of hot rocks that are weaker than the rocks around them. Their weakness allows magma rising at some time in the future to push them aside and rebuild the magma chamber ahead of a fresh eruption in the same place.

Volatiles

Magma is held under great pressure while it remains in the mantle or at the base of the crust, and substances that would be gases at lower pressures are held in solution in the rocks. These substances are called volatiles. Water, carbon dioxide, and sulfur dioxide are among the compounds commonly present in magma. However, the magma may contain far more of these compounds than is needed to saturate it. The Pinatubo lava contained much more than this, proving that there were bubbles of gas in the magma 3–6 miles (5–10 km) below the surface or possibly lower.

As the rising lava approaches the surface it starts to cool, and minerals within it begin to form crystals. Crystallization "squeezes" the dissolved volatiles out of solution. They form bubbles, adding to the bubbles that exist already, and as the crystals continue to grow the bubbles are compressed into a smaller and smaller volume. The pressure increases until some of the gases blast an opening to the outside and escape through the vent. Immediately after this happens, the sudden reduction in pressure causes the remaining volatiles to come out of solution and explode into the air as a froth of gas and molten rock. This kind of frothy mass is called a *nuée ardente* ("blazing cloud"), and a very powerful explosion can send the top of it all the way to the stratosphere. The temperature inside the cloud is 480–930°F (250–500°C). It is made from material that is denser than the surrounding air, so it sinks and flows downhill at the surface at speeds up to 125 MPH (200 km/h), destroying everything in its path. A cloud of ash and fire racing along at this speed is possibly the most terrifying kind of storm a volcano can produce.

Types of volcano

Pinatubo is a stratovolcano. This is the same type of volcano as Mount Vesuvius, Mount Fuji, Krakatau in Indonesia, and Mount Egmont in New Zealand. Lava pouring from a central vent solidifies around the vent, building a conical mountain with steep sides. At the time of its 1991 eruption, the top of Pinatubo was about 5,725 feet (1,745 m) above sea level. The eruption blasted away almost 500 feet (150 m) from the top.

The lava that produces a volcano of this shape contains more than 55 percent silica, but it also contains a high percentage of volatiles. They cause violent explosions, so the eruption comprises intermittent explosions alternating with flows of fairly viscous lava. The rocks and ash, the pyroclastics, ejected in the explosions fall back onto the solidifying lava, building up a cone of alternating layers—or strata, hence the name—of lava and pyroclastics. The diagram shows a cross-section through a stratovolcano such as Pinatubo.

Pyroclastics can build cones by themselves called pyroclastic cones. A pyroclastic cone has even steeper sides than a stratovolcano, but it is smaller. Paracutín, Mexico, is a typical pyroclastic cone and is only about 1,350 feet (412 m) high.

Truly giant volcanoes, such as Mauna Kea (13,797 feet; 4,205 m) and Mauna Loa (13,682 feet; 4,170 m) on Hawaii, are shield volcanoes. They

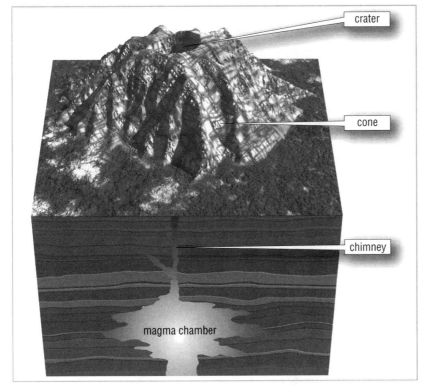

crater

cone

chimney

magma chamber

Cross section of a volcano

are made from more fluid lava containing less silica than are stratovolcanoes. Because it is more fluid, the lava flows farther before it solidifies and builds a broad cone with sides that slope less steeply than the sides of a stratovolcano.

Shield volcanoes are built from lava that solidifies to form the rock basalt. Basalt lava can also ooze from a fissure in the ground and spread to the sides without forming a cone. This results in a basalt flood that can cover a very large area. A flood of this kind happened in the western United States 14 to 17 million years ago. It is called the Columbia basalt flood. The map shows its location, with the Columbia River flowing across it. It covers about 85,000 square miles (220,000 km²), but it is far from being the world's largest: the Karroo flood in South Africa covers 772,000 square miles (2 million km²).

Columbia basalt flood. The shading marks the area covered by the basalt flood on the borders of Washington, Oregon, and Idaho.

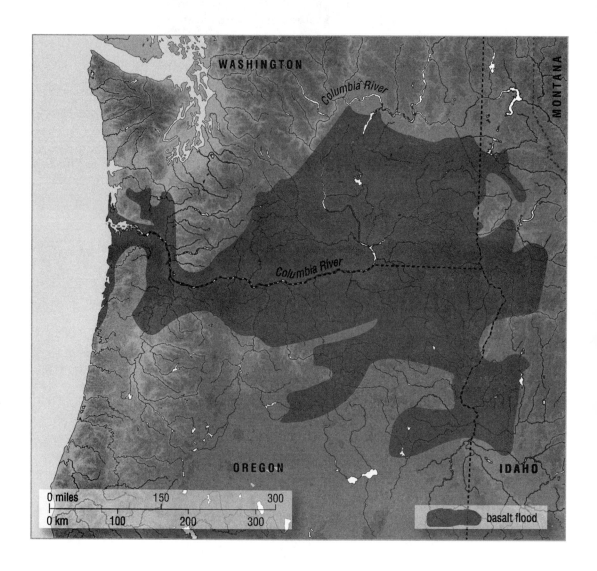

Types of eruption

Mount Pinatubo exploded in very much the same way as did Vesuvius in the year 79 C.E. That eruption buried the city of Pompeii so quickly beneath ash that the inhabitants had no time to escape. One of the victims, killed on a nearby beach and not in the city, was a Roman scholar named Gaius Plinius Cecilius Secundus, born in 23 C.E. and better known as the writer and naturalist Pliny the Elder. Volcanic eruptions of this type are called plinian in his honor.

Plinian eruptions are one of a number of types of volcanic eruptions. Vesuvius usually erupts less violently than it did in 79 in what are known as subplinian or vesuvian eruptions. These are explosive and happen after the volcano has been dormant for a very long time. During this period of dormancy, gas pressure builds up in the lava chimney until it is powerful enough to blast the plug sealing the top of the chimney high into the air. The initial explosion is followed by a flow of frothy lava, with clouds of ash and gases.

The most violent eruptions of all are called peléean, after Pelé, the Hawaiian goddess of volcanoes. They are often preceded by the appearance of a lava dome, and they usually produce *nuées ardentes*. Shield volcanoes also occur in Hawaii. These do not erupt explosively, but they often produce spectacular fire fountains—literally, fountains of molten lava up to 650 feet (200 m) high that continue for some time. Eruptions of this type are called hawaiian.

In 1963 an eruption off the coast of Iceland created a new island, called Surtsey, which gave its name to the type of eruption that produced it. A surtseyan eruption occurs when water floods into an open volcanic vent. The water at the base of the column boils and vaporizes, but it is prevented from expanding by the weight of the water above it. Pressure builds up and the volume of water vapor increases until the whole vent explodes, throwing a column of material up to 12 miles (20 km) into the air.

In Roman mythology Vulcan, the son of Jupiter and Juno, was thrown out of heaven by his parents and fell to earth on the island of Lemnos in the Aegean Sea. His fall, which took an entire day, left him lame. He became the god of fire, called on to prevent fires as well as capable of starting them, and from time to time he caused volcanoes to erupt. Vulcanian eruptions are explosive and occur when gas pressure in a fairly viscous magma blows off the overlying solid crust. The eruption ejects gas, ash, and rocks of all sizes, but no new lava. Eruptions of this type often continue for some time.

Stromboli, the island volcano off the Italian coast in the Tyrrhenian Sea, has also given its name to a type of eruption. Strombolian eruptions produce frequent but only moderately violent explosions that throw lava into the air. It falls back to build a steep-sided cone.

Where the volcanoes are

Volcanoes erupt at places where magma is able to rise through the rocks of the crust. There are two kinds of places where this can happen: at plate margins and above hot spots.

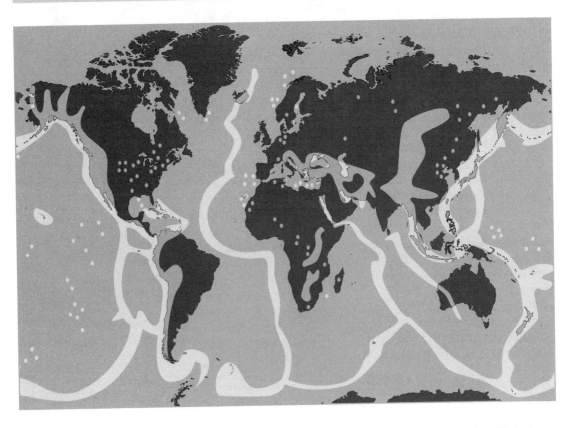

Major volcanic and
earthquake zones

Earth's crust is composed of large, rigid blocks of rock called plates, which rest above the denser material of the mantle. Convection currents in the mantle cause the plates to move in relation to one another, and it is at the boundaries between them, called plate margins, that magma may be able to rise to the surface. These are the regions where earthquakes are most likely to occur and where volcanoes are most likely to erupt. The map shows how they are distributed around the world.

Hot spots are places away from plate margins where magma penetrates the crust beneath the ocean floor. They are caused by convection currents that bring a plume of mantle rock up against the base of the crust. The plume remains in the same place while the plate slowly moves over it. This produces a chain of submarine volcanoes and, if the volcanoes are big enough, volcanic islands. The Hawaiian Islands lie at the end of a volcanic chain of this kind. They form part of the Hawaiian-Emperor chain, extending from the Meiji Seamount off the coast of the Kamchatka Peninsula to Hawaii, that began forming about 70 million years ago. A seamount is an isolated volcanic mountain rising from the ocean floor that is not high enough to project above the surface of the sea. The map shows the position with respect to the stationary hot spot that the moving plate had reached 50, 40, 30, 20, and 10 million years ago. Hawaii moved over the hot spot less than 2 million years ago.

Why volcanoes affect the weather

Not every volcanic eruption affects the climate. In order to do so an eruption must eject a large amount of fine particles into the stratosphere. There is very little vertical movement of air in the lower stratosphere, but air does move horizontally. This means that material injected into the lower stratosphere spreads horizontally but falls only very slowly, so it remains in the upper atmosphere for months or even years.

The climatic effect is greatest if the volcano is close to the equator. That allows the material it places in the stratosphere to spread into the opposite hemisphere, and once it has done that it can affect the climate in both hemispheres.

The climatic effect is due to reflection. Every surface reflects light. The percentage of the light falling upon it that a surface reflects is called

Hawaiian-Emperor chain. The hot spot has remained in the same place while the plate has moved. The hot spot is now directly beneath Hawaii.

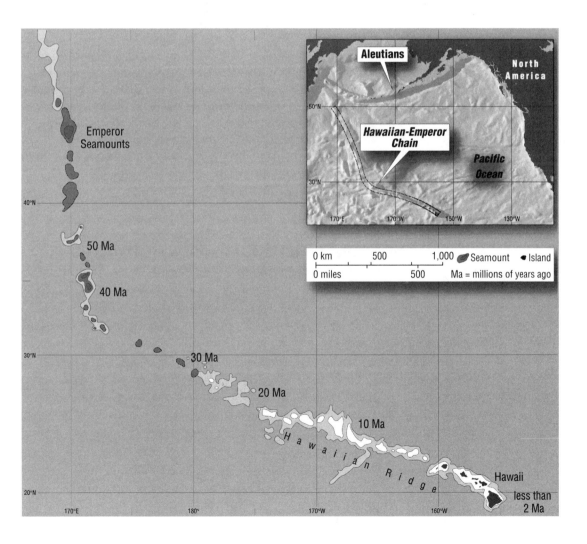

its albedo. If it reflects all of the light it has an albedo of 100 percent, written as 100 or, more often, as 1. If it absorbs all the light, reflecting none at all (although there is no such surface), it has an albedo of 0. The average albedo for the Earth as a whole is about 0.3, or 30. Freshly fallen snow has an albedo of 0.75 to 0.95, and a black road surface has an albedo of 0.05 to 0.10. Ordinarily, the stratosphere has no albedo at all because air is transparent. Small particles do reflect light, however, and so they add to the planetary albedo by reflecting incoming light. They form a veil that is too high and too thin to be visible but that shades the surface just a little. This has a cooling effect.

The veil is invisible, but the particles have another effect that can be seen. Volcanic dust produces spectacular sunsets. They happen because the particles scatter some of the light that collides with them in all directions. How much of the light is scattered depends on its wavelength. Short-wave light—violet and indigo—is scattered so thoroughly by air molecules in the upper atmosphere that these colors disappear completely. Air molecules in the lower atmosphere scatter blue light. Scattering makes the light reach us from all directions, so that a clear daytime sky is blue. Fine particles also scatter yellow, orange, and red light, and soon after dawn and just before sunset, when the sun is low in the sky, they scatter it the most. This is because when the sun is low its light has to pass through a greater thickness of air than it does when higher. The air itself scatters the blue and green light to such an extent that it filters it out, and the light reaching the surface is yellow, orange, and red, the colors of dawns and sunsets. Red dawns and sunsets happen occasionally, but for months after a major eruption they are commonplace.

Volcanic eruptions and climate

Without the particles that Mount Pinatubo injected into the stratosphere when it erupted in 1991, the summers of 1992 and 1993 would have been warmer than they were, but the Pinatubo eruption was a very minor affair compared with the biggest eruption of the 20th century. That was the eruption of Mount Katmai, and it was so violent that when it subsided it left a lava dome that is now a volcano in its own right called Novarupta.

The Katmai eruption began on June 6, 1912, and lasted for 60 hours. Katmai lies at the center of the Katmai National Park in Alaska, created in its honor in the Valley of Ten Thousand Smokes. The map shows its location.

Valley of Ten Thousand Smokes was the name Robert Griggs gave it when he visited the valley in 1916 on behalf of the National Geographic Society. His was the first visit since the eruption to what was then a remote area—Mount Katmai is about 265 miles (425 km) southwest of Anchorage, at 58°N, 155°W. Griggs found that the valleys of Knife Creek and the

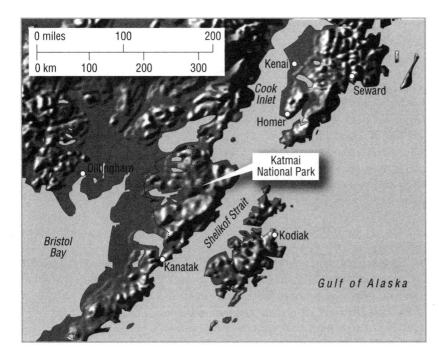

Katmai, Alaska

Ukak River had been covered by ash. Altogether, ash covered more than 40 square miles (104 km²), and in some places it was 700 feet (214 m) thick. As much as a foot (30 cm) of ash had fallen 100 miles (160 km) away. There were countless small cracks in the ash through which steam and gas were escaping from the water below ground that had been heated by the lava. These were the ten thousand smokes. The water has cooled now, of course, and the smokes are no longer to be seen.

The eruption apparently began about 10 miles (16 km) from Katmai at a vent situated where Novarupta is today. As this eruption died down it raised the lava dome that is now Novarupta, 1,300 feet (395 m) across at the base and 2,760 feet (841 m) high. This eruption excavated a space in the rocks that caused Katmai itself to collapse, forming a caldera about 2 miles (3 km) across and 1,970 feet (600 m) deep.

Pinatubo ejected about 1.2 cubic miles (5 km³) of magma. Novarupta-Katmai ejected an estimated 3.5 cubic miles (15 km³). The column of dust, ash, and hot gas from Pinatubo reached a height of about 18.6 miles (30 km). The plume from Novarupta-Katmai rose higher than 16.8 miles (27 km).

Sulfur dioxide and other gases ejected by Novarupta-Katmai produced acid rain over a vast area (see "Acid Rain, Snow, Mist, and Dry Deposition," page 90). It tarnished brass in Victoria, British Columbia, 1,500 miles (2,400 km) away, and it weakened the fibers of clothes hanging to dry on clotheslines in Vancouver, on the mainland opposite Victoria, to such an extent that the clothes partly fell to pieces. Their owners accused store-keepers of selling shoddy goods.

The particles hurled so high into the air also affected the weather. They shaded out so much sunlight that on Kodiak Island, a few miles away across the Shelikof Strait, it remained almost pitch dark for two days after the eruption. The haze became visible in Washington, D.C., a few days later, and eventually it was visible as far away as Africa. It reduced the amount of solar radiation reaching the surface by 20 percent, according to measurements made in California and Algeria that probably represent the effect over all of the Northern Hemisphere. That summer the average temperature over the Northern Hemisphere was about 1.8°F (1°C) below normal. It was a "year without a summer."

Mount Agung is a volcano on the island of Bali, Indonesia, that erupted in March 1963. The eruption was violent, although nothing to compare with the eruption of Katmai. It ejected 0.07 to 0.14 cubic miles (0.3 to 0.6 km³) of magma to a height of 11 miles (18 km), and the plume contained about 11 to 22 million tons (10 to 20 million tonnes) of sulfate particles. After six months these had spread through the stratosphere to blanket the entire Earth, reducing the temperature by about 1°F (0.5°C). This was too small a temperature drop to have any measurable climatic effect, but the dust produced spectacular sunsets over the next few years.

Tambora and Frankenstein

There have been other "years without summers." The most famous—or notorious—was in 1816. That was the year when snow fell over eastern North America in June and covered the ground as far south as Pittsburgh. Connecticut had frosts every month of the year, and in Quebec City there were days in June when the temperature failed to rise above freezing. The killing frosts came to New England in September.

The changed weather altered wind patterns and the way weather systems tracked across the Northern Hemisphere, with some curious results. Ukraine enjoyed a heat wave, and while most of Europe shivered and the harvests failed, there was a fine summer in the north of Scotland. In England the temperature in July and August was 4.8°F (2.7°C) below average, and there was a fairly heavy fall of snow in the eastern part of the country on September 22, with severe frost in London. Southern England rarely experiences snow before January. It was one of the most disastrous harvests ever known in England, and there were food riots. Approximately 92,000 people died worldwide in the famine that fol-lowed the eruption.

There were also other results from that dismal summer. A group of friends had planned a vacation in a house they had rented near Geneva, Switzerland. The party consisted of the poet Percy Bysshe Shelley, his wife Mary, and Mary's stepsister Claire Claimont, and Lord Byron, who was staying at another house nearby. The weather was so bad that there were many days when they were unable to go outdoors at all, so they devised ways to pass the time. They read ghost stories aloud to one another, and then Byron suggested that each of them should write one. Byron and Shelley soon tired of this and gave up, but Mary persevered. The result of her effort was published in 1818 with the title *Frankenstein or, The Modern Prometheus.*

It was dust from a volcano that robbed the world of its summer that year. Mount Tambora, in what is now Indonesia, had erupted in April 1815, and it had taken this long for the veil of particles to blanket the Earth. The winter of 1815–16 and spring of 1816 were unremarkable. It was not until May that the effects started to become apparent, as the temperature failed to rise as it should.

The eruption was one of the most violent in the past few thousand years. It ejected more than 12 cubic miles (50 km^3) of magma to a height of more than 25 miles (40 km). The material it ejected included about 220 million tons (200 million tonnes) of sulfate crystals, and it was the sulfate that reflected sunlight, lowering surface temperatures by about 2°F (1°C).

At the time Tambora erupted, the stratosphere still carried a load of particles from earlier eruptions, so the Tambora particles added to the stratospheric pollution that was already present. Volcanoes had erupted in 1812 on the island of St. Vincent, in the Caribbean, and one of the world's most active volcanoes, Mount Awu, on the Sangihe Islands, Indonesia, had also erupted—for the first time since 1711, after its longest quiet period ever. There were further eruptions in 1814 in the Philippines.

Krakatau

Krakatau (formerly known as Krakatoa) is a small volcanic island in the Sunda Strait, between Djawa (Java) and Sumatera (Sumatra), Indonesia. In 1883 several volcanoes in the vicinity became active, and Krakatau began erupting on August 26 and continued until August 28. A series of increasingly violent explosions hurled more than 2.4 cubic miles (10 km^3) of rock, ash, dust, and gases more than 25 miles (40 km) into the sky. This was the second largest volcanic eruption in recorded history, after that of Tambora.

The Krakatau eruption is remembered mainly for the huge tsunami that swept over the coast of Djawa, killing more than 36,000 people. It also produced brilliant sunsets and unusually cool weather across the world, although the fall in temperature was slight and occurred too late in the year for it to affect harvests.

Lakagígar

Benjamin Franklin (1706–90), who had a life-long interest in meteorology, was the first scientist to suggest a link between volcanic eruptions and bad weather in comments he made on the weather of 1783. These were published in 1784 as "Meteorological Imaginations and Conjectures," a paper he submitted to the Literary and Philosophical Society of Manchester (see "Acid Rain and Manchester Air," page 85). Franklin wrote:

> During several of the summer months of the year 1783, when the effect of the sun's rays to heat the earth in these northern regions should have been greater, there existed a constant fog over all Europe, and a great part of North America. This fog was of a permanent nature; it was dry, and the rays of the sun seemed to have little effect towards dissipating it, as they easily do a moist fog, arising from water. They were indeed rendered so faint in passing through it, that when collected in the focus of a burning glass they would scarce kindle brown paper. . . .
>
> The cause of this universal fog is not yet ascertained. Whether it was adventitious to this earth, and merely a smoke, proceeding from the consumption by fire of some of those great burning balls or globes which we happen to meet with in our rapid course round the sun, and which are sometimes seen to kindle and be destroyed in passing through our atmosphere, and whose smoke might be attracted and retained by our earth; or whether it was the vast quantity of smoke, long continuing to issue during the summer from Hecla in Iceland, and that other volcano which arose out of the sea near that island, which smoke might be spread by various winds, over the northern part of the world, is yet uncertain.

Franklin's "fog," which was really a haze of particles, extended from Iceland to Syria, North Africa, and the Altai Mountains in western Siberia. The eruption responsible for it is unlikely to have been that of Hekla, which erupted in 1768. It is almost certain to have been Lakagígar, which is a fissure in the rocks rather than a single volcano, extends for 25 miles (40 km) and comprises about 100 individual craters (*Lakagígar* means "Laki craters"). Mount Laki, 2,684 feet (818 m) high, is the volcano that stands near the center of the fissure.

Franklin reported that it resulted in a particularly severe winter, but he was not in a position to say how severe. In fact, the temperature that winter over the Northern Hemisphere as a whole was about 2°F (1°C) below the average, but in eastern North America the effect was much worse. There the winter was 8.6°F (4.8°C) colder than the 225-year average, and it was 1790 before winter temperatures recovered to their preeruption levels.

In England there was a wet summer and then a blizzard lasting from December 7 to 9, followed by severe frost. Gilbert White (1720–93) noted in his *Natural History and Antiquities of Selborne* (published in 1789) that "This frost killed all the furze and most of the ivy, and in many places stripped the hollies of all their leaves" (furze is gorse, *Ulex europaeus*). White also reported that two men in the village of Selborne suffered frostbite in their feet and two others in their fingers.

Lakagígar began to erupt on June 8, 1783, and the eruption continued for about 50 days, during which it ejected about 3 cubic miles (12.6 km³) of lava, rocks, and ash. This was the biggest lava flow recorded in historical time (there were much larger ones in prehistoric times), and it covered 218 square miles (565 km²). More significantly, the eruption released huge amounts of sulfur dioxide. Some of this formed an estimated 88 million tons (80 million tonnes) of sulfuric acid. The acid poisoned crops, and fluoride compounds that were also among the gases condensed, settled to the ground, and contaminated the pasture, fatally poisoning around 53 percent of all the cattle, 72 percent of the horses, and 83 percent of the sheep. The resulting famine, known as the Haze Famine, caused the deaths of about 9,000 people—approximately one-quarter of the Icelandic population at the time. The cloud of gases and ash drifted as far as France, where some of that year's crops were lost and some livestock were poisoned. The unrest this produced may have contributed to the discontent that led to the French Revolution of 1789.

Lakagígar may not have been the sole cause of the haze affecting areas far from Iceland. Mount Aso-san in Japan also erupted in August 1783, ejecting particles that very probably added to those from Iceland.

El Chichón and Mount St. Helens

Volcanic eruptions continue to pollute the air and affect the weather. El Chichón in Mexico had lain silent for centuries. Then, in March 1982, it awoke. The eruption commenced on March 26 and continued until the middle of May, with especially violent explosions on March 29 and April 4. The March 29 explosion killed 100 people, and the one on April 4 released a huge cloud of dust and gas. The full death toll amounted to approximately 2,000.

El Chichón ejected 0.07 to 0.08 cubic miles (0.3 to 0.35 km³) of material to a height of 16 miles (26 km). The ejected matter included up to 3.6 million tons (3.3 million tonnes) of sulfur dioxide. All of this was converted to sulfuric acid, and by May 1 the cloud had encircled the Earth. By June it had reduced surface temperatures by about 0.4°F (0.2°C). A year later it covered almost all of the Northern Hemisphere and much of the Southern Hemisphere.

Mount St. Helens in the Cascade Range, Washington State, exploded on May 18, 1980. It ejected 0.8 cubic miles (0.35 km³) of material to a height of 13.7 miles (22 km). Ash that remained in the lower atmosphere settled to the ground as the plume crossed the United States. The map shows the area affected by it. It was a major eruption, but the climatic effect was to reduce the average temperature for a few months by only about 0.2°F (0.1°C).

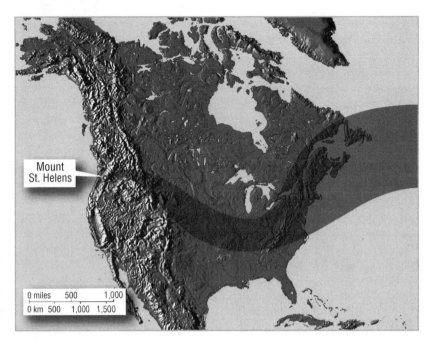

0 miles   500   1,000
0 km 500   1,000 1,500

Mount St. Helens. The shading indicates the area of North America covered in ash fallout from the 1980 eruption.

Volcanoes are a major natural source of atmospheric pollution, and, as these examples show, they can have catastrophic consequences. We think of volcanoes as sending rivers of molten lava to destroy fields and villages or producing spectacularly beautiful fireworks in the night sky. They do these things, of course, but they can also have more sinister effects. The dust and gases they release into the stratosphere can cause famines in which thousands of people lose their lives.

Killer trees?

When we think of acid rain or smog, the pictures that spring to mind are of factory smokestacks, power plants, and freeways crammed with six lanes of nose-to-tail cars. The pictures are accurate, but they tell only part of the story—albeit the part we can do something about—because nature also pollutes the air. The previous section described how volcanoes can cause acid rain, and this is not difficult to imagine. After all, an erupting volcano is not that different from a factory chimney. It is just a great deal bigger, and there are no controls to limit its emissions. It is a polluter without a license.

It is more difficult to accept that parts of the natural environment that we like and think beautiful and worth preserving are also major polluters. We love forests, and we are quite right to do so. Forests confer all kinds of benefits. They support a wide range of plants and animals and also help in moving water from the ground to the air and in reducing the force of the wind. We enjoy walking through them. Many of our folk tales and fairy stories are set in them, although in fairy stories they are often dark and dangerous places where humans easily lose their way and where fierce animals, evil witches, and malevolent goblins dwell. Images of forests are deeply embedded in our culture. It comes as a shock, therefore, to learn that they are a major cause of smog—but they are.

Similarly, we love the ocean, even those of us who live in the center of a large continent thousands of miles from the coast. We may never see the sea, but tales of seafaring and exploration are an integral part of the culture of most peoples. The sea is clean and represents nature at its purest. We worry about overexploiting the resources it contains and polluting it with our wastes. It seems wrong to suppose that the ocean—or, more correctly and even worse, certain of the organisms that inhabit the ocean—cause acid rain, but they do.

Clouds over the ocean

Water vapor will condense to form cloud droplets only if there are cloud condensation nuclei present (see the section Evaporation and Condensation). The nuclei are needed to provide surfaces onto which the liquid can collect. This is not a problem over land, because there is always a certain amount of dust in the air. On average there are 80,000 to 100,000 cloud condensation nuclei in every cubic inch of air (5 to 6 million per liter). That is ample for the condensation of vapor. When the relative humidity approaches 100 percent, clouds form without difficulty.

Over the open ocean, thousands of miles from the nearest land, the situation is rather different. Ocean air is very clean. This means it is dust-free. Each cubic inch of ocean air contains an average of only 16,000 cloud condensation nuclei (1 million per liter). This is not enough for clouds to be able to form at all easily. Therefore, we should expect the sky over the oceans to be largely clear of clouds but the air to be very moist. As every satellite picture shows, however, there is as much cloud over the oceans as there is over land. How can this be?

The sulfur cycle

The answer to the puzzle was discovered by James Lovelock, the English chemist who is best known for being the principal author of the Gaia hypothesis (see sidebar, page 131). Like many scientific discoveries, it arose almost serendipitously out of a quite different investigation.

Elements that are biologically important, such as nitrogen, carbon, phosphorus, and sulfur, move constantly in biogeochemical cycles that take them from the ground to water to the air and back again. Living organisms use these elements—our bodies are made from them—and drive the cycles along by moving the elements around. Most of the major cycles are fairly well understood, but Lovelock was not happy with the description of the sulfur cycle.

At some point in their cycles, each of these elements finds its way to the sea. In order for the cycle to continue, there must be a way for it to return to the land, and the only way that is possible is through the air. Each element must return to the air, drift over land in the moving air, and then adhere to solid surfaces or dissolve in water and fall to the ground in raindrops. Bacteria living in the mud of estuaries and coastal waters use sulfur and produce hydrogen sulfide (H_2S) gas as a by-product. Some of the hydrogen sulfide escapes into the air, and scientists supposed that it returned to land in this form. There is a difficulty with this, however, because hydrogen sulfide smells very strongly of rotten eggs. If sulfur were traveling as hydrogen sulfide, the air near estuarine and coastal muds would stink of bad eggs, but it does not. (It would also be poisonous to breathe, rather than invigorating.)

Lovelock discovered that what really happens is more interesting, more complicated, and produces a strong, distinctive smell. It is the fresh, clean smell of the sea. Sulfur is returned to the air not as hydrogen sulfide from mud-dwellers but by single-celled plants that drift near the ocean surface—the phytoplankton.

Many of these plants contain a compound called dimethylsulfoniopropionate (DMSP), which they make from precursor compounds. They are not the only plants that contain DMSP. It is also found in seaweeds, marsh grasses, and other plants that grow in salty places. DMSP regulates the movement of water across the membrane enclosing the cell, and the amount of it in the cell varies according to the salinity of the water surrounding the cell. This is vital to the survival of the cell. If the salinity inside and outside differ, water will enter or leave the cell, either dehydrating it or bursting it, and if the salt content rises too high the cell will die. When the plant dies or is eaten, the DMSP is released into the water, where enzymes break it down into acrylic acid (also called propenoic acid, $CH_2{:}CH.COOH$) and dimethylsulfide ($(CH_3)_2S$, or DMS. Other plant compounds also decompose to DMS, but DMSP is the most important and best known.

The substances themselves had been known for a long time. DMS was first identified and analyzed in 1935, and it was not long after that DMSP was identified as its precursor. DMSP was first extracted and its characteristics described in 1948. There was no secret about the compounds. What Lovelock discovered was their "Gaian" role in cloud formation and the cycling of sulfur.

Some DMS escapes into the air, where it is rapidly oxidized by hydroxyl (OH) or nitrate (NO_3) radicals. The products of this oxidation are sulfur dioxide (SO_2), sulfuric acid (H_2SO_4), dimethylsulfoxide (DMSO; CH_3SOCH_3), methanesulfinic acid (MSIA; $CH_3(O)OH$), and methanesulfonic acid (MSA; CH_3SO_3H). All of these form particles in the air

The Gaia hypothesis

While working as a consultant to NASA (the National Aeronautics and Space Administration) during the preparations for the Viking program to place two landers on the surface of Mars, James Lovelock, philosopher Dian Hitchcock, and others discussed how it might be possible to detect whether a planet supports life. Extraterrestrial life is likely to be utterly different from any kind of life on Earth, so how would we recognize it? They reasoned that any living organism must absorb certain substances (nutrients and a source of chemical energy) obtained from its environment and excrete metabolic waste products into its environment. These activities would alter the chemical composition of the environment. Such alterations should be detectable, because the composition of the environment would then be different from the equilibrium it would reach if it were subject only to physical and chemical laws.

The idea that living organisms inevitably alter their environment led to the realization that, having altered it, their activities—respiration, feeding, excretion—inevitably maintain it in its altered state. This is the state that is congenial to them, and so it follows that conditions on a planet that supports life are significantly altered and managed by the living organisms to their own advantage. In fact, life takes over the running of the planet.

This can be seen clearly in the case of Earth, where in the absence of life the atmosphere would contain very little nitrogen and methane if it also contained oxygen, because both nitrogen and methane would be oxidized and disappear. With the help of energy supplied by lightning, nitrogen would form soluble nitrates and be washed to the surface in rain, and methane would be converted to carbon dioxide and water. Their presence indicates that these gases are constantly being returned to the air, and because no inorganic chemical reactions are capable of this, biological processes are most likely responsible—and, of course, they are. Venus and Mars, in contrast, have atmospheres that are in chemical equilibrium, and their compositions are easily explained. Living organisms also regulate the temperature of the lower atmosphere by adding or removing carbon dioxide and the salinity of the oceans by adding or removing salt.

Lovelock discussed this idea with a friend, the novelist William Golding, who suggested that the new concept be called "Gaia." In Greek mythology Gaia (or Ge) represents the Earth. Lovelock's proposal has since become known as the Gaia hypothesis. (A hypothesis is a proposed explanation for certain phenomena that awaits testing by experiment.)

There are two versions, called "weak" and "strong." The weak version holds that the cycles through which elements move are driven mainly by the action of living organisms. These cycles involve carbon, nitrogen, phosphorus, sulfur, iodine, and other elements, which move between the rocks of the solid Earth, the atmosphere, and the oceans. The strong version takes this further and holds that the Earth is itself a living organism.

Bioremediation, in which bacteria are used to clean up pollution, and the suggestion that the addition of iron to ocean water might stimulate marine algae (phytoplankton) to remove more carbon dioxide from the air and thus modify the climate are both "Gaian" ideas. The hypothesis has also proved very fruitful in directing scientific thought toward the possibility of biological explanations for phenomena. Nevertheless, it remains controversial, and many scientists find it unacceptably vague or reject it outright.

either by themselves or by linking to other compounds. The resulting particles form ideal cloud condensation nuclei, and it is onto them that water vapor condenses.

This is how it is possible for clouds to form freely over the open ocean. It is also the chemical route by which sulfur moves from the ocean to the air. Once airborne, some of the sulfur is carried over land in drifting clouds, and some unoxidized DMS released close to the shore just drifts through the air to produce the smell people associate with seaside vacations.

DMS and acid rain

Sulfur dioxide reacts with water to form sulfuric acid, adding to the sulfuric acid that forms directly by the oxidation of DMS. Sulfuric acid is a strong acid. When particles of it act as cloud condensation nuclei the resulting cloud droplets are acid, and the precipitation that falls from the cloud is also acid.

MSA (methanesulfonic acid) is another strong acid. It forms mainly during the day by reactions between DMS, hydroxyl, and oxygen. At night DMS reacts mainly with nitrate radical. MSA is a major product of DMS oxidation, and it, too, exists as particles that act as cloud condensation nuclei. Consequently, it also triggers the formation of acidic clouds and acid precipitation.

Plants are not the only source of DMS. Cattle also release it as a gaseous by-product of their digestion of proteins (all of which contain sulfur), and if cattle do so the chances are that other ruminant animals—sheep and goats—do so as well. Farms are therefore contributing to acid rain.

Acid rain from DMS is probably unimportant in urban areas where there are other and bigger sources of acid. In remote areas, however, far from any source of industrial pollution, DMS can acidify the rain and snow significantly. That is how ocean plants can and do cause acid rain.

Killer trees

Photochemical smog—the yellow-brown haze with the acrid smell—is a feature of large cities with sunny climates (see "Photochemical Smog," page 55). We associate it with Los Angeles, where it was first identified, Mexico City, and Athens, although it is common in many other cities as well. Those are not the only places where you are likely to encounter it, however. You may find it out in the countryside. Your immediate reaction might be to suppose the pollution has been carried on the wind from some distant city, so you blame the city for setting you coughing and rubbing your eyes, but you would be wrong. Rural smog is produced by the countryside itself—by the plants. It is smog, all right, but it is entirely natural.

Professor Reinhold A. Rasmussen, now at the Oregon Graduate Institute of Science and Technology, was the first scientist to draw attention to the role of plants in causing air pollution. It was his research that led President Ronald Reagan to make his famous off-the-cuff remark about trees and volcanoes generating more pollution than automobiles, the remark critics dismissed as some ludicrous reference to "killer trees." The president overstated the case, but we now know that Professor Rasmussen was correct.

It has even given a range of mountains their name. The Blue Mountains, near Sydney, Australia, are named for the blue haze that often hangs over them. That is natural smog. A similar haze often hangs over the Dandenong Ranges in Victoria, Australia, and the Blue Ridge and Great Smoky Mountains in the United States are probably named for the blue haze or "smoke" that often colors them.

The haze is caused by terpenes emitted from pine needles. These react rapidly with ozone to produce minute particles less than 0.1 μm (0.000000004 inch) across. Particles of this size scatter sunlight, and blue is the color they scatter most efficiently. Scattering makes blue light fly off in all directions, so it reaches your eyes from all directions, and that is why you see a blue haze over the mountains—in fact, over the forests that grow on the sides of the mountains.

Isoprene and terpenes

Terpenes are a group of chemical compounds. You can smell many of them (although some are odorless), and all the odors are pleasant. When you walk through a pine forest, for example, there is a distinctive smell of pine. Pine wood often retains it, and pine resin also has it. What you smell are two substances, alpha-pinene and beta-pinene, belonging to the terpene group.

It is not only pine trees that produce terpenes. The smell of citrus fruit is due to limonene. Celery smells of beta-selinene. Camphene gives both ginger and citronella oil their odor. All of these are terpenes or derivatives of them, as are the smells of turpentine, camphor, sage, eucalyptus, aniseed, oil of wintergreen, sandalwood, rose, and menthol.

No one knows precisely why these plants produce their delicious smells. Some attract pollinating insects, and some of the oils that release the smells may protect the plant against fungal disease. Monoterpenes are known as essential oils and are found in small reservoirs inside leaves and pine needles. They deter animals from eating the leaves or needles by making them ill. Insects, rabbits, and hares are deterred in this way.

Terpenes released by leaves may help regulate the internal temperature and the loss of water by transpiration. It is possible, however, that many terpenes are incidental by-products of plant metabolism.

Terpenes in animals have definite biological functions. Vitamin A (retinol) is a terpene, and so is rhodopsin, the pigment found in the rod cells of the eye retina that allows us to see in dim light. There are also terpenes in shark oil and cod liver oil.

Plants manufacture acetic acid (also called ethanoic acid, CH_3COOH); it is the raw material (the fatty acid) from which the amino acid glycine is assembled. Molecules of acetic acid combine to form mevalonic acid ($C_6H_{12}O_4$), which is converted to isopentenyl pyrophosphate, a compound that contains the basic unit of isoprene (C_5H_8). Terpenes consist of isoprene molecules joined together forming monoterpenes ($C_{10}H_{16}$), sesquiterpenes ($C_{15}H_{24}$), diterpenes ($C_{20}H_{32}$), and so on. Rubber is a polyterpene with more than 1,000 isoprene units. Carotenes, the pigments that give carrots and tomatoes their color, are probably made from isoprene units.

But pollutants?

Plants release isoprene and terpenes in response to sunlight, and the amount they release increases with rising temperature. They vaporize readily and are therefore classed as volatile organic compounds, or VOCs. In fact, isoprene and terpenes from plants are by far the largest source of atmospheric VOCs. They are also soluble, so those that fail to evaporate are soon washed away by the rain.

Deciduous trees (trees that shed all their leaves in winter) emit more isoprenes and terpenes than do evergreen trees, despite the associations these compounds have with pine forests. The amount released varies greatly from one tree species to another: some emit up to 10,000 times more VOCs than others. Scarlet (*Quercus coccinea*), red (*Q. rubra*), and willow (*Q. phellos*) oaks emit large amounts, as do London plane (*Platanus acerifolia*), California sycamore (also called Californian plane, *P. racemosa*), liquidambar (*Liquidambar styraciflua*), poplars (*Populus* sp.), and eucalyptus (*Eucalyptus* sp.).

What happens to these VOCs once they are in the air depends on the amount of nitrogen oxides (NO_X) present. In bright sunlight ultraviolet radiation drives the reactions that convert NO_X into ozone (see sidebar, page 59). If VOCs are also present, the ozone reacts with them to produce the range of compounds that make up photochemical smog—including more ozone.

Unburned hydrocarbons, mainly from gasoline and diesel engines, are the principal source of VOCs in towns and cities, but even there isoprene and terpenes make a significant contribution. In the countryside virtually all the VOCs are produced naturally. Not only is the natural VOC contribution much greater overall than that from burning fossil fuels, it is also more effective, because isoprene and terpenes are much more chemically reactive than are unburned hydrocarbons. Their high reactivity makes terpenes extremely flammable. They make Christmas trees (real ones, of course) smell good, but they also make them a fire hazard.

Obviously, the fact that VOCs emitted by plants can contribute to the production of smog and ground-level ozone does not mean we should pave over our city parks and cut down the trees that line our streets. Trees do much more good than harm. It does mean, however, that perhaps we should choose carefully which species we plant in warm, sunny regions where trucks and autos may supply the NO_X they need to set us coughing.

Pollution from wildfires

There is nothing we can do to prevent pollution that occurs entirely naturally. We cannot seal volcanoes to prevent them from erupting, and we cannot alter the biochemistry of plants to stop them from emitting isoprene and terpenes. These things are beyond our control. We can reduce the pollution caused by substances we release into the air ourselves, however, from our factories, farms, homes, and cars. These sources of pollution are within our control.

Between these two there is a third source of air pollution. Forest, bush, and grass fires emit smoke and a wide range of gases that can react in sunlight to generate photochemical smog. A wildfire is like a big factory pouring its wastes into the air without even a tall chimney to help disperse them. Not surprisingly, a wildfire can cause serious pollution locally and, if it is big enough, sometimes on a regional scale, covering a substantial part of a continent, for example. Wildfires also destroy homes, farms, and other property, and they cost human lives.

They occur naturally, of course. There have always been fires of this kind, most of them ignited by lightning. We cannot eliminate them, but we can try to prevent those fires that are ignited by people either deliberately, which is a criminal offense, or inadvertently. We can discourage criminal behavior and educate people to be careful with matches, campfires, cooking stoves, and bottles left lying on the ground that can act as "burning glasses" by focusing sunlight.

Unfortunately, reducing this risk or even removing it entirely fails to address the much bigger problem of the way we manage the land in regions that are dry for part of the year. Poor management does not cause fires directly, but it does create the conditions in which, once ignited, they can blaze out of control.

When a forest burns

Trees shed their leaves or needles, and from time to time certain species of older trees shed branches. Smaller plants, such as grasses and herbs, die down at the end of their growing season, leaving dead and withered material lying on the surface. Plants including trees, grow old and die, and when they die they fall to the ground. In a forest or any other area of natural vegetation, dead plant material accumulates on the ground, where it can dry out thoroughly—so thoroughly that it crunches when you walk over it.

Once it is in this condition, it is highly flammable. It needs only a spark to ignite it, and it is usually lightning that supplies the spark. Electrical storms that produce lightning but no rain are quite common. The fuel catches fire, but often only at ground level. Most natural fires are ground fires. These burst into flame from time to time, but mainly they smolder through the fuel lying on the ground and just below the surface.

They consume the fuel together with grasses, herbs, shrubs, and small saplings. It is not a hot fire. The highest temperature at ground level is usually around 194 to 248°F (90–120°C). Large fallen logs and fully grown trees are superficially charred, but the fire is not fierce enough to destroy them. After a time the fire dies out, either because rain extinguishes it or because it exhausts its supply of fuel.

Sometimes, however, a fire can leap upwards and ignite the crowns of the trees. A crown fire is much more serious. Occasionally one starts when lightning strikes a tree and ignites its foliage, but a ground fire can also spread upward. This is likely to happen if there are trees with crowns that extend downward, so they begin at a fairly low level, or when there is a large accumulation of suitable fuel. This includes many tall saplings, dead saplings that are still standing, and tall shrubs. These sources of fuel provide a "ladder" the fire can climb.

Once the canopy is alight, a crown fire spreads rapidly. Hot air, rising by convection high above the forest, carries burning fragments and sparks that it scatters into the canopy downwind. Air near the surface is drawn spiraling in to replace the rising air. This can generate winds of hurricane force—a firestorm—that feeds oxygen to the flames like a bellows, intensifying the fire, and blows burning material onto new stocks of fuel. It can even become so hot that radiant heat from the flames is able to ignite dry material some distance away. When that happens the fire leaps unpredictably from place to place.

The Yellowstone fire

This is what happened in Yellowstone National Park in 1988. There are fires in the park every summer, and there always have been. Lightning ignites them during the dry season. There were 235 fires between 1972 and 1987. All of them were allowed to die down naturally.

Fires were less frequent in the 1980s, however, because of a series of unusually wet summers. Consequently, dead plant material accumulated unburned until 1988. The spring of 1988 was very wet, and there were few fires, but a severe drought had set in by June. By the third week in July fires were breaking out in many places. The authorities decided to bring them under control, but this proved almost impossible. On the worst day, August 20, more than 150,000 acres (60,700 ha) were burning. The fires continued to blaze until September 11, when the first snowfall began to suppress them. They continued to smolder until November. By then the fires had burned almost 1 million acres (400,000 ha), about 45 percent of the park area.

The Bambi effect

Ecologists recognized in the 1940s that fires are entirely natural in areas like Yellowstone and that the plants and animals of the region are adapted to them. In some places land managers used carefully controlled fires as tools to clear away old, dead plant material and encourage new growth. Since 1972 it had been policy in Yellowstone to keep natural fires under control, but not to extinguish them.

Nevertheless, many members of the public thought all fires should be suppressed. They were influenced by the famous Disney movie *Bambi*, which depicted forest animals fleeing in terror from a rapidly advancing wall of fire. Consequently, for several decades it became the practice to extinguish all forest fires as quickly as possible in response to public opinion. This allowed dead, flammable plant material to accumulate rather than being removed periodically by natural fires. When a fire did occur, the added supply of fuel ensured that it was a big one and difficult to control.

This became known as the "Bambi effect." The movie depiction is very misleading. Birds simply fly away from fires. Most mammals have ample time to move out of the way. Reptiles, amphibians, insects, and other smaller animals find places to shelter below ground in burrows or beneath logs. The heat of the fire is felt only at and above the ground surface; the temperature is quite comfortable an inch or two below ground level. The fire passes over or past them. In fact, for many species it is safer to stay put than to make a run for it: predators lie in wait for animals fleeing in blind terror. Yellowstone has a population of around 31,000 elk (also called wapiti, *Cervus elaphus*). About 250 died from smoke inhalation during the 1988 fire. Some animals die, obviously, but fire is not a serious threat to wildlife.

After a few years a fire-devastated area makes a full recovery. Young trees were emerging in Yellowstone by the spring of 1989. Not only did the park recover, but it was invigorated. A fire leaves the surface cleared of plants but covered in a layer of ash. This is a valuable fertilizer that is washed down into the soil by the first rain.

Fires out of control

Fire has always been used to clear land. Our prehistoric ancestors also used it to drive game. Repeated burning killed trees but encouraged grasses and herbs that cannot tolerate shade and that grow rapidly after a fire. Increasing the area of grassland allowed grazing animals to thrive, and these, in turn, destroyed emerging tree seedlings. This is how some of the world's grasslands were formed out of the open woodland that preceded them.

All fires pollute the air, but the pollution is local and temporary if only a limited area is burned and the fire is extinguished after a short time. Most fires in temperate climates burn safely, even if they are unpleasant for people living nearby, because rain will usually quench them after a few hours. This is much less likely in climates with a pronounced dry season.

In 1997–98 the strongest El Niño event in many years occurred. During an El Niño there is usually drought in Indonesia (see sidebar, pages 138–139), and when farmers and logging companies lit fires to clear away

El Niño

At intervals of between two and seven years, the weather changes across much of the Tropics and especially in southern Asia and western South America. The weather is drier than usual in Indone-sia, Papua New Guinea, eastern Australia, north-eastern South America, the Horn of Africa, East Africa, Madagascar, and in the northern part of the Indian subcontinent. It is wetter than usual over the

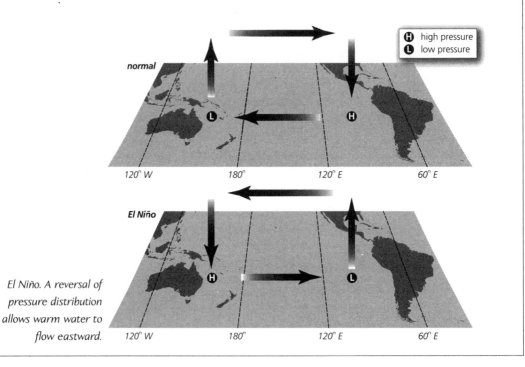

El Niño. A reversal of pressure distribution allows warm water to flow eastward.

unwanted vegetation in September 1997, as they do every year, the fires spread and were soon burning out of control (see sidebar, pages 140–141). Most of the fires are lit to clear forest in order to provide land for com-mercial tree plantations and farms. That year they were exacerbated by the large amount of dead, dry wood that logging companies had left lying on the ground. Those fires produced the most serious air pollution parts of Asia had seen in half a century.

Wildfires also burned out of control in Mexico in 1998. They, too, were linked to the El Niño drought and covered about 1,875 square miles (4,856 km²). The fires were mainly in the south of the country, but the smoke spread to Mexico City and then into the southern United States.

Even without the help of El Niño, fires can quickly blaze out of control in dry weather and turn into wildfires. In January 2002, for example, bush fires raged through New South Wales, Australia, destroying nearly 200 homes, approaching the suburbs of Sydney, and covering about 740,000 central and eastern tropical Pacific, parts of California and the southeastern United States, eastern Argentina, central Africa, southern India, and Sri Lanka. The phenomenon has been occurring for at least 5,000 years.

The change is greatest around Christmastime—midsummer in the Southern Hemisphere, of course. That is how it earned its name of El Niño, "the Christ child," in Peru, where its effects are most dramatic. Ordinarily, the western coastal regions of South America have one of the driest climates in the world, but El Niño brings heavy rain. Farm crops flourish, but many communities rely on fishing, and the fish disappear.

Most of the time the prevailing low-level winds on either side of the equator are the trade winds, blowing from the northeast in the Northern Hemisphere and from the southeast in the Southern Hemisphere. At high level the winds flow in the opposite direction, from west to east. This is known as the Walker circulation, in memory of Sir Gilbert Walker (1868–1958), who discovered it in 1923. Walker also discovered that air pressure is usually low over the western side of the Pacific, near Indonesia, and high on the eastern side, near South America. This pressure distribution helps drive the trade winds, and the trade winds drive the Equatorial Current that flows from east to west, carrying warm surface water toward Indonesia. The warm water accumulates around Indonesia, in a warm pool.

In some years, however, the pressure distribution changes. Pressure rises over the western Pacific and weakens in the east. The trade winds then slacken. They may cease to blow altogether or even reverse direction, so they blow from west to east instead of east to west. This causes the Equatorial Current to weaken or reverse direction. Water then begins to flow out of the warm pool, moving eastward, and the depth of warm water increases off the South American coast. This suppresses upwelling cold water in the Peru Current and deprives fish and other marine life of the nutrients in the cold water. Air moving toward South America is warmed and carries a great deal of moisture. This brings heavy rain to the coastal region. This is an El Niño.

In other years the low pressure deepens in the west, and the high pressure in the east rises. This accelerates the trade winds and Equatorial Current, increasing the rainfall over southern Asia and the dry conditions along the South American coast. This is called La Niña. The periodical change in pressure distribution is known as the Southern Oscillation, and the complete cycle is an El Niño–Southern Oscillation (ENSO) event. The diagram illustrates how this happens.

acres (300,000 ha). The fiercest of all Australian wildfires broke out on February 16, 1983. That was Ash Wednesday in the Christian calendar, and so they are known as the Ash Wednesday fires (see sidebar, page 142).

Wildfires are distressingly common events in Southern California. The worst in recent years blazed in October and November 1993, fanned by a dry Santa Ana wind blowing from the mountains into the Los Angeles Basin, an area of 7,000 square miles (18,130 km^2) surrounded by mountains on three sides. Those fires burned more than 300 square miles (777 km^2), and in the course of 10 days they destroyed more than 1,000 buildings.

Acts of war

Fires also result from acts of war. In 1991 Iraqi forces retreating at the end of the Gulf War set fire to 613 oil wells, storage tanks, and refineries in

Kuwait. These fires produced a huge pall of black smoke that covered most of the Persian Gulf region for several months.

The tragic September 11, 2001, attack on the World Trade Center also produced a large cloud of smoke from burning aviation fuel as well as the aircraft and buildings themselves. Those fires continued burning, although not fiercely, for many weeks after the event.

Pollution from fires

Smoke from the Kuwait oil fires shaded the surface. This caused the air temperature to fall by 18°F (10°C), and the sea-surface temperature fell by several degrees. Once the smoke cleared, temperatures returned to their former levels.

Soot settled over nearly 370 square miles (958 km²) of desert. Most of the soot was washed down by rain. Scientists discovered that the soot particles acted as cloud condensation nuclei, triggering the formation of clouds and increasing rainfall.

There were no long-term consequences to the environment or to the health of people living in the area from the smoke and gases released by

Asian fires of 1997–1998

In the middle of September 1997, forest fires blazed out of control in Sumatra and Kalimantan and on a smaller scale in Java, all in Indonesia. A mixture of photochemical smog and a pall of smoke settled over parts of Malaysia, Singapore, Brunei, Indonesia, and Papua New Guinea. It also spread, but less severely, over Thailand, Hong Kong, and the Philippines. On September 17 the Indonesian environment minister, Sarwono Kusumaatmadja, considered evacuating the entire population of 45,000 from Rengat, a port in Sumatra, but a change in the wind direction brought an improvement in the air quality. On September 19 the authorities declared a state of emergency in the Malaysian state of Sarawak and the bordering Indonesian province of Kalimantan (both on the island of Borneo). The visibility was so poor that on September 20 two ships collided in the Strait of Malacca. The map shows the area that was affected.

When the air pollution index (API) registered 635 in Kuching, capital of Sarawak, the authorities closed the airport, ordered schools and shops to close, and advised the 1.9 million residents to remain indoors. An API value greater than 500 denotes an extreme risk to health. On September 23 the API reached 839 in Kuching. This was possibly the highest pollution level ever recorded anywhere in the world. In the worst affected areas breathing the polluted air was equivalent to smoking 80 cigarettes a day.

All 234 persons on board were killed when poor visibility caused an airliner to crash as it approached to land at Medan, Sumatra, on September 26. By the end of September the fires had spread to Malaysia, and the smoke reached Jakarta.

The fires died down in November with the arrival of a short rainy season but broke out again in January and continued burning until May 1998. The API reached 500 in Borneo on April 12, and on April 30 the Malaysian authorities announced that the city of Kuala Lumpur was to be hosed down from the roofs of skyscrapers to wash the smog from the air.

the Kuwaiti fires. Following the September 11, 2001, attack in New York, there were fears that the collapse of the buildings had injected enough asbestos dust into the air to constitute a health hazard, especially to members of the emergency services and workers clearing the Ground Zero site. This hazard did not result from the fires, however. They caused only local and short-lived pollution.

Fires resulting from acts of war are too localized to cause serious or widespread air pollution. Wildfires, on the other hand, are very much larger. They can and do pollute the air.

The 1997–98 Indonesian fires released substantial amounts of carbon monoxide from the inefficient combustion (incomplete oxidation) of peat from the peat-swamp forest that covers about 20 percent of the affected area. They also released carbon dioxide (CO_2), methane (CH_4), other hydrocarbon compounds, and nitrogen oxides (NO_X). These gases reacted in the strong sunlight to produce the range of compounds associated with photochemical smog, including ozone (see "Photochemical Smog," page 55). The Mexican fires of 1998 also raised ozone levels to more than twice the limit that is considered safe and held them above the safe limit for a week. Schools kept their students indoors,

Borneo and Sumatra,
where destructive fires
occurred in 1997–98

The Ash Wednesday fires

There was a drought in eastern Australia that lasted from April 1982 through January 1983. By February 1983 the ground in Victoria and South Australia was parched, and the trees and grasslands were tinder-dry. February, the middle of the summer in the Southern Hemisphere, was hot. On February 16, Ash Wednesday in the Christian calendar, the temperature reached 109.4°F (43°C). Winds averaging 30 MPH (50 km/h) and gusting to 60 MPH (100 km/h) were blowing from the northwest, bringing dust and extremely dry air from the desert interior of the continent. Later in the day a cold front passed over the region, and the wind direction changed to southwesterly.

That afternoon about 180 bush fires broke out. Most were in Victoria, but a number were in South Australia, in the Adelaide Hills and on farmland in the southeast of the state. Some started when power lines crashed together in the wind, showering sparks onto the dry vegetation. Others ignited when trees were blown into power lines. A few were started deliberately. The cause of many of the outbreaks was never discovered.

Most of the fires were brought under control by the end of the day, and all of them were extinguished within two or three days. In Victoria the fires burned more than 770 square miles (1,995 km^2)—an area twice the size of metropolitan Melbourne. The fires in South Australia burned about 614 square miles (1,590 km^2). A total of 75 people lost their lives, 47 of them in Victoria, including 12 volunteer firefighters, and 28 in South Australia. Hundreds of others were injured. Several hundred homes were destroyed in South Australia and more than 2,000 in Victoria.

factories reduced their production, and restrictions were imposed on traffic in order to reduce the effects of the smog generated by the fires.

This is pollution we should be able to reduce. During the Indonesian fires the government banned the use of fire to clear land, but by then the land was already ablaze. Twice President Suharto apologized to the people of Malaysia and Singapore for the inconvenience the fires were causing them. It was an environmental catastrophe that should not be repeated.

In many countries farmers and landowners are permitted to use fire to clear land, but only under certain conditions. They must do so only when weather conditions minimize the risk of the fire spreading out of control. They must not light fires when the wind will carry smoke over populated areas. They must not light fires unless they have the materials and equipment on hand to bring them under control if they threaten to spread outside the area designated for burning. If their fires cause damage to property or injury to others, they are liable to pay compensation and may be guilty of criminal offenses. If such constraints were applied everywhere and then enforced, the damage from wildfires might be reduced, although it is impossible to prevent all wildfires.

CURING THE AIR

Pollution and health

During the 1997–98 forest fires in Indonesia and Malaysia, tens of thousands of people had to be treated for smoke inhalation, and several of the victims died (see the section Pollution from Wildfires). The World Health Organization (WHO) estimates that about 3 million people die each year as a result of air pollution, but it admits the estimate is uncertain. The true figure could be anywhere between 1.4 and 6 million persons. In some places air pollution may trigger 30 to 40 percent of all attacks of asthma and 20 to 30 percent of all cases of other respiratory illnesses. Air pollution can kill. An official total of 4,700 people died as a result of air pollution during the London smogs of 1952 and 1962, and the true total may have been much higher (see "Pea Soup: The Original Smog," page 37).

It takes more than a bad smell to make someone ill, however, and the WHO sets guidelines for the maximum concentrations that are considered safe for just five pollutants: carbon monoxide (CO), lead (Pb), nitrogen dioxide (NO_2), ozone (O_3), and sulfur dioxide (SO_2). National environmental agencies, such as the Environmental Protection Agency in the United States, refer to the WHO guidelines when calculating the pollutant limits they should set within their own countries. The limits take account of the length of time a person is exposed to the pollutant. The longer you continue to breathe the polluted air, the greater is the chance that it will make you ill, so the limit is set lower for longer exposure.

The WHO guidelines are set out in the table. The concentrations are given in micrograms per cubic meter ($\mu g\ m^{-3}$). This is the unit that is customarily used; $1\ \mu g\ m^{-3} = 0.000001$ ounces per cubic foot. The annual ambient concentration is the concentration present in the air anywhere in the world averaged over a year.

These are the most widely distributed pollutants, but they are not the only ones. Ammonia (NH_3) is poisonous if inhaled, but it is emitted only in certain places and remains in the air for only a very short time before it dissolves or reacts with airborne acids, such as sulfur dioxide (to form ammonium sulfate [$(NH_4)_2SO_4$], a useful plant fertilizer). It has such a strong smell that it is rather unlikely that anyone would inhale enough of it to suffer any injury. Hydrogen sulfide (H_2S) is also poisonous, but it, too, is emitted only in certain places, such as stagnant water and mud, and in amounts that are too small to cause harm. It smells strongly of rotten eggs, so anyone exposed to it is likely to hurry out of the way.

Interpreting the guidelines

The WHO guidelines are just that—guidelines. They are useful to governments in setting permitted emission limits for industry and vehicle

WHO AIR POLLUTION GUIDELINES

Pollutant	Annual ambient concentration $\mu g\ m^{-3}$	Guideline value $\mu g\ m^{-3}$	Effects observed at $\mu g\ m^{-3}$	Time
CO	500–7,000	100,000	N/A*	15 min.
		60,000		30 min.
		30,000		1 hour
		10,000		8 hours
Pb	0.01–2.0	0.5	N/A	1 year
NO_2	10–150	200	365–565	1 hour
		40		1 year
O_3	10–100	120	N/A	8 hours
SO_2	5–400	500	1,000	10 min.
		125	250	24 hours
		50	100	1 year

*Not Applicable

exhausts, but first they must be related to the effect that each pollutant has in a particular place. In other words, the guidelines need interpretation. They need still more interpretation to translate them into a form that can be released for public information.

The Environmental Protection Agency (EPA) has developed the Air Quality Index (AQI). This is a set of numbers that indicate the quality of the air in relation to its effects on human health. It is based on the National Ambient Air Quality Standards (NAAQS). These are maximum values for the concentration of each of a number of pollutants. If a standard is exceeded, the air is deemed to be injurious to health, and emission limits are based on calculations of the maximum amount of a pollutant the air can receive without breaching the NAAQS for that substance. When a company applies for a permit to emit waste gases, the environmental authority calculates how much the surrounding air can absorb before an NAAQS is breached and bases the permit on that figure.

The pollutants included in the NAAQS are carbon monoxide (CO), sulfur dioxide (SO_2), nitrogen dioxide (NO_2), ozone (O_3), and small particles known as PM_{10} and $PM_{2.5}$. The NAAQS are: CO, 10 mg m^{-3} for 8 hours; SO_2, 365 μg m^{-3} for 24 hours; NO_2, no value set; O_3, 235 μg m^{-3} for 1 hour; PM_{10}, 150 μg m^{-3} for 24 hours; $PM_{2.5}$, 40 μg m^{-3} for 24 hours. Lead is not included because leaded gasoline is the principal source of airborne lead, and only unleaded gasoline is now sold in the United States and Europe. The WHO continues to include it because leaded gasoline is still used in some countries.

When calculating the AQI for a particular area, the agency responsible measures the actual atmospheric concentration of each pollutant. Air is monitored at a number of sites, and the highest concentration found is taken as the value overall. These values are then related to the NAAQS. This involves weighting the pollutants and allotting a simple numerical value to each. The highest value for any of the pollutants measured is then taken as the AQI for the area. The result can then be compared to the standard AQI table. The calculation is quite complex, because it must take account of the length of time a person is likely to be exposed to each pollutant but then reduces these to a single overall index number.

If the color is green, the air is clean and it is safe to engage in any kind of outdoor activity, however energetic. If the color is yellow, most people are safe, but some people may have slight breathing difficulties due to ozone. If you suffer from asthma or heart or lung disease, you should avoid exercising very strenuously, especially in the late afternoon and early evening. Children should also take care at these times.

If the color is orange, you should avoid prolonged exercise in the late afternoon and early evening if you suffer from asthma or heart or lung disease. Children should also play quietly at these times.

If the color is red, many people may experience breathing difficulty or discomfort. Exercise outdoors mainly in the early morning and late evening.

If the color is purple, the air is considered very unhealthy, and most people will experience breathing difficulty or discomfort. You should exercise outdoors only in the early morning and late evening.

If the color is maroon, the air is considered dangerous to breathe. Everyone should avoid strenuous outdoor activity.

Does air pollution cause cancer?

Airborne hydrocarbons other than methane are not included in the NAAQS. They are emitted mainly by road vehicles and from solvents used in such products as paints and adhesives. They are what give gasoline and

AIR QUALITY INDEX		
Index	Description	Color
0–50	Good	Green
51–100	Moderate	Yellow
101–150	Unhealthy for sensitive groups	Orange
151–200	Unhealthy	Red
201–300	Very unhealthy	Purple
301–500	Hazardous	Maroon

paints their distinctive smells, and they are worrisome because some of them are very poisonous. Benzene (C_6H_6) and 1,3-butadiene ($CH_2:CH.CH:CH_2$) can cause cancer, for example, and formaldehyde (HCHO), acetaldehyde (or ethanal, $CH_3.CHO$), and particles of unburned diesel fuel are suspected of doing so. Hydrocarbons are also involved in the reactions that lead to the formation of photochemical smog (see "Photochemical Smog," page 55).

Just because a pollutant is known to cause cancer, it does not follow that it will necessarily do so in the amounts present in the air. Carcinogenicity, the ability of a substance to cause cancer, is determined in the laboratory by measuring the effect on cultured tissue or laboratory animals or by studying the health records of individuals exposed to large amounts of the substance, usually in the course of their work. In both cases the doses that confirm the link are much higher than those present in the air outside the laboratory or workplace. Members of the public are exposed to doses that are much lower, and no one can be certain whether there is a level below which the substance has no effect. The evidence suggests that if air pollution does cause cancer, the effect is very small.

It is difficult to establish a link. This is because "cancer" is not one illness but many different ones, and several events must take place before any of them becomes established. Usually there must be a first exposure to initiate the damage that leads to cancer, then a second, involving other substances, to promote development of the disease. It may be necessary for these events to be repeated a number of times and in a particular way, and even if disease does begin it may be decades before it becomes apparent. This complicated sequence of events and prolonged time scale mean that tracing the effect—a cancer—back to a cause requires a very large research program continued over many years, and that is only the start of the problem.

An air pollutant must be inhaled in order for it to cause any illness. Cancers that result from inhaling substances are either very common, such as lung cancer, or very rare. If the illness is common, it is almost impossible to separate the effect of a small exposure to a pollutant from much bigger exposures to other factors that may cause it. Cigarette smoking is the principal cause of lung cancer, for example, and the inhalation of tobacco smoke also affects nonsmokers. This makes it very difficult to measure the very much smaller effect that might result from air pollution. Rare cancers may not occur frequently enough to establish a statistical relationship to pollution, so that if there is a link it may be impossible to detect. Benzene is known to cause a certain type of leukemia, and it is one of the carcinogens present in tobacco smoke. That link is very well established. Nonsmokers absorb much less benzene than smokers, and no link to cancer has been found in them, but this does not mean no link exists. Measuring the relationship is complicated by the extreme rarity of the disease: between four and five people out of every million in the population can expect to contract this form of leukemia over a lifetime of 70 years.

It seems that the risk is extremely small of contracting cancer from benzene when it is present in small amounts as an air pollutant, rather than in much larger amounts from smoking or occupational exposure. The same is true for other known or suspected carcinogens that are contained in the gases emitted when fossil fuels are burned inefficiently. They certainly cause cancer in people exposed to high doses, but the risk to the general public is small.

Overall, scientists have calculated that fewer than 5 percent of all cases of lung cancer that occur among city dwellers in the United States can be attributed to air pollution of all kinds. City dwellers are exposed to much more pollution than are people who live in rural areas. The risk of contracting one of the rare forms of cancer from air pollution is too small to be measurable.

Effects of other pollutants

Carbon monoxide

Hemoglobin is the pigment that gives blood its red color. It has a weak affinity for oxygen. This property allows it to absorb oxygen in the lungs, becoming oxyhemoglobin, and to give it up in tissues where the oxygen concentration is low. Hemoglobin transports oxygen around the body.

It has a strong affinity for carbon monoxide. When it absorbs this gas to become carboxyhemoglobin, it forms a stable compound, thus losing its capacity to transport oxygen. It can be harmful to people with heart disease and to fetuses and newborn infants, but it is rare for concentrations to reach harmful levels outdoors.

Carbon monoxide can be a risk indoors. Appliances that burn oil or gas may emit carbon monoxide if they burn fuel inefficiently, so the carbon in the fuel is not fully oxidized to carbon dioxide (CO_2). It is very important to ensure that indoor gas and oil appliances are properly maintained by qualified technicians.

Carbon monoxide is colorless and odorless, so it can accumulate unnoticed in an enclosed space until it reaches a concentration high enough to cause headaches and make people feel tired and confused. This stage occurs when the blood contains about 30 percent carboxyhemoglobin. At 40 percent people become confused, and at 60 percent they lose consciousness and may die unless they are removed into fresh air. Victims who are revived, even after losing consciousness, usually make a full recovery with no aftereffects.

Ozone

A pale blue gas with the pungent smell associated with electric sparks, ozone is poisonous at very low concentrations. It causes inflammation throughout the respiratory system, making people cough and wheeze. It can also cause chest pains.

Some people are especially sensitive to ozone, but persons who suffer from heart or respiratory illness or are prone to asthma attacks are particularly at risk. People who do strenuous exercise are also affected badly. They may have difficulty breathing at quite low ozone concentrations.

Nitrogen dioxide and sulfur dioxide

These gases irritate the respiratory tissues. Nitrogen dioxide (NO_2) is fairly insoluble, but it can damage tissue by oxidizing surface molecules, although this causes breathing difficulties only at levels much higher than those found in ordinary air. If pollution is severe and nitrogen dioxide levels exceed about 565 μg m^{-3}, people with asthma and children under five years of age may have problems.

It is possible that if young people undergo prolonged exposure to low levels of nitrogen dioxide their lungs will be damaged and that the damage will become evident when they are older. This is not certain, however.

Sulfur dioxide constricts the air passages after exposure for only a few minutes, and people with asthma are especially sensitive to it. Exercise increases the effect. Prolonged exposure causes thickening in the lining of the lungs as well as other changes that allow mucus to accumulate in the lungs.

Lead

Lead, in the form of tetraethyl lead (Pb (C_2H_5)$_4$), was formerly added to gasoline to improve its antiknocking properties. The lead remained in the engine exhaust fumes and entered the air with them as a spray of fine particles. When these were inhaled they penetrated deep into the lungs, from where lead could enter the bloodstream. Being a heavy metal, airborne lead remained close to the ground and tended to accumulate in partially enclosed areas, such as city streets.

Scientists have known for many years that lead and its compounds are extremely poisonous in large doses. They damage the immune system as well as the blood, brain, nerves, kidneys, and reproductive organs. The effect of the small doses present in the air were much more difficult to ascertain, but eventually it was established that these can impair brain function in children and raise blood pressure in middle-aged men. Most countries have phased out the use of tetraethyl lead as an ingredient of gasoline, and this has removed the principal source of this pollutant, although its health effect was not the reason for removing it. Lead destroys the catalysts that are used in the catalytic converters fitted to car exhausts. If the exhaust gases contain lead, the catalytic converter will not work and so is unable to remove the other pollutants.

Lead is still contained in emissions from lead smelters and plants that incinerate old lead–acid batteries (such as car batteries) and in waste oil that has been contaminated with lead. These contribute only minute amounts of lead and are not considered to present a pollution problem provided emissions from the plants are strictly controlled.

Small particles

Minutely small particles are now thought to be one of the most serious air pollutants of all. Breathing air polluted by them is almost as harmful as breathing air thick with tobacco smoke.

The risk they pose is firmly established. Studies involving extremely large numbers of people in several different cities have found that deaths from heart and lung complaints increase on days when the air contains high concentrations of particles. The most impressive study compared data on the causes of death of 500,000 people older than 16 years with data on air pollution. The researchers allowed for the effects of smoking, obesity, diet, and differences related to where the individuals lived. They found that increasing the mass of small particles in 1 cubic meter of air by one microgram is associated with a 6 percent increase in deaths from heart and lung disease and an 8 percent increase in deaths from lung cancer. Los Angeles was the city where the risk was highest, with an average of 20 μg m^{-3} in 1999 and 2000, with Chicago second at 18 μg m^{-3}, and New York City third with 16 μg m^{-3}. Some smaller towns have even higher levels because they are close to coal mines or other sources. Subsequent research revealed, however, that an oversight in applying the computer program to process the statistics had approximately doubled the apparent risk. The harmfulness of small particles is therefore much less than had originally been supposed.

How small is a "small" particle? At first, the risk was believed to come from particles that are between 2.5 μm and 10 μm across—it would take about 25 particles 10 micrometers across to equal the thickness of a human hair. These particles are known as PM$_{10}$; PM stands for "particulate matter." They enter the air in smoke and also as dust, pollen, and fungal and bacterial spores. They remain airborne for up to several hours and can travel up to 30 miles (50 km). When inhaled they penetrate the respiratory passages and enter the lungs, where they can cause damage.

Particles less than 2.5 μm across, known as PM$_{2.5}$, are now considered to be much more dangerous. These are up to 100 times smaller than the thickness of a hair. This means they can remain airborne for longer—days or weeks—and travel for hundreds for miles. They penetrate much deeper into the lungs and can reach the smallest, most delicate lung tissues, but their composition makes them even more hazardous. They tend to consist of metal particles, especially poisonous heavy metals, and organic compounds, some of them carcinogenic.

Healthy air

There are many other harmful substances that sometimes pollute the air, especially in enclosed spaces. As well as ammonia and hydrogen sulfide, normally encountered outdoors, there are radon and asbestos, for example.

Radon, a radioactive gas that is a natural product from the radioactive decay of radium-226, enters the air from soil. Most of our exposure to radiation comes from radon. It can cause cancer if it accumulates in the air, as it may do in buildings that have tightly fitting doors and windows to prevent drafts and people inhale it. Walls and floors can be sealed to prevent radon from entering from below ground. Asbestos fibers can damage lung tissue, but only workers exposed to them on demolition sites are likely to be at risk.

We often think of air pollution in terms of the air outdoors, but the most serious pollution occurs indoors. Any pollutant that is released into the air indoors is about 1,000 times more likely to penetrate someone's lungs than the same pollutant released outdoors. In the United States the limit that is set for PM_{10} pollution is 150 µg m^{-3}. In many developing countries poor people burn wood, grass, crop residues such as straw, and cow dung to heat their homes and cook their food. Often there is no proper chimney to remove the smoke, and PM_{10} concentrations can reach 10,000 µg m^{-3}. The World Health Organization estimates that approximately 2 billion people live in this way.

That is not to say that outdoor air pollution is harmless. It is not. In most of the industrial countries levels of air pollution have been reduced substantially over the last few decades, and governments and industry are striving to reduce them further. We must hope that these efforts succeed. If they do, public health will improve, and the costs of illness—in treatment and lost working times as well as the misery and disruption it causes—will fall.

Trapping pollutants

Once a pollutant has entered the atmosphere, there is no practical way to remove it. Eventually the air will cleanse itself, of course. There are natural chemical reactions that convert pollutants into harmless substances. Other pollutants settle onto surfaces and adhere to them or are washed to the surface by rain or snow. Polluting gases and particles seldom remain in the air for more than a few hours, or at the most days.

This is of little help to us, unfortunately, because despite their short residence times the pollutants are likely to remain airborne long enough to cause harm, and as fast as natural processes remove them our factories, homes, cars, and trucks add more. If we wish to enjoy cleaner air, we will have to prevent the pollutants from entering it in the first place. We will have to trap them before they can escape.

That is the way pollution control works. It uses technological devices to mimic the natural processes that cleanse the air, but it applies them to air that has not yet left the source of pollution. As new and more effective control devices become available, many manufacturers take advantage of them to cleanse the emissions from their plants or products. After all, factory managers have to breathe the same air as does everyone else. Setting legally enforceable emission limits compels their more reluctant competitors to install controls as well. This leads to improved air quality, and it ensures that irresponsible industrialists are not permitted to gain a commercial advantage by saving on the cost of emission control. Emission limits create a level playing field.

Cleaning gasoline

An individual car is not a particularly polluting machine. The trouble is that there are so many cars, and together they cause a great deal of pollution. The first source of that pollution is the fuel they use.

Gasoline evaporates, releasing hydrocarbons into the air and giving gasoline its distinctive odor. The warmer the fuel is, the faster it evaporates and the more of it that enters the air. As well as causing pollution, this wastes fuel.

Vaporization occurs when the tank is being filled. As fuel enters it forces out the vapor that is always present in the tank. Fuel vapor escapes even when the tank is closed. Fuel tanks must be ventilated in order to allow the fuel to leave them freely. During a warm day vapor escapes through the vent even when the car is not running.

Manufacturers have reduced these losses by installing canister systems. The vent on the fuel tank and those parts of the engine that leak gasoline fumes are covered, and vapors from them are fed into pipes. These lead to a container, the canister, where they are stored. While the car is running the vapors are fed back into the engine to be burned.

Gasoline itself has also changed. Limits have been imposed on the volatility of fuel—the ease with which it vaporizes—and the benzene content has been reduced. Reducing volatility has reduced losses by vaporization, and reducing the benzene content has reduced emissions of the most harmful hydrocarbon (see "Pollution and Health," page 143). Since 2000 gasoline sold in the most polluted cities of the United States has had to emit 20 percent less hydrocarbons than the fuel that was being sold in 1995. Limits to the amount of sulfur in fuel were introduced in 1993 to reduce emissions of sulfur dioxide, and the sale of leaded gasoline was banned from the beginning of 1996.

Catalytic converter

Most vehicle emissions are from the exhaust. Nowadays cars are fitted with a device called a three-way catalytic converter to reduce them, and every car in most states must be inspected regularly to make certain that the vehicle is safe to drive and that the converter is still working. It is called a three-way converter because it reduces emissions of three substances: carbon monoxide, volatile organic compounds (hydrocarbons), and nitrogen oxides. It is catalytic because it uses catalysts, substances that accelerates a chemical reaction while remaining unaltered.

A catalytic converter looks like a box wrapped around the exhaust pipe, located between the engine and the muffler. As the diagram shows, it has two compartments. Each of these is filled with a honeycomb structure made of ceramic that contains a catalyst.

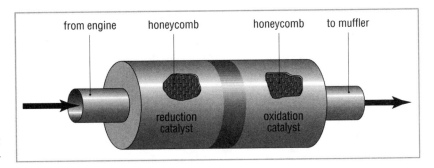

Three-way catalytic converter

Exhaust gases from the engine enter the first chamber, which contains platinum and rhodium, the reduction catalysts. As they flow through the honeycomb, the gases are exposed to the catalysts. The reduction catalysts reduce nitrogen oxide (NO) and nitrogen dioxide (NO_2), releasing nitrogen and oxygen:

$$2NO \rightarrow N_2 + O_2$$
$$2NO_2 \rightarrow N_2 + 2O_2$$

The gases then proceed to the second chamber, which contains platinum and palladium, the oxidation catalysts. These catalysts oxidize carbon monoxide (CO) to carbon dioxide (CO_2) and burn the unburned hydrocarbons using oxygen contained in the exhaust.

How much oxygen the exhaust contains depends on the ratio of fuel to air that is fed into the engine cylinders. A sensor mounted in the exhaust flow between the engine and the catalytic converter monitors the oxygen concentration in the exhaust gases and feeds this information to the engine computer. The computer adjusts the fuel–air ratio, ensuring an adequate supply of oxygen to the oxidation chamber while at the same time making the engine burn its fuel efficiently.

Scrubbers and filters

Factories also emit polluting gases. Sulfur dioxide (SO_2) is the most important of these. It is produced when a fossil fuel containing sulfur is burned. Coal is the fuel that contains the most sulfur. The process for removing sulfur dioxide is called flue gas desulfurization (FGD). Two basic types of FGD devices are available, wet scrubbers and dry scrubbers, and they are used worldwide in coal-burning factories and power plants.

Wet scrubbers are the kind of FGD most widely used. A slurry mixture containing water and limestone, a substance that reacts with SO_2, is injected into a vessel, and the flue gas is passed through it. In some scrubbers the slurry is sprayed through nozzles into a tower. In others it floods across perforated plates or is poured onto the top of packing material that fills the chamber. As the flue gas passes through the slurry, the SO_2 reacts with the limestone (calcium carbonate, $CaCO_3$) to produce calcium sulfate

(CaSO$_4$). Air is added, either in the scrubber or in a separate chamber, to remove unwanted calcium sulfite (CaSO$_3$) by oxidizing it, and the water in the slurry combines with the calcium sulfate to produce hydrated calcium sulfate, or gypsum (CaSO$_4$.2H$_2$O). The overall reaction is:

$$SO_2 + CaCO_3 + 1/2O_2 + 2H_2O \rightarrow CaSO_4.2H_2O + CO_2$$

Gypsum can be sold commercially and is used in the construction industry. The wastewater from the process must then be treated before it can be discharged or reused.

Other versions of wet scrubbers use different materials. These include fly ash, very fine-grained ash from furnaces, sea water, ammonia (NH$_3$), caustic soda (sodium hydroxide, NaOH), sodium carbonate (Na$_2$CO$_3$), potassium hydroxide (KOH), and magnesium hydroxide (Mg(OH)$_2$). A wet scrubber can remove up to 99 percent of the sulfur in the flue gas.

Dry scrubbers use the same reaction but produce no wastewater. They are the second most widely used variety of FGD device. Fine droplets of a lime slurry (calcium hydroxide, Ca(OH)$_2$), called lime milk because of its appearance, are sprayed into the reaction chamber. Hot flue gases are also directed through the chamber, and the lime milk vaporizes. Vaporization takes about 10 seconds, and during this time the lime reacts with SO$_2$, sulfur trioxide (SO$_3$), hydrochloric acid (HCl), and other acids. The reactions produce a powdered mixture of calcium sulfate and calcium sulfite, together with lime that did not react. This is removed and used again.

A dry scrubber can remove more than 90 percent of the sulfur in flue gases, and under ideal conditions it can remove as much as 95 percent.

Filters

Solid particles are filtered from the gas stream. The filters used are similar to those in a domestic vacuum cleaner, tumble dryer, or air conditioning system, but they must be able to withstand the high temperatures they encounter in an industrial environment.

Bag filters are the most widely used variety. As its name suggests, a bag filter is a cylindrical bag with an open end that is fastened over the end of a gas pipe. It can be up to 30 feet (9 m) long and three feet (1 m) wide. Some filters simply fasten over the end of the pipe—they may even be tied in place. Others are equipped with a ring at the mouth that fits very precisely over the gas pipe, and there are also bags that sit inside their own carbon steel or stainless steel housings. The housing attaches to the gas pipe.

Filters are made from a range of materials. The most popular are polyester felt and polypropylene felt, but nylon, woven polypropylene, canvas, cotton drill, flannel, and army duck are among the others. Teflon is also used.

Two factors influence the choice of material: the size of the mesh and the temperature of the gas. Obviously, the mesh size determines the size of the particles the filter will trap. A modern filter will trap more than 99 percent of the particles of its own mesh size or larger.

Natural fibers, such as cotton, cannot be used if the gas temperature is greater than 195°F (90°C). Nylon cannot be used at temperatures higher than 390°F (200°C). Glass fiber, sometimes impregnated with graphite and treated with silicon to increase its durability, can tolerate temperatures above 500°F (260°C).

Electrostatic precipitators

There is yet another way to remove particles from a stream of flowing air. It exploits the fact that opposite electrical charges attract each other.

When you comb your hair does it ever crackle and move toward the comb? This is due to static electricity (see sidebar), and you can easily produce it. Inflate a toy balloon, then draw it gently across a sweater several times, always in the same direction. Now place it gently against the wall, and you will find it stays there. Rubbing against the rough fibers of your sweater strips electrons away from the atoms on the surface of the balloon, leaving the surface with a positive charge. When you place the balloon against the wall it attracts electrons in the atoms on the surface of the wall, but those atoms refuse to relinquish their electrons, so the balloon atoms must share them. That is what keeps the balloon in place. In the same way, when you comb your hair the comb captures electrons from the hair, giving the comb a positive charge and your hair a negative charge. If your body acquires a static electric charge—this can happen when you shuffle about on a wool or nylon carpet wearing leather-soled shoes—it can discharge if you touch a metal object. The charge can be strong enough to produce a visible spark and to give you a slight shock.

This is the principle the electrostatic precipitator uses. The general arrangement is shown in the drawing. As the gas or air enters the device it crosses wires set at right angles to the direction of flow. The wires, called electrode wires, carry a current of several thousand volts. This large current causes the wires to discharge electrons into the air around them, so that each wire is surrounded by an electrostatic field, called a discharge corona. The coronas are represented by disks in the drawing, but they surround each wire and are actually cylindrical in shape. In most industrial precipitators the gas remains close to the wires for more than one second. This allows plenty of time for electrons in the coronas to attach themselves to particles in the gas—in fact, this takes less than one-tenth of a second. Having gained electrons, the particles carry negative charge.

There is a slight drawback, however. The powerful field around the wires also breaks the bonds between the two atoms in diatomic oxygen molecules ($O_2 \rightarrow O + O$), producing single oxygen atoms (O) that attach to other oxygen molecules to form ozone ($O + O_2 \rightarrow O_3$). The ozone quickly breaks down again and causes no problems in an industrial plant, but it can pollute the air around electrostatic precipitators that are sited in office or apartment buildings, where people are nearby. Ozone is very poisonous (see the section Pollution and Health), and the risk of contaminating the air in this way restricts the use of these devices mainly to industrial settings.

Static electricity

An electric current comprises a flow of electrons, particles that carry a negative charge, through a conducting medium, called a conductor. They move rather like waves. Each electron moves only slowly and for a short distance, like the water molecules moving with a wave on the surface of a pond, but their motion is transferred to adjacent electrons in the conductor. Electrons repel each other. Consequently, if there is an excess of electrons at one end of a conductor, mutual repulsion will drive electrons along the conductor. This is called electrostatic repulsion, and the force driving the electrons in an electrostatic force.

If the electrons are evenly distributed throughout the conductor, however, and their charge balances the positive charge on the protons in the nuclei of the atoms that make up the conductor, then all the electrons in the conductor will be at rest. No current will flow because there is no electrostatic force to drive it.

All the electrons in a conductor may be at rest, and the conductor itself may be isolated. However, another conductor may have more or fewer electrons. In that case, although there is no electrostatic force within either conductor, there is an electrostatic force between them. The electrons are unable to flow from one conductor to the other because there is no contact between the two. The electricity is therefore static. This is static electricity.

If the potential difference, the difference in charge between the two conductors, is strong enough and the two are close enough to one another, the electrons may overcome the resistance of the medium separating them and flow between them. The result in air is a spark. Lightning is the biggest natural example.

In the second part of the precipitator the gas, with its charged particles, flows across collecting plates, metal plates that are grounded so an electric current is able to flow through them. The plates attract the charged particles. After a time the plates are covered with dust. Mechanical rappers tap the plates at regular intervals to shake the dust free. It falls into containers below the precipitator and is removed.

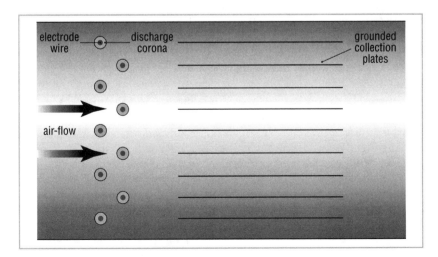

Electrostatic precipitator

The gas leaves the precipitator stripped of the dust particles. An efficient installation can remove close to 95 percent of particles from 0.000004 to 0.0004 inch (0.01 to 10 μm) in size. This is highly efficient, and electrostatic precipitators are very useful for cleaning the air leaving coal-fired furnaces and factories that produce a large amount of dust. They will capture mites and protozoa as well as mineral grains, but not bacteria or viruses.

Smaller precipitators, sometimes used domestically, are less efficient. This is because they are not fitted with mechanical rappers, so they must be cleaned manually, and they may not allow the particles to remain in the vicinity of the coronas for long enough to become fully charged. There is also a risk that the ozone they produce may cause breathing difficulties for people who are especially sensitive to it.

Accidents

Most pollutants form as an inevitable by-product of a process. Other pollutants are occasionally released accidentally.

Fires at industrial plants can release copious amounts of black smoke, but mixed with the smoke may also be substances derived from the materials being used in the factory. These can be extremely poisonous. Many of the organic compounds used in the plastics industry contain chlorine. If this is released as chlorine gas, people must be evacuated from the area. Chlorine is a yellowish gas that is heavier than air, so it sinks to ground level. It was used in World War I as a poison gas.

Burning plastics may also release carbonyl chloride (Cl_2CO). This is a colorless gas and is also very poisonous. It, too, was used as a poison gas in World War I and called phosgene.

Dioxin (the popular name for 2,3,7,8-tetrachlorodibenzo-*p*-dioxin) can also be produced when organic materials containing chlorine are burned. The worst incident of dioxin pollution occurred in July 1976 at the village of Seveso, near Milan, Italy. An explosion at a factory manufacturing the herbicide 2,4,5-T released a huge cloud of gas heavily contaminated with dioxin. All 700 inhabitants had to be evacuated from the village, more than 600 domestic animals were destroyed, and all the vegetation within a five-mile (8-km) radius had to be removed and incinerated. There were no human deaths, but people who were heavily exposed to dioxin suffered from chloracne, a distressing skin ailment. Prolonged exposure to fairly low levels of dioxin is believed to cause cancer. Industrial plants are not permitted to emit it.

The most serious incident of air pollution the world has ever seen did not involve dioxin, however, but methyl isocyanate (MIC). This is an intermediate product used in the manufacture of certain pesticides, and the Indian subsidiary of Union Carbide made MIC for this purpose at its factory to the north of the city of Bhopal, India. It is extremely poisonous.

On the night of December 23, 1984, a large amount of water entered a storage tank at the factory containing MIC. This triggered a reaction that released MIC. Workers first detected the leak at about 11:30 P.M., when their eyes began to smart. They told their supervisor, but the leak continued for two hours. By that time about 40 tons (36 tonnes) had escaped, and the gas had poured over the nearby residential area where people were sleeping.

MIC is about twice as heavy as air. It flowed close to the ground, spreading downwind for about five miles (8 km). At least 3,000 people died, perhaps more, and hundreds of thousands of people were injured. Many of the survivors were left with chronic illnesses, mainly affecting the eyes, muscles, lungs and respiratory system, digestive system, and nervous system, as well as psychological difficulties.

Accidental pollution is treated as an emergency. Depending on the extent and nature of the incident, people may be advised to remain indoors or be evacuated until the danger has passed. Sometimes, though, as the cases of Seveso and Bhopal illustrate, events move too fast, and an industrial accident results in injury or death to large numbers of people.

Fortunately, such incidents are extremely rare. Most accidental pollution of the air lasts for only a short time—air has a powerful natural capacity for cleansing itself—and the cause of the accident is soon discovered and remedied. The few serious accidents also provide lessons. The Seveso incident gave rise to the Seveso Directive, for example, a law that applies in all member nations of the European Union. It requires factory managers to notify local people, local authorities, and the emergency services of the chemical substances they store on their premises. This allows proper precautions to be taken, controls to be imposed, and conditions inside the factory to be monitored.

Provided the lessons are learned, each accident allows us to ensure that it never occurs again. We cannot be certain there will never be another Seveso or Bhopal, of course, but it is very unlikely. Accidents can be prevented once we know what caused them.

The pollution resulting from routine emissions of gases is less dramatic but more difficult to prevent. Removing pollutants from the outside air is impossible. Removing them from waste gases before these are discharged is possible and can be done efficiently, but it is rather expensive. It is well worth the cost, of course, and the production, marketing, installation, and maintenance of the control devices generates employment and adds to the prosperity of the nation.

All the same, there is another way: to avoid generating the pollutants in the first place. This requires a more advanced approach involving quite radical changes to the technologies we use, but it is the direction that research has already taken.

New cars for old

Pollution is a type of inefficiency. It is wasteful. In some cases, the pollutant itself might have a use. If it could be recovered there might be a commercial market for it, so that simply discharging it into the environment is a waste. In other cases it may be possible to reduce the amount of material a process discharges by making the process itself more efficient and obtaining more useful work for each unit of fuel or raw material.

Automobile manufacturers have made considerable progress in improving fuel economy. At one time a family automobile would cruise at around 40 MPH (64 km/h), with a top speed of around 50 MPH (80 km/h), and consume fuel at the rate of about 15 miles to the gallon (4 miles, or 6 km, to the liter). A modern family car cruises comfortably at 50 MPH (80 km/h), has a top speed of more than 90 MPH (145 km/h), and travels around 37 miles for every gallon of gasoline (9.8 miles, or 15.7 km, to the liter). It is also easier and much safer to drive than earlier models. A vehicle that achieves better performance while consuming less fuel is more efficient and, because it burns less fuel, causes less pollution. Automobiles do cause serious pollution where traffic is congested, but an equivalent number of cars from the 1930s or 1940s would cause very much more.

It is also possible to burn cleaner fuel. Engines that run on liquefied petroleum gas (LPG) are very similar to gasoline engines apart from their system for storing fuel. LPG is a mixture of propane (C_3H_8) and butane (C_4H_{10}) that occurs naturally in gas fields and as a by-product of petroleum refining. It is cleaner to burn than gasoline, and hundreds of companies use fleets of LPG cars and delivery vans. The gas is delivered at a filling station from a pump, just like a gasoline pump, and is stored in the vehicle as a liquid held under pressure.

Natural gas can also be used. It, too, is much cleaner than gasoline, but storage is much more difficult. The gas is about 92 percent methane (CH_4). Methane does not liquefy easily, so it must be stored either as a gas compressed at about 200 times atmospheric pressure or as a liquid at about –310°F (–190°C). Natural gas is used for some large trucks and buses, but it is not practical for private cars because of the size and weight of the fuel tank.

More improvements are probably possible, but they are limited. The efficiency of the internal combustion engine, both gasoline and diesel, is approaching a ceiling. This affects not only automobiles but also trucks, buses, and diesel railroad locomotives. Electrifying railroad systems solves the problem for rail transport and improves efficiency. Trains that use electric motors powered from lines above or beside the track run more reliably than do those with a diesel engine, and electricity can be generated from central power plants with little pollution. Electrification is possible because trains run on a limited number of fixed tracks. Electrifying road transport in the same way works satisfactorily for streetcars running in cities, but using the same system to drive private cars and trucks would be much more difficult and costly.

Aircraft jet engines also consume large amounts of fuel and emit the same gases as do internal combustion engines. There is a limit to the improvements that can be made to their efficiency.

In response to this approaching ceiling, manufacturers are looking in radically new directions. They are reinventing the automobile engine. Some are even looking critically at air transport and are reviving a technology most people thought completely obsolete.

Electric motors

Electric motors are the cleanest of all engines. They emit nothing whatsoever while they are running. Critics point out that this is because the pollution is concentrated around the power plants that generate the electricity they use, but the criticism is not really valid. Emissions from a large factory, such as a power station, can be controlled. A modern power station causes an extremely small amount of pollution for each unit of energy it produces, and even this is being reduced. Electricity from one power plant can run thousands of electric motors. If each of those motors had to generate its own power by burning fuel, and supposing it did this as efficiently as possible, each motor would still emit something. All of those "somethings" would add up to a great deal more pollution than is emitted from a power station.

What is more, and in some senses more important, electrically driven vehicles cause no pollution in city centers, residential areas, and near freeways—the places where pollution can harm people. Power plants can be sited away from homes, schools, and shops.

Automobiles driven by electric motors are therefore nonpolluting, even when pollution from the power station is included. They are also very quiet. In some countries, such as Britain, they have been used for many decades for doorstep milk deliveries and are a very familiar sight. Known as "milk floats," they travel at around 10 MPH (16 km/h) with a gentle whirring sound, stopping outside each house. What the customers do not see is that the delivery round is quite short, and at the end of it the float travels to the nearby milk depot where its batteries spend the rest of the day recharging. Nevertheless, running cars the same way sounds like a good idea, and the idea of exchanging internal combustion engines for electric motors has aroused great interest.

Unfortunately, there is a problem. Storing electricity is difficult. Batteries are the only devices that will do this. They convert chemical energy into electricity. Ordinary car batteries usually contain lead and sulfuric acid, but lead-acid batteries are heavy in relation to the power they deliver. This makes them unsuitable for electric vehicles. Nickel-cadmium, nickel-metal hydride, and lithium ion batteries are preferable.

Even then, the batteries take up a considerable amount of space, account for a considerable percentage of the weight of the vehicle, and must be recharged frequently. Electric cars are being marketed, many of them made by Peugeot and Citroën, but the current models have a range of only around 50 miles (80 km) before their batteries need recharging; they have a top speed of only around 56 MPH (90 km/h). Other manufacturers are seeking to improve on this performance, but it seems that milk delivery remains the best use for battery-powered vehicles.

Hybrids

This does not mean that electricity cannot be used to power cars, but only that we need more power and a better way to charge the batteries. These problems can be solved, and one solution is called the hybrid vehicle. A hybrid combines two or more technologies.

Hybrid vehicles are popular with manufacturers because the technologies they combine are already well established. Hybrids can be developed fairly quickly and offer very real advantages.

Any engine runs most efficiently if its speed remains constant, and it can be designed to operate this way. It requires no additional power capacity to allow for acceleration, and it wastes no power by slowing down. This is far from the situation with an ordinary car, bus, or truck engine. The engine speed changes constantly. The vehicle must move from a standstill to its cruising speed. When it moves through traffic it accelerates and slows repeatedly and stops at traffic lights then starts again. When it leaves the city limits it accelerates to a higher cruising speed. These frequent changes consume fuel and mean the engine must be more powerful—and therefore burn more fuel—than one that would maintain a constant speed.

A hybrid vehicle has a small conventional engine, with about one-tenth to one-quarter the output of the engine in an ordinary vehicle of the same size. This runs at a constant speed, achieving a fuel consumption in a typical family car of more than 60 miles per gallon (15.8 miles, or 9.8 km, per liter). The engine drives a generator that produces electricity that is used to charge the batteries. The batteries power the electric motor that drives the car. In other words, the hybrid is an electric car in which the batteries are kept fully charged at all times.

There are two ways a hybrid can be configured. A series hybrid uses its internal combustion engine to drive a generator, the generator to charge the batteries, the batteries to drive the electric motor, and the electric motor to turn the wheels. The car propulsion system is entirely electric. In a parallel hybrid both the internal combustion engine and the electric motor are connected to the driveshaft. There is no generator because when the car is being powered by the internal combustion engine the driveshaft spins the electric motor without taking power from it. This converts the electric motor into a generator, and it charges the batteries. A parallel hybrid can be driven by the internal combustion engine, the electric motor, or the two combined.

A series hybrid has a much greater range than a purely electric vehicle, but in other respects its performance is similar. It is not fast, it has difficulty with steep hills, and its acceleration is slow. On the other hand, its fuel efficiency is high. A parallel hybrid is somewhat less economical with fuel but much more like a conventional car to drive. It can take hills and accelerate to pass other cars easily.

Flywheels

Batteries may be the only way electricity can be stored, but they are not the only way to store energy. A flywheel can also do that. The flywheel car is another type of hybrid—it combines two technologies.

A flywheel has most of its mass concentrated around its rim, like a toy gyroscope. If the flywheel is made to spin at high speed, the inertia due to the mass at the rim will keep it spinning for a long time. Energy is used to spin the flywheel up to speed, but most of that energy can be recovered from the spinning wheel.

In a flywheel car there is a conventional engine. This may be an ordinary internal combustion engine, but a gas turbine can also be used—and is used in one successful car design. The gas turbine is similar to the type used in jet aircraft, but it is small and burns unleaded gasoline. A catalytic converter (see "Trapping Pollutants," page 150) reduces the emissions almost to zero. The gas turbine drives an electrical generator and also provides power for the car during cruising. Electricity from the generator maintains the rotational speed of the flywheel. The flywheel also drives a generator. The vehicle has two ordinary 12-volt car batteries.

The flywheel is mounted on gimbals. These allow it to move freely without affecting the movement of the car. It is housed inside a vessel in a partial vacuum, with a vacuum pump to remove air. This reduces aerodynamic drag on the flywheel. Drag would slow the wheel, and the friction it causes would also generate heat. The containment vessel for the flywheel assembly is designed to withstand the force exerted by the debris that would be thrown outward if the flywheel were to fail.

It takes about two minutes for a stationary flywheel to reach its full speed, driven by the gas turbine. Once it is up to speed, the flywheel should continue spinning for several weeks or even months.

When the driver turns the ignition key, the flywheel starts the gas turbine engine. Pressing the accelerator transmits energy from the flywheel to the wheels of the car. Pressing the brake slows the car, but the energy removed from the wheels is transferred to the flywheel. The flywheel is used for acceleration. This means the engine can be small and run at fairly constant speed, the most efficient way to operate an engine. The engine supplies power for cruising and to recharge the flywheel.

Fuel cells

Hybrid vehicles overcome one of the inconveniences of batteries by charging them constantly. Flywheels abandon batteries entirely and store energy in a different way. There is a third alternative. This is to abandon conventional batteries and the internal combustion engine and generate electrical power by an entirely different means. That is what a fuel cell does.

The fuel cell is like a battery that never needs charging, but that consumes fuel—hence the *fuel* in its name. It is a cell because it is an enclosed unit. Like a battery, a fuel cell converts chemical energy into electrical energy. Fuel cells are assembled into stacks in order to provide enough power to drive a car or van.

Hydrogen (H_2) is fed in under pressure at one side of the cell. The other side of the cell is filled with air. The hydrogen makes contact with a catalyst, a substance that facilitates or accelerates a chemical reaction but is not altered by it. The catalyst separates the electrons (e^-) from hydrogen atoms, leaving the atomic nuclei. A hydrogen nucleus consists of a single proton, so the reaction is $H_2 \rightarrow 2H^+ + 2e^-$.

A membrane separates this side of the cell from the other side. The membrane allows protons (H^+) to pass but prevents electrons from doing so. The electrons are removed through an external electrical circuit, and the protons pass through the membrane. On the other side of the membrane, oxygen (O_2) molecules in the air are also exposed to a catalyst. This separates the molecules into single atoms, each bearing negative charge ($O_2 \rightarrow 2O^-$). The protons combine with the oxygen to form water ($2H^+ + O^- \rightarrow H_2O$). Water is the only exhaust product (see sidebar).

It is not quite so simple, because there must be a source of hydrogen. This can be supplied as hydrogen gas and stored on the vehicle, either as a gas under very high pressure or as a liquid at a temperature below –423°F (–253°C). Neither of these alternatives is attractive, and engineers are working to develop a different way to store hydrogen by absorbing it in a substance that will hold and release it as required. Metal hydrides, for example, are combinations of metal alloys that absorb up to about 2 percent of their own weight of hydrogen and release it when the tank is warmed.

Current fuel cells use a fuel that contains hydrogen, such as natural gas, methanol, ethanol, LPG, or even gasoline. The fuel is passed through a reformer, a device that removes the hydrogen. This is fed to the fuel cell, and the residue is discharged. The residue is polluting, of course, but a fuel cell emits much less pollution for each unit of power than does even the most efficient internal combustion engine.

Hydrogen

Hydrogen is the perfect fuel. Burning it releases more energy than does burning gasoline, weight for weight, and the only by-product is water. It is also safer than gasoline. If it escapes it rises rapidly upward because it is much lighter than air. A hydrogen fire rises away from the ground, so the chances of being burned by it are low, and, not being a liquid, it cannot cling to skin and clothing, as blazing gasoline does.

The difficulty with it concerns storage, but some manufacturers are working to solve this. There is a prototype BMW car with a 5.4-liter,

Fuel cells

A fuel cell is like a battery, but a battery that does not run down and that never needs recharging provided fuel is fed to it. Like a battery, it converts chemical energy into electricity and heat. Its fuel is hydrogen.

The cell has two porous electrodes separated by an electrolyte. This is a thin plastic sheet that allows protons (particles with positive charge) to pass, but blocks the passage of electrons (particles with negative charge). It is also called a polymer electrolyte membrane or proton exchange membrane. The electrolyte membrane is in contact with the surface of the cathode.

Hydrogen (H_2) fuel is fed under pressure into the anode (negative electrode). Oxygen (O_2) from the air is fed into the cathode (positive electrode).

In the anode, the hydrogen atoms encounter a catalyst, a substance that facilitates or accelerates a reaction but is not altered by it. Various substances are used, but most fuel cells use powdered platinum attached to cloth or a special kind of paper. The catalytic reaction separates electrons (e^-) from the hydrogen atoms, leaving the positively charged hydrogen nucleus, or proton (H^+).

$$2H_2 \rightarrow 4H^+ + 4e^-$$

The electrons travel around an external electrical circuit to the cathode, doing useful work on their way, such as running an engine.

The protons pass through the electrolyte membrane and enter the cathode. Oxygen also enters the cathode, where it meets the catalyst. The catalyst drives a reaction that separates oxygen molecules (O_2) into separate atoms, each of which possesses negative charge ($O^- + O^-$). When hydrogen reaches the cathode it reacts with the oxygen, and two electrons from the external circuit to form water.

$$2O^- + 4H^+ + 2e^- \rightarrow 2H_2O$$

Water vapor is released. It is the only product of the reaction. The diagram illustrates the arrangement of the components.

Fuel cells operate at temperatures higher than room temperature. The type described here operates at about 176°F (80°C), but others operate at up to about 390°F (200°C). Cells of this type produce 37 to 186 horsepower (50 to 250 kW).

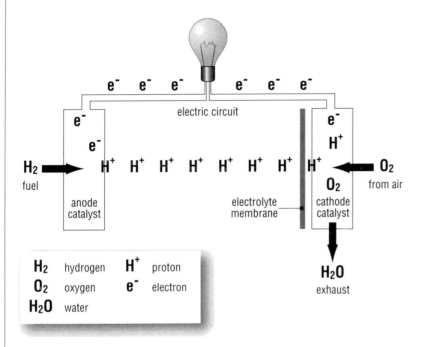

H_2	hydrogen	H^+	proton
O_2	oxygen	e^-	electron
H_2O	water		

Fuel cell

12-cylinder V-engine that runs on hydrogen. Its fuel tank, with a capacity of 37 gallons (140 liters), contains 70 layers of aluminum and fiberglass. The car has a top speed of 140 MPH (226 km/h) and a range of 217.5 miles (350 km) between refuelings.

Airships

Since heavier-than-air flight came to dominate air transport in the late 1930s, the emphasis has been on capacity and speed. Airships, the predecessors of modern civil airliners, were almost forgotten, their demise accelerated by a number of spectacular accidents. The accidents were attributed to the use of hydrogen as a lifting gas (see sidebar), and airships

Airships

An airship consists of a rigid frame covered with a skin to provide a large, enclosed space that is filled with a lifting gas. This is a gas that is lighter than air. The earliest airships used hydrogen as a lifting gas. All modern airships use helium because, although it provides less lift and is much more expensive, it is nonflammable. The vessel is powered by engines and is equipped to carry passengers, freight, or both, either suspended beneath the vessel in a gondola, or accommodated inside the frame. It is the rigid frame and the fact that it can be steered that distinguish an airship from a gas-filled or hot-air balloon and the powered balloon known as a blimp.

The first airship was designed and built by the French engineer Henri Giffard (1825–82). It was 144 feet (44 m) long, 52 feet (12 m) in diameter, and held 88,300 cubic feet (2,500 m³) of hydrogen. It was powered by a 3 horsepower (2 kW) steam engine with a three-bladed propeller 11 feet (3.4 m) in diameter turning at 110 r.p.m. On September 24, 1852, Giffard took it on its maiden flight from the Hippodrome in Paris, flying at about 6 MPH (10 km/h) in a light wind.

Airships possess positive buoyancy. That is to say, the total mass of the airship, including its lifting gas, is less than the mass of the air that its volume displaces. Therefore, the airship experiences a buoyancy force acting upward.

At 32°F (0°C) and an atmospheric pressure of 29.92 inches of mercury (1,000 mb), 1,000 cubic feet of air weigh 80.72 pounds (1,000 m³ weigh 1.29 tonnes), and 1,000 cubic feet of helium weigh 11.14 pounds (1,000 m³ weigh 178.6 kg). Hydrogen is about half as heavy as helium. Consequently, 1,000 cubic feet of helium will lift 62 to 65 pounds (1,000 m³ will lift 994 to 1,042 kg).

Its buoyancy means that the engines of an airship are not required to raise it from the surface or to propel it at a sufficient speed for it to experience lift from aerofoil surfaces. The engines need only propel the vessel at a speed that is convenient, so they can be quieter than those of a conventional aircraft and consume much less fuel.

Rigid airships do not depend on the internal gas pressure to maintain their shape. There are openings in the hull to allow air to enter and leave freely in order to equalize the pressure inside and out. Ballonets are containers filled with air and separated from the lifting gas by flexible diaphragms. Varying the pressure in the ballonets accommodates the changes in the volume of the lifting gas due to changing temperature. There are usually two ballonets, located fore and aft, and they are also used to trim (control the attitude of) the vessel.

acquired a reputation for being dangerous. The reputation was undeserved—hydrogen was not the cause of most of the accidents, and airships were no more dangerous than the aircraft that replaced them—but defending airships was of no avail. They vanished, most people thought forever.

Now they are promising to return in an updated version. Many companies are building or developing airships, but the most famous name in airship history is leading them. On August 5, 1908, an airship landed at the German city of Echterdingen. Later the same evening a gust of wind tore it from its mooring. The ship burst into flames and was totally destroyed. Undaunted, its designer and builder made more—eventually more than 100. He was Count Ferdinand von Zeppelin, and his airship was called Graf Zeppelin (*Graf* is German for "count").

Three decades later the airship died, zeppelins disappeared, but the Zeppelin company survived by making other products. Then, on September 18, 1997, a new zeppelin, built by Zeppelin Luftschifftechnik GmbH, flew over the city of Friedrichshafen. In May 2002 the Zeppelin NT LZ N07 (NT stands for "new technology") gave people short trips over Berlin.

The LZ N07 is 246 feet (75 m) long and holds about 29,000 cubic feet (8,200 m^3) of helium. It has three engines mounted on its internal frame but extending outside the envelope. Two of the engines are set on the sides of the airship and drive propellers that can turn to direct their thrust through 120°. The third engine drives a tail propeller that can move through 90°, giving thrust from horizontally to the rear to vertically downward, and also a small propeller directed to the side. The tail propellers help maneuverability. The vessel cruises at 80 MPH (129 km/h), carrying a crew of two and 12 passengers in its gondola. It is much smaller than the giants of the 1930s, but larger ships are planned, eventually with a volume of about 1,059,000 cubic feet (30,000 m^3) that can carry 84 passengers.

Airships are not fast, but they are friendly. The engines can be relatively small—reducing fuel consumption and exhaust emissions—and quiet. Those of the LZ N07 are contained in carbon fiber housings that dampen the noise they make, and their propellers turn at only 1,250 r.p.m. This also reduces noise. 21st Century Airships, Inc., a Canadian company based in Newmarket, Ontario, is developing spherical airships powered by turbo diesel engines with long propellers that turn slowly.

An airship does not need airfields in the conventional sense. It lands by descending low enough for ground technicians to catch its mooring line, like a ship docking. The technicians clip the line to a winch, and the winch winds the airship down until its gondola touches the ground. It can embark and disembark passengers in a city park or any other convenient open space. It needs hangar facilities for maintenance, but these can be sited in a remote spot far from the city.

Airships are ideal vessels for tourists, who can travel at a comfortable speed while enjoying the view from the large windows of the gondola. The vessel can set them down safely in places far from the nearest airport, then re-embark them at the end of their visit—like cruise passengers visiting a port. Airships are also suitable for carrying cargo from city center to city center, and they could be used for emergency and rescue operations. They are able to remain stationary in the air, to rise and descend vertically, and to turn through a circle with the nose of the vessel at the center.

A modern version of an old invention

None of these ideas is new. The first airship flew in 1852. W. R. Grove, a Welsh engineer, invented the fuel cell in 1839. H. Piper, an American engineer, filed for a patent on a hybrid vehicle on November 23, 1905. Designers have been experimenting with flywheels at least since the 1970s.

What is new is the application of new materials and new technologies to these old ideas. Modern airships use aluminum and carbon fiber, and they are controlled electronically. Their crews have the Global Positioning System to help them navigate and computer displays to monitor every aspect of the vessel's performance.

For 150 years after its invention, the fuel cell was no more than a curiosity. It could not be made to work usefully and economically. Now it can, because hydrogen can be supplied to it fairly easily, and there are modern polymer materials to make effective membranes.

Hybrid vehicles were always feasible, but while petroleum was cheap and plentiful and pollution was not a problem, they could not compete. Now they are seen as a straightforward means for reducing fuel consumption and therefore pollution.

The pollution we experience today can be prevented. In years to come—and not too many years—we will use vehicles that cause almost none.

Heat without fire

Using an electrical device, such as a power tool, freezer, or hair dryer, produces no gaseous or particulate pollution whatsoever. It is perfectly clean, although the electromagnetic field around it worries some people. Pollution results from burning fossil fuels, and when we use electricity this pollution occurs at the power station. Power generation is very much cleaner than it was years ago, but it is impossible to reduce it to zero. Combustion is oxidation, a chemical reaction, and like any reaction it changes compounds into other compounds. It does not destroy or remove them.

Pollution from power plants can be minimized, but the ideal solution would be to generate electricity using a technology that emits nothing. This sounds impossible, but it is not. Capturing solar radiation and extracting energy from the wind, tides, and waves and converting these to electricity leaves no chemical by-products (see "Sun and Wind," page 176). Harnessing the energy of falling water leaves no residue in the water or in the air, and although nuclear power generation does leave waste, the power plant itself emits nothing harmful into the air. Fusion power, a technology of the future, emits nothing and creates no hazardous waste.

Hydroelectric power

Bhutan, a small country of 633,000 people in the Himalayas sandwiched between India to the south and Tibet to the north, has a self-sufficient economy. It pays for the goods it imports by selling electricity to India. The electricity is generated by hydropower, the energy of falling water. There is so much falling water in Bhutan that the country is able to satisfy its own needs and export the surplus.

Laos, in southeastern Asia, is a much larger country. It sells hydro-electricity to its neighbor, Thailand. This is its largest source of foreign exchange.

Hydropower accounts for more than 95 percent of all power genera-tion in Laos, and all of the electricity in Bhutan is generated in this way. As the table shows, many other countries are highly dependent on hydropower. About 7 percent of the electrical power used in the United States is generated in this way.

People have used falling water as a source of power for thousands of years, and it has been used to generate electricity since about 1910. By 1907 hydropower was supplying about 15 percent of U.S. electricity, by 1920 it reached 25 percent, and it reached 40 percent by 1940. U.S. hydropower generating capacity tripled between 1921 and 1940 and tripled again between 1940 and 1980. Its relatively small contribution to the current power supply is not due to a decline in output, but to the much faster expansion of other types of generation.

Waterwheels to turbines

A traditional waterwheel, usually made from wood, turns slowly, and its rotary motion is transmitted by a driveshaft and gears to the machinery it operates. Because the "fuel"—the falling water—is free, the wheel does not need to be efficient, and it is not. This type of wheel is not suitable for power generation. That requires a turbine capable of spin-ning at high speed.

There are several types, two of which are illustrated in the drawing. The Pelton wheel comprises a set of buckets mounted around the rim of a wheel. Water is discharged into the buckets under pressure from a nozzle. Each bucket is divided in the center to allow it to deflect the water to the sides, out of the way of the jet heading for the next bucket.

COUNTRIES DEPENDENT ON HYDROPOWER

Country	Hydropower as % of total generation
Albania	94.9
Bhutan	100.0
Brazil	90.6
Burundi	98.4
Cameroon	96.7
Democratic Republic of Congo	99.6
Republic of Congo	99.3
Costa Rica	85.7
Ethiopia	94.2
Georgia	84.3
Ghana	99.9
Iceland	93.2
Kyrgyzstan	89.0
Laos	96.5
Malawi	97.8
Nepal	94.7
Norway	99.4
Paraguay	99.9
Rwanda	97.6
Tajikistan	97.9
Tanzania	86.3
Uganda	99.1
Uruguay	90.7
Vietnam	83.0
Zambia	99.5

(Source: *Encyclopaedia Britannica Book of the Year 2002*)

There are two versions of the Francis wheel. One, shown on the right in the opposite drawing, is encased in a spiral container called a volute. This distributes the water evenly around the wheel. The other version is open. A Francis turbine is fitted with adjustable guide vanes. These direct the water onto the runner blades around the edge of the spinning wheel. Adjusting the guide vanes alters the force with which the water strikes the runner blades and therefore regulates the output.

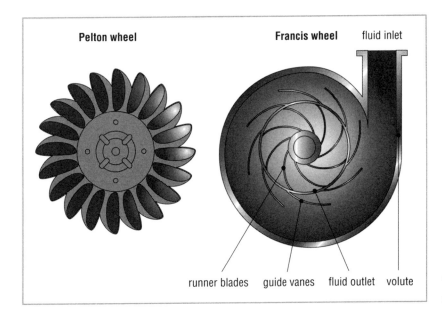

Pelton wheel   **Francis wheel**   fluid inlet

runner blades   guide vanes   fluid outlet   volute

Two widely used types of turbine

Pelton wheels are impulse turbines. These are installed in the air and are driven by the force of the jet of water striking the buckets. The Turgo wheel is a different type of impulse turbine that spins faster than a Pelton. The jet of water is directed to strike just one side of the buckets. The height from which water falls to reach the turbine is called the head. Impulse turbines are used at sites where the head is high, not less than 50 feet (15.25 m) and up to 6,000 feet (1,830 m). Each turbine delivers up to 200 MW (megawatts; 1 MW = 1 million [10^6] watts).

The Francis wheel is a reaction turbine. It operates while fully immersed in water and enclosed inside a pressure casing. Differences in water pressure across the runner blades generate a force similar to the lift generated by an aerofoil, and it is this force that spins the wheel. Other types of reaction turbines include the propeller and Kaplan wheels. The propeller is like a ship's propeller. It has three to six fixed blades driven by water flowing over them. The Kaplan is also a propeller, but the pitch of its blades—the angle between the blades and the following water—is variable. This allows the propeller to continue turning at a constant speed if the speed of the flowing water varies. Reaction turbines are used where the head is from 10 feet (3 m) to 2,000 feet (610 m), and they can deliver up to 800 MW. A propeller turbine works with a head of 10 to 300 feet (3 to 91.5 m) and delivers up to 100 MW, and a Kaplan turbine delivers up to 400 MW.

Hydropower plants

Large hydroelectric installations are built into the walls of dams. The dam impounds water in a reservoir, and it is released at a variable rate depending on electricity demand. Alternatively, a river or part of a river can sometimes be diverted through a canal or feeder channel called a penstock. The water passes the turbines and returns to the river. A diversion requires no dam, but it is feasible only where the river flows reliably and the diversion can provide a sufficient head.

Pumped storage systems are different. There are two components to electricity supply: base load and peak load. Base load is the power that is generated all the time, day and night, through the year. It can be varied, but usually not very quickly. At times when demand suddenly increases— around mealtimes, when everyone is cooking, for example, or when the weather turns cold and all the heating systems switch on—other generating capacity is required to satisfy this peak load. Pumped storage systems use surplus base load power, usually at night, to pump water from a low reservoir to another reservoir at a higher elevation, where it is stored. At times of peak load the water is released to flow through a penstock, past turbines, and back to the low-level reservoir.

Large hydropower plants are capable of generating more than 30 MW of power. Many generate a great deal more than this. Small installations generate 0.1 to 30 MW, and micro hydropower plants, used to provide electricity for single buildings or small communities, have a capacity of up to 100 kW (1,000 watts).

Hydropower is clean, but it can alter the quality of water downstream of the installation, and it will kill or seriously injure any fish that collide with the turbines. The construction of impoundment reservoirs involves flooding valleys, with the consequent loss of land, sometimes inhabited farmland, and natural habitat.

The technology is also restricted by the availability of suitable sites. Most of those that can be exploited are already in use, so there may be limited opportunity for further expansion.

Nuclear power

People fear nuclear power stations. They are unpopular in many parts of the world, especially in the United States and Europe, where there is a large and powerful antinuclear movement. The fact is, however, that nuclear power stations are very safe. During the 50 years in which nuclear reactors have been operating, there have been very few mishaps, and only two of these have caused deaths. Only six have released radioactive substances into the outside environment.

Hydropower is much more dangerous. Two hydroelectric dam failures in India in 1979 and 1980 killed 3,500 people. A dam failure in Colombia killed 160 people in 1983, and in 1991 a dam failure in Romania killed 116. Between 1970 and 1992 in the world as a whole, a total of about 4,000 people died through hydroelectric dam failures, 1,200 people died in accidents involving natural gas, and 6,400 died in accidents involving coal mining. Altogether, 41 people were killed by accidents at nuclear power plants.

The first fatal accident was at a U.S. experimental military reactor in 1961. Three workers at the reactor died, and there was a small release of radiation. The other fatalities occurred in 1986 at the Chernobyl-4 reactor in Ukraine. That accident involved a major radioactive release that affected much of Eastern Europe and Scandinavia. One worker at the plant was killed by falling debris, one by steam burns, and a further 29 from radiation exposure. Since the accident there have been up to 10 further deaths from thyroid cancer due to radiation exposure. According to the official United Nations report into the aftermath of the accident, there is no scientific evidence of any other deaths due to radiation exposure or of significant health effects to most of the people who were exposed. An accident in 1957 at the Windscale-1 reactor in the United Kingdom at the site now known as Sellafield caused widespread contamination. The reactor in question was producing plutonium for military use. There was a very minor release of radiation from an experimental reactor at Lucens, Switzerland, in 1969, of minor, short-lived radiation from the Three Mile Island-2 reactor in the United States in 1979, and a minor release in 1980 from the Saint Laurent-2 reactor in France. There were other accidents and some fatalities, most at military facilities, before 1980, but these occurred during the preparation or handling of fuel and were not due to reactor failures. An accident at Tokai-mura, Japan, in 1999, in which two people died, also occurred at a fuel preparation plant.

Radioactive waste

Although nuclear power plants release no particles or gases into the air, when reactor fuel is changed the old fuel remains as waste. Radioactive waste is classified as high, intermediate, and low level, depending on the level of its radioactivity. Intermediate-level waste originates mainly in nuclear reactor facilities and comprises materials that have been heavily irradiated. It can be processed into low-level waste. Low-level waste also includes contaminated clothing and materials that have been exposed to radioactive sources, not all from power plants. Low-level waste is disposed of safely in special landfill sites. About 90 percent of all radioactive waste is intermediate or low level.

High-level waste is produced by nuclear reactors and comprises either spent fuel in solid form or a liquid residue that remains at the end of spent-fuel reprocessing. The purpose of reprocessing is to recover uranium and plutonium from spent fuel. These are then recycled. The process begins by stripping the cladding from the fuel containers, then dissolving the fuel in strong acid. This is what liquefies the fuel, resulting in the highly radioactive liquid residue.

High-level waste is very hot. It is placed in containers and stored under water in large ponds. The water absorbs radiation as well as removes heat. It remains there for a number of years until it has cooled. At present, high-level waste is still held in ponds while a final decision is being made on permanent storage. Before storage the liquid waste can be converted into a type of glass or a synthetic rock called synrock. The solidified waste is then sealed in containers that corrode at a known rate, so that scientists can predict how long it will be, under the worst possible conditions, before the contents could escape from containment. The containers will then be stored in a permanent facility, probably below ground in a geologically stable structure, where they must remain isolated from the outside environment until their radioactivity has decayed to a level similar to that of natural rock containing radioactive elements, such as granite. This is likely to take several thousands years, but not millions, as some people have suggested. Finland is likely to be the first country to store high-level waste in a permanent underground facility. This will be near Eurajoki, where 78 percent of the population support the plan.

Although the disposal of high-level radioactive waste presents a problem, it is a problem that has already been solved technically and that can be solved politically. The amount produced by nuclear power plants is quite small. About 99 percent of all high-level waste results from weapons manufacture and from spent fuel from military reactors, such as those powering submarines. Research reactors, used in universities and industry, also generate waste.

Radioactive decay

Certain elements are unstable. Their atomic nuclei divide naturally. The splitting process is known as fission, and it transforms one element into another in a series of steps. These involve the emission of particles, electromagnetic radiation, or both. The emissions constitute radioactivity, and the effect on the element is called radioactive decay. Eventually, radioactive decay leads to nuclei that are stable, and decay ends. The time it takes for half of the atoms in a sample of an element to decay and lose their radioactivity is called the decay constant or half-life. This is extremely regular for any radioactive element.

An atomic nucleus is made of protons, carrying positive charge and neutrons, carrying no charge. The number of protons in its nucleus determine the chemical characteristics of an element, because it is the charge on the protons that governs the way the element reacts with other elements. Most elements occur in varieties, called isotopes, with different numbers of neutrons in their nuclei. Varying the number of neutrons alters the mass of the nucleus but has no effect on its chemistry. Isotopes are identified by their atomic mass, as, for example, oxygen-16, usually written as ^{16}O.

Uranium, for which the symbol is U, has three isotopes. ^{238}U, with a decay constant of 4.51 billion years, constitutes 99.27 percent of natural uranium, ^{235}U, with a decay constant of 713 million years, constitutes 0.72 percent, and ^{234}U, with a decay constant of 247,000 years, constitutes 0.006 percent. When ^{238}U decays, ^{234}U is one of the daughters in a series that leads to ^{206}Pb (lead). ^{235}U decays first to ^{227}Ac (actinium) and finally to ^{207}Pb. ^{233}U also exists and can be used as a reactor fuel, but it does not occur naturally. It is manufactured from ^{232}Th (thorium), a nonfissile element that is naturally abundant.

When uranium nuclei decay they emit neutrons. These have a great deal of energy and are known as fast neutrons. ^{238}U absorbs fast neutrons, but when a neutron strikes a ^{235}U atom it destabilizes the nucleus. This promptly decays, releasing two or three more neutrons, each of which may strike another ^{235}U nucleus and so on in chain reaction. The chance of a neutron striking a nucleus depends on the total mass of atoms in its vicinity. If there is less than a certain mass, many of the neutrons will escape. The critical mass is the minimum mass needed to sustain a chain reaction. It must be a critical mass of ^{235}U, however, because ^{238}U absorbs neutrons so fast it will not sustain a chain reaction.

Nuclear fission releases energy. Mass for mass, uranium fission releases about 2.5 million times more energy than the combustion of carbon.

Inside a reactor

A nuclear reactor harnesses the energy of radioactive decay. The most widely used fuel is enriched uranium. This is uranium that has been processed to increase the content of ^{235}U to about 3 percent. Effectively, this reduces the amount of ^{238}U and the percentage of neutrons ^{238}U isotope absorbs. The uranium, in the form of uranium oxide, is made into ceramic pellets sealed inside metal cylinders called fuel rods. The fuel rods are bundled together to make a fuel assembly.

In order to increase further the likelihood that neutrons will strike a ^{235}U nucleus, the fast neutrons must be slowed down. This is achieved by embedding the fuel assembly in a moderator, a substance that slows fast neutrons when these collide with its atoms.

The rate of the chain reaction must also be controlled. This is achieved using a substance that absorbs neutrons, commonly boron. The absorbing material is formed into control rods that can be raised or lowered as required into spaces in the fuel assembly. The fuel assembly, control rods, and moderator together make up the reactor core. The reactor must then have a means of removing the heat produced inside the core and using it to produce steam to drive the turbines that operate the electrical generators.

There are several types of reactors, but most commercial reactors for power generation use water both as a moderator and to remove heat from the core. These are pressurized water reactors (PWR). The water inside the reactor is held under high pressure. Boiling water reactors (BWR), the most widely used alternative, allow the water in the reactor to boil and use the steam directly to drive the turbines.

The diagram shows the layout of a PWR. Water is pumped under high pressure through a primary water loop. It moderates the reaction in the reactor and at the same time is heated. The hot water then passes to a

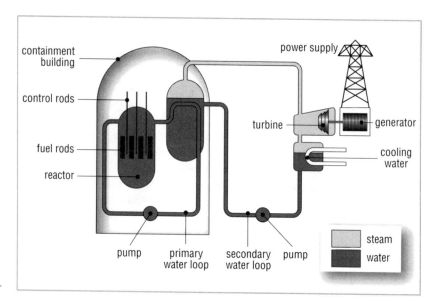

Pressurized water reactor

chamber where it is piped through a heat exchange in a tank of water. It passes heat to the surrounding water. This is held under lower pressure, allowing it to boil, and the steam is fed to the turbines. After passing the turbines the steam is cooled by contact with pipes carrying cold water and is pumped back to the chamber to be heated again. This constitutes the secondary water loop. The turbines are connected to the generators.

Safety

Reactors are designed to minimize the risk of radiation leakage. The fuel pellets are held inside cladding that prevents material leakage, and the reactor itself is contained inside a very solid reactor vessel.

In the case of commercial plants, the reactor vessel is located inside a containment building. This consists first of the reactor building, which is designed to prevent radioactivity from escaping into the environment outside. It must also withstand violent events, such as a major failure in which most of the contents of the reactor core escape from the reactor vessel, an explosion within the reactor, or an outside occurrence such as an earthquake. Consequently, the reactor building is housed inside a containment structure made from thick steel covered with concrete. Not all research and military reactors have containment buildings.

In addition, a reactor has devices to prevent a major accident from causing the core temperature to rise out of control. The control rods can be lowered rapidly and fully to shut down the reaction. Emergency core cooling systems—there are several, so that if one should fail another will not—automatically cool the core using cold water, and an emergency power system is activated automatically if the main power supply should fail. It ensures that pumps and valves continue to function.

Nuclear fusion

A conventional reactor exploits the energy released by nuclear fission, the splitting of an atomic nucleus into two approximately equal parts. A fusion reactor exploits the energy that is released when two nuclei merge, or fuse. Stars shine and radiate heat because of the fusion reactions that take place inside them.

When two nuclei fuse a small amount of their combined mass is converted into energy. The amount is small, but the relationship between mass and energy is described by Einstein's equation $E = mc^2$, where E is energy, m is mass, and c is the speed of light. This suggests that a small amount of fuel is capable of releasing an extremely large amount of energy.

The fuels for a fusion reactor are deuterium (D) and tritium (T). Deuterium, or "heavy hydrogen," is an isotope of hydrogen with a nucleus comprising one proton and one neutron. About one water molecule in every 3,000 contains a deuterium atom. Deuterium is therefore very abundant. If all the power on Earth were generated from deuterium, there would be enough to last for several million years. Tritium is an isotope of hydrogen with one proton and two neutrons in its nucleus. Tritium does not occur naturally, but it can be manufactured from lithium, a plentiful metal. Using the deuterium–tritium reaction, 132 gallons (500 liters) of water producing 0.35 ounce (10 g) of deuterium, and 1.05 ounce (30 g) of lithium producing 0.525 ounce (15 g) of tritium, could produce enough electricity to supply all the needs of one American for a lifetime. The reaction is

$$D + T \rightarrow {}^4He + n + energy$$

^{4}He is an isotope of helium produced by fusion and n stands for neutron.

The difficulty is that atomic nuclei carry positive charge, and like charges repel one another. Consequently, it is very difficult to achieve fusion. The atomic nuclei, stripped of their electrons to form a plasma, must be brought together at high speed, and a large number of nuclei must take part. Deuterium and tritium will not fuse at temperatures below 180 million degrees F (100 million degrees C). They must be raised to this temperature and at the same time isolated from the walls of their container, because contact with the walls would cool them. There are several designs for containment. The most advanced—in the sense that scientists and engineers have been working with it for longer than with any of the others—is called a Tokamak. It is toroidal (doughnut-shaped) and contains the fuel inside an intense magnetic field. So far, there is no commercial fusion reactor. Research has continued for several decades, and scientists hope that the technology will start to produce power before the middle of the 21st century.

If they are right and fusion power becomes a reality, it will bring important advantages. Its fuel is abundant and will not be exhausted for a very long time. A fusion reactor is inherently safe. The reaction cannot run away because if anything goes wrong it shuts itself down. There are no gaseous or particulate emissions of any kind, so the reactor is incapable of polluting the air. The reactor structure does become radioactive because it is bombarded by neutrons, but the extent of this can be minimized by choosing the right materials. In any case, the radioactivity decays quickly. There is no waste that requires long-term disposal.

Sun and wind

Sunshine and wind are free. The Sun radiates energy that bathes the Earth and that also drives all the movements of the air and oceans. It produces the wind and waves as well as supplying us with light and radiant heat. This source of energy is there for the taking. It costs us nothing, it causes no pollution, and it is inexhaustible.

When people talk about "renewable energy," this is what they mean. There are several ways solar energy can be harnessed for our use. These are based on a variety of technologies.

Some people also count geothermal energy as a renewable source of "natural" energy. In fact, however, geothermal energy is quite different. It is not derived from solar energy, it is not inherently clean, and it is not inexhaustible.

Geothermal energy

The temperature of the rocks beneath our feet increases with depth. This rise in temperature is due mainly to the heat released by the radioactive decay (see "Heat without Fire," page 166) of elements present naturally in the rocks. In a sense, Earth's crust is a huge nuclear reactor.

The rate of temperature increase is called the geothermal gradient. This averages 58 to 116°F for every mile of depth (20 to 40°C km^{-1}), but it can be considerably greater in volcanic regions. There are places, however, where locally the gradient is unusually high, and there is a body of hot water or rock fairly near the surface.

If a hole is drilled into such a pool of hot water, the water will rush to the surface, where its heat can be used. Hot rock is exploited rather differently. Two holes are drilled into it some distance apart. Explosive charges are then detonated at the bottom of the two holes. The explosions shatter the rock between the holes, forming small spaces where water can pass. Water is then pumped down one hole under pressure. It flows through the shattered hot rock, is heated by contact with it, and rises through the second hole and into pipelines that carry it to where its heat is extracted.

This is not clean water, however. Substances that are present in the rock dissolve into the hot water that washes past them. Whether the water is from a subterranean reservoir that has been there for millions of years or was pumped down recently, it reaches the surface as a solution of mineral compounds. It is highly corrosive and would cause serious pollution if it should mix with surface waters. It requires careful treatment and must not be allowed to mix with other water. When its heat has been extracted from it, the water requires careful disposal.

Extracting heat from a localized area below ground cools the rocks. After a number of years, the hot water will be gone and the hot rocks will have cooled to the temperature of the surrounding rock. The source of energy will then be exhausted.

Geothermal energy is extracted from hot water. It can be used to preheat water that will then be heated further for industrial use or to generate electricity. It can also be piped through a group of buildings to provide space and water heating. Hot water must be used locally, however, because it cools rapidly as it passes along pipes. Geothermal energy is useful only if it occurs in an area where it can be used. Consequently, it is of very limited value.

Biomass

Sunlight supplies the energy for photosynthesis and therefore for plant growth, and that is the most obvious way to exploit it: allow the sunlight to grow plants, and then use the plants as fuel. All the plants growing in a particular area, or all those of a particular species, constitute the biomass in that area. Biomass fuel is fuel derived from plants that were grown for that purpose.

It is hardly original, of course. We have been burning wood since prehistoric times, and fossil fuels were originally made by photosynthesis. Before coal became the preferred fuel, industry used wood or charcoal. The wood, for direct use or for making charcoal, was grown for the purpose in plantations where trees were cut at ground level at intervals of 10 to 12 years. The stumps then regenerated by growing shoots all around the edge. The shoots were harvested as tall poles when they reached suitable size. The technique was called coppicing, and it is being revived in some places by conservationists because coppiced woodland provides an excellent habitat for wildlife.

Modern biomass fuels are more diverse. Fast-growing tree crops, such as various willow *(Salix)* species, are grown where the ground is suitable. Crop residues, such as leaves, stems, and husks, can be burned. Conventional farm crops also supply fuel, although the varieties used are bred for this purpose and in future may be modified genetically to improve their characteristics. These varieties are not usually edible. Potatoes and corn (maize) are the crops most widely grown for fuel. The sugars and starches they contain are converted to ethanol (alcohol) by fermentation. Ethanol can be used as a fuel like gasoline.

Biomass fuel is renewable because after one crop has been harvested another can be sown. Producing it calls for no new technologies or skills. Farmers grow the crops using ordinary farming methods. Burning the fuel can pollute the air, however, although it does not contribute to global warming because the carbon dioxide its combustion releases was taken from the air a few months earlier by the growing plants. It is simply being recycled.

There are disadvantages to biomass fuel production. Growing the crops occupies land that would otherwise be growing conventional farm crops. Crops grown for food or industrial uses, such as oils and fibers, command a higher price than do crops grown for fuel. Farmers will therefore grow fuel crops only if they are subsidized to do so or if there is no market for alternative crops and they must choose between growing fuel or leaving the land fallow. This does not rule out biomass fuels as a significant source of energy. As agriculture becomes increasingly productive, less land is needed to supply the food and raw materials we need. Land can be taken out of agricultural production in parts of North America and Europe and could be devoted to producing biomass crops. This may not be an option in the less-developed countries of Africa, Asia, and Latin America, however, where all the available farmland is needed to grow conventional crops.

Solar warmth

We can use the warmth of the sunshine directly. Solar collectors are a familiar sight. Usually mounted on the roof but sometimes on the ground, they help to heat the household water supply.

A solar collector is a shallow box containing a pipe that carries water back and forth to form a heat exchanger. The pipe is connected to a second heat exchanger inside the hot water tank, and a small pump drives the circulation. Inside the collector the pipe sits on an insulated base to minimize the loss of heat and is covered by a matte black material that maximizes the absorption of heat. The collector is mounted so that it faces the noonday Sun. Water in the collector becomes hot and is carried to the hot water tank, where it gives up its heat. The device is simple and effective, but it requires warm sunshine. It is less effective in winter, and it is uncertain whether it can capture enough heat in high latitudes to warrant the cost of installing it.

A solar chimney converts solar heat into electricity on an industrial scale. The technology has been tried experimentally. Several research teams are developing it, but at present there is no operational solar chimney.

In the desert an area of about 14 square miles (37 km²) is covered by a glass or plastic roof, like a greenhouse, about 6.5 feet (2 m) above the ground but rising toward the center. Beneath the roof the ground is covered with

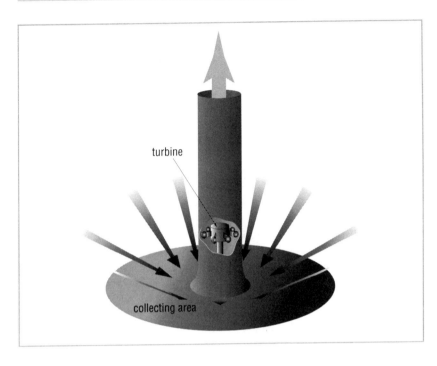

turbine

collecting area

Solar chimney

gravel that colors it matte black. At the center of the "greenhouse" is a tall cylindrical structure, resembling a chimney. A turbine is located inside the chimney. The diagram shows how the components are arranged.

The covered ground acts like a solar collector. The ground heats up, heating the air in contact with it. The hot air rises toward the center of the roof, where it flows up the chimney. As it rises, more air is drawn in to replace it, and the flow accelerates. Air rising up the chimney spins a turbine, and the turbine is linked to a generator.

An experimental solar chimney operated in Spain for seven years, and there have been other demonstration chimneys. These prove that the concept works.

A solar pond also traps solar heat, but it has no moving parts. Salt water is denser than fresh water, and so fresh water that is poured carefully over the top of a layer of salt water will float there without mixing. A solar pond uses a layer of fresh water to insulate a layer of salt water.

The pond is lined with black plastic to absorb heat. Water saturated with salt forms a layer over the bottom, and a layer of fresh water lies over it. The Sun heats the plastic lining, which heats the salt water. Convection currents mix the salt water, ensuring that it heats evenly, but they do not rise into the overlying fresh water. It remains at the same temperature as the air. Hot salt water is piped from the pond through a heat exchanger in a tank containing fresh water, then returned to the bottom of the pond to be heated again. The hot fresh water can then be heated further to raise steam for power generation. The fresh water layer in the pond must be replenished from time to time to replace the water lost by evaporation.

Solar cells

Solar collectors, solar chimneys, and solar ponds trap the heat of the Sun. This restricts them to regions with a warm climate. Solar cells are different. They trap light itself and convert it directly into electricity. Solar cells, mounted as arrays, usually of 36 cells, provide power for spacecraft. Closer to home they are used to power some pocket calculators, illuminated road signs, traffic lights, and buoys at sea. In years to come arrays mounted on roofs may provide electricity for the building below. They could do so now—the technology is firmly established—but the electricity would be too expensive to be economical.

Although solar cells can function in high latitudes and at high elevations in winter as well as in summer, they do have limitations. They need sunlight, so they will not work at night, and winter nights are long in the far north. This means either that electricity generated during the day must be stored for use at night or there must be an alternative supply.

Electricity can be stored in batteries. Batteries that are suitable for the purpose are expensive—ordinary car batteries will not do—and require additional equipment to maintain them in good order. A small generator or the ordinary power grid can provide an alternative supply.

Solar cells and batteries deliver direct current (DC). Electrical appliances use alternating current (AC), and that is also what the grid supplies. Consequently, electricity from solar cells and batteries must be converted from DC to AC before it can be used. The device that converts it is called an inverter.

Essentially, a solar cell is a semiconductor, usually made from slices cut from a crystal of very pure silicon that has been modified by adding small amounts of particular impurities. A semiconductor is a substance intermediate between a conductor and an insulator. Electrons move freely through a conductor but cannot move through an insulator. They will move through a semiconductor when "pushed" by an electric field.

A silicon atom contains 14 electrons arranged in three shells. The two inner shells are filled, but the outer shell has only four electrons (although it could hold eight). Consequently, the atom shares electrons with four of its neighbors. This locks the atoms together into the lattice structure of the crystal. To convert the silicon into a semiconductor material, a few atoms of phosphorus are added to one layer of silicon and a few atoms of boron to another. The addition of phosphorus and boron is called doping. Silicon with added phosphorus is known as n-type silicon, and that with boron is p-type silicon.

The outer shell of a phosphorus atom contains five electrons. The atom can form four bonds with silicon, but one electron remains unattached. When a photon of light strikes the silicon, its energy is absorbed, allowing an electron to break free. The free electron moves around the crystal in search of a vacancy—a "hole" into which it can fall.

Boron has only three electrons in its outer atomic shell. Consequently, each boron atom has a vacancy for an electron—a free hole. Holes can also

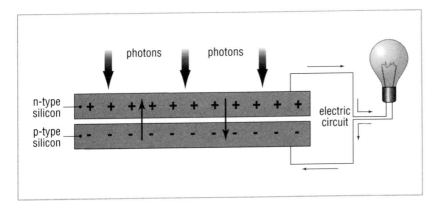

Solar cell. When photons strike the n-type silicon, they free electron-hole pairs. Some of the electrons pass from the p side to the n side. They leave the n side by flowing through the circuit, doing useful work on the way, and then return to the p side.

move around, because each time an electron moves it leaves a hole that is quickly filled.

Place a layer of n-type silicon—"n" for negative, because it contains free electrons—next to a layer of p-type silicon—"p" for positive, because it contains free holes—and an electric field will form, separating them. The field will push electrons from the p-side to the n-side, but not in the other direction. The technical term for this type of device is *diode*.

A striking photon frees one electron, thus creating one free electron and also one hole. If the electron–hole pair approach the electric field between the two layers, the field will send the electron to the n-side and the hole to the p-side. The n-type silicon then carries a negative charge, the p-type silicon a positive charge, and if a circuit connects them a current will flow, returning the electrons to the holes on the p-side. The diagram shows how this works.

The semiconductor with a p–n junction lies at the heart of a solar cell. To complete the device, the semiconductor is sandwiched between other layers, as shown in the diagram. The cover glass protects the cell. The antireflective coating below it maximizes the absorption of light. Then, above and below the two semiconductor layers, there are layers containing the electrical contacts that link the cell to its neighbors in the array and to the supply.

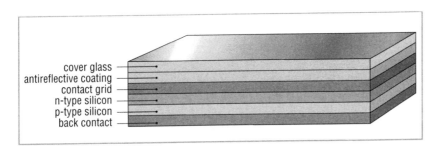

The layers in a solar cell

Wind and water

Wind generation is the most advanced of all the technologies for producing electricity directly from solar energy. Its principle is very simple. A large rotor, or wind turbine, resembling an aircraft propeller is mounted on top of a high tower, where it is free to turn so that it always faces into the wind. As it turns in the wind, a system of gearing links it to a generator mounted directly behind the rotor. Sensors detect the wind direction, and a small electric motor ensures that the rotating blades remain oriented at right angles to the wind direction. In most designs the pitch of the rotor blades—the angle they make with the wind—can be varied, allowing them to turn at a constant speed despite variations in wind speed. The blades can also be feathered, or turned so they are edge-on to the wind. This stops them from turning when it is necessary to shut down a turbine for maintenance or when the wind speed exceeds their designed tolerance.

The rated capacity for wind turbines varies from about 4 kW to about 5 MW, depending on the design. Single generators are used to supply power to individual buildings or small, isolated communities. Generators that feed power into the supply grid are arranged in arrays called wind farms. Most wind farms comprise about 10 to 40 generators, but large offshore wind farms that are being planned in northern Europe will have more than 100.

Wind farms are built on the windiest sites available, but even there the air is occasionally calm. That fact, together with the time lost for repairs and maintenance, means that a wind generator operates at no more than 40 percent of its rated capacity. A conventional modern power station has a capacity of about 1 GW and operates at 80 percent of capacity, so its actual output is 800 MW. A wind farm with an actual output of 800 MW and turbines rated at 500 kW—about the average capacity—would need to comprise about 4,000 turbines. Wind turbines must be sited some distance apart so they do not "steal" the wind from one another. The usual spacing is five to seven rotor diameters. Consequently, wind farms occupy large areas. Livestock can graze the land between the turbines, and some other types of farming are possible, although the turbines may make it difficult to maneuver farm machines if the land is to be cultivated. The public is not allowed unrestricted access to the sites for safety reasons—there is always a remote risk that a rotor blade could become detached and fall—and to guard against sabotage.

The output from a wind turbine is proportional to the area swept by the rotors and to the cube of the wind speed. This means that if the wind speed doubles, the output increases eightfold. That is why the windiest sites are chosen and the turbines are large.

At present the total capacity of the wind turbines installed in the United States is more than 425 GW. The American Wind Energy Association estimates that wind power could contribute 20 percent of U.S. demand from a land area of about 16,000 square miles (41,440 km^2). This sounds large, but it is equal to less than 1 percent of the total land area, and it would be distributed throughout the country.

Moving water can also be used to generate power. Tidal flow provides the most reliable movement, but a tidal power station requires a large tidal range, the vertical distance between the sea level at the highest and lowest tides. The biggest tidal power plant in the world is located on the River Rance in northern Britanny, France, and it has been operational for more than 30 years. Its 24 turbine generators are housed inside a dam, called a barrage, nearly half a mile (0.8 km) long with a road along the top linking the towns of St. Malo and Dinard. As the tide rises water flows through the dam and into a bay where it is held. As the tide falls the water is released and flows back through the dam and past the turbines. The La Rance plant is being upgraded by installing new turbines that spin on both the incoming and outgoing tides. This will double the output of a plant that already supplies 90 percent of the electricity used in Britanny.

Tidal power plants are restricted by cost, the availability of sites, and environmental impact. They can be installed only on large river estuaries with a large tidal range. The cost of building a tidal barrage is high compared with the cost of building other types of power station. Scientists also worry about the effect of the barrage on the river downstream and its wildlife. The barrage alters the way water flows out to the sea, and this alters the way it deposits sediment. This might affect the use of the estuary by shipping. Many invertebrate animals inhabit estuarine mud, and many wading birds feed on them. Altering the flow might radically disturb this habitat. Although they sound attractive and La Rance is clearly a success, tidal barrages are unlikely to contribute significantly to future power requirements.

Waves can also be harnessed, at least in theory. There are two ways to approach the task. The first exploits an oscillating water column (OWC). This is a device that is firmly fixed to a coastal rock face below sea level. It contains a column of air that is compressed when water rises from the bottom. Compression drives the air past turbines that generate power. Each time a wave arrives, the turbines are given a fresh spin. The first OWC device was installed in Japan to provide power for the light on top of a buoy, but some years later a much bigger one was installed in a fjord at Tofteshallen, Norway. It generated 500 kW of power and continued doing so for several years, but it was finally wrecked by a severe storm in 1998. An experimental OWC device has since been built on the island of Islay, Scotland. It produces 180 kW.

The alternative approach involves a device that floats on the surface. As it rises and falls with the waves, its vertical motion is converted to a rotary motion and used to generate power. The most advanced type is the "Salter duck," invented in the 1970s by Professor Stephen Salter of Edinburgh University. It is a tear-shaped device that rests on the water surface. As the drawing indicates, the ducks are linked in strings, usually of 25, to a rod running through the thicker end. As the waves pass, they alternately

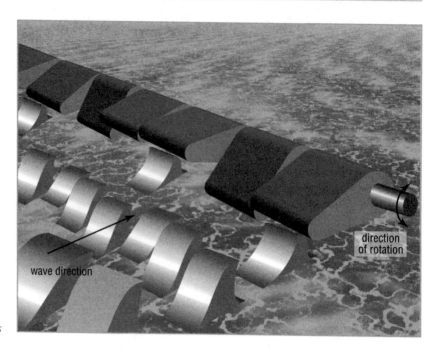

Salter ducks

raise and lower the unattached end, causing the ducks to nod. The nodding motion is converted into electrical power.

As with the OWC devices, a duck installation, including the linkage to the generator and the cable carrying the power, must be able to withstand fierce storms. Achieving this is difficult. As with a wind farm, a set of duck arrays big enough to generate a useful amount of power would occupy a very large sea area. It could be sited far enough from the coast to be out of sight, but ships might have to divert a long way to avoid it.

It is also possible to exploit the difference in temperature between water near the ocean surface and water at a greater depth. This is not a new idea. It was first proposed in 1881 by the French physicist Jacques-Arsène d'Arsonval (1851–1940), although he did not live to see it built. The first working device was built by Georges Claude (1870–1960) in 1930.

The technology requires a temperature difference of at least 36°F (20°C) between the surface water and water at a depth of 3,300 feet (1,000 m). If there is less difference than this, so that cold water is at a greater depth, more energy is expended pumping cold water to the surface than the system generates. A suitable temperature difference can be found only between latitudes 32°N and 25°S. It is essentially a tropical method for generating power.

Ocean thermal energy conversion (OTEC) is applied as a closed-cycle, open-cycle, or hybrid system. In the closed-cycle design, as originally conceived by d'Arsonval, warm surface water is used to heat a working fluid with a low boiling point, such as ammonia, thus converting it to steam that drives a generating turbine. Cold sea water then condenses the working fluid for it to be vaporized again.

Claude used an open-cycle design in which warm surface water is the working fluid. This is vaporized under a partial vacuum, producing low-pressure steam that drives the turbine. The steam can then be condensed in a heat exchanger, as in the closed cycle, or simply mixed with cold water.

Hybrid plants combine both approaches. Warm sea water is vaporized in a partial vacuum, and the steam is used to vaporize a working fluid.

OTEC systems can be built offshore or onshore, provided the coast shelves steeply to a sufficient depth. The efficiency is extremely low—no more than about 2 percent of the available energy is converted to electricity—but there is a limitless volume of ocean water available. Consequently, the potential yield of OTEC devices could be large.

The Sun supplies us with heat and light. It provides the energy that moves the atmosphere, generating the winds, and the winds generate ocean waves. Heat, sunlight, wind, and waves can all be used to obtain energy. The potential is huge, but so are the limitations. Natural energy is widely dispersed. Concentrating it is necessary because we require differences in energy, not simply an even spread of energy, and this is costly. Nevertheless, as the technologies advance our reliance on these sources of energy will increase.

Laws and treaties

Air pollution is not a new problem. We have been polluting the air for as long as we have been using fire. That is not surprising, because the burning of fuel is the major cause of air pollution, nor are we the first to recognize the problem. People realized something was wrong centuries ago when they noticed that the air smelled bad, made them cough, and made their eyes run.

As long ago as 1273 King Edward I of England passed a law that forbade the cooking of food over a coal fire. Coal smoke imparts a distinctive flavor to food, and the king was responding to a popular belief that it could make people ill and even kill them. It is doubtful whether the law had much effect, and it seems that it did little to improve the quality of London air, because in 1306 the same king issued a proclamation that banned the burning of coal in London. That law was enforced, at least for a time. One manufacturer who disobeyed was tried and beheaded.

Modern attempts to address the problem began in the late 19th century. Smoke abatement laws were passed in the United States in the 1880s. These dealt with smoke from factories, railroads, and ships and were administered by local boards of health. In Britain the Public Health (London) Act of 1891 aimed at controlling smoke emissions, but its effect was quite limited because, like the American legislation, it failed to deal with the principal source of city smoke, domestic fires. A second attempt to clean the air made the same mistake. The Public Health (Smoke Abatement) Act of 1926 recognized that smoke was harmful to health, but lawmakers shrank from dictating what people should do in the privacy of their own homes. Householders went on burning coal for heating, hot water, and cooking until the middle of the 20th century.

Clean air laws

Despite the lack of progress, more was being discovered about the effects and extent of polluted air. The year of the feeble British legislation, 1926, also saw the first large-scale survey of air pollution in the United States, centered on Salt Lake City, and two years later the public health service began monitoring air quality in the eastern industrial cities. It found that pollution over New York City was reducing the amount of sunshine by 20 to 50 percent. A further survey in 1937 showed that conditions in New York were worsening.

A serious smog incident (see "Pea Soup: The Original Smog," page 37) in St. Louis in 1939 led to a vigorous campaign to reduce smoke by switching to a higher grade of coal and oil. In 1941 St. Louis adopted the first regulations in the United States aimed at controlling smoke emissions. The first Air Pollution Control District was formed in 1947 in Los Angeles, and the first national conference on air pollution was held in 1949, sponsored by the public health service. The first international conference on air pollution was held in New York City in 1955, and an International Clear Air Congress was held in London in 1961.

Congress passed the Air Pollution Research Act in 1955. After several smog incidents had caused deaths—between 170 and 260 people died during a smog in New York City in November 1953—legislators began to act. California was the first to impose limits on automobile emissions in 1959.

Rapid industrialization caused very severe air pollution in the Soviet Union during the 1930s and 1940s. This led the Soviet government to enact what may have been the first modern law dealing with air pollution. It came into force in 1949, but like British and American laws of the time, it was not very effective.

The first really effective law was the Clean Air Act of 1956 passed by the British government following the London smog of 1952. The law succeeded because at last legislators were prepared to impose restrictions on domestic fires. The law established "smokeless zones," urban areas where it was forbidden for anyone to emit smoke. That meant that coal fires were banned in most British towns and cities. It did not end air pollution, because people were still permitted to burn smokeless fuels, such as coke, but it almost eliminated smoke. As it turned out, the politicians' fears were not justified. People soon saw the benefit as the skies cleared for the first time in centuries. What is more, smoke is highly visible, and so the law was simple to enforce.

Establishing the EPA

U.S. federal legislation followed a parallel route. The Air Quality Act of 1967 empowered the Department of Health, Education and Welfare to designate areas within which air quality would be controlled. The department was authorized to implement this by setting standards for air quality by specifying the technologies to be used in reducing pollution, and it was given powers to prosecute persistent offenders if local agencies failed to do so.

In 1970 the Clean Air Act was passed. This strengthened the Air Quality Act. It was amended in 1990 to deal more specifically with acid rain, urban air pollution, and emissions of toxic substances (see the section Pollution and Health). The amendments also instituted a national program of permits to make it easier to apply the law and improved the mechanisms for enforcement.

The Clean Air Act is one of the pieces of legislation that established the authority of the Environmental Protection Agency (EPA), formed in 1970. Other relevant legislation includes the National Environmental Policy Act of 1970, the Asbestos Hazard Emergency Response Act of 1986, the Asbestos Information Act of 1988, and the Asbestos School Hazard Abatement Act of 1982.

International air pollution

Air moves, and it does not respect international frontiers. This means that pollution generated in one country can drift across the border into an adjacent country. What is worse, the pollution generated close to a frontier may create no difficulties in the country producing it but serious problems for its neighbor.

Scientists studying the movement of air discovered in the 1970s that airborne pollutants sometimes travel long distances. At the time they were principally concerned with acid rain (see "Acid Rain, Snow, Mist, and Dry Deposition," page 90), but it was clear that other forms of pollution were also implicated. The scientific findings led to intergovernmental discussions and then to negotiations held under the auspices of the United Nations Economic Commission for Europe (UNECE). These culminated in 1979 with the Convention on Long-range Transboundary Air Pollution. The convention was signed by 35 countries, including all the European nations, Canada, and the United States.

It became the framework for later legislation dealing with particular aspects of the main issue. In 1985, for example, 20 of the signatory nations signed a protocol to the convention committing themselves to reducing their national annual emissions of sulfur dioxide to a level 30 percent lower than it had been in 1980. These nations came to be nick-named "The 30-Percent Club," and, having committed themselves, they urged other nations to join them.

A blanket 30-percent reduction sounded impressive, but the approach was flawed. Some environments are much more sensitive than are others to a particular form of pollution, and some reductions can be achieved more quickly and cheaply than others. When the "30-percent" agree-ment—its correct title is the Sulfur Protocol—became due for revision in 1989, the UNECE recommended using a computer model called RAINS, developed by the International Institute for Applied Systems Analysis, to help in assessing how to reduce pollution most effectively. The second Sulfur Protocol was signed in 1994, based on information obtained from the model. The model is also being used within the European Union to develop comprehensive limits on emissions of ammonia, nitrogen oxides, and volatile organic compounds.

Ozone

Concern about the depletion of the stratospheric ozone layer over Antarc-tica led to the establishment in 1977 of the United Nations Consultative Committee on the Ozone Layer. Its purpose was to assess the scientific evidence for depletion of the ozone layer and to secure international agreement on steps to halt and then reverse the depletion.

The consultative committee continues to meet. It prepared the way for the UN Convention to Protect the Ozone Layer, signed in March 1985 by 49 countries. The convention called on nations to cooperate in monitoring the ozone layer and to agree on ways to halt its depletion. In 1987 appropriate measures for achieving this were laid out in the Montreal Protocol on Substances That Deplete the Ozone Layer, usually shortened to Montreal Protocol. The Montreal Protocol has since been strength-ened by amendments agreed to in London in 1990, Copenhagen in 1992, Vienna in 1995, Montreal in 1997, and Beijing in 1999. The Beijing amendments came into force on January 1, 2000.

Progress continues

The United Nations Environment Program, established following recom-mendations to do so from the United Nations Conference on the Human Environment held in Stockholm in 1972, is the UN agency that brings governments together to devise ways of reducing air pollution. As aware-ness of the economic and social costs of pollution has grown, so has the willingness of politicians to address them. This has made it possible not only to secure token agreement to international treaties seeking to reduce pollution, but to ensure that the resulting laws are effective and enforced.

The progress continues. Leaded gasoline was banned some years ago throughout North America and the European Union, but its use continues in some countries. In March 2002 a call for the ban to be extended through-out Asia came from the First International Conference on Environmental Risks to Children's Health, held in Bangkok, Thailand, and attended by more than 300 health and environmental experts.

International action has also helped to stimulate national and regional action. On October 24, 2001, the European Parliament agreed to new measures to reduce pollution by smog. These will ensure that by 2010 the maximum level of ozone recommended as safe by the World Health Organization will not be exceeded more than 25 times in each year, except where it proves impossible to achieve the necessary reduction.

Irish cities also suffer from pollution, and in October 2001 the Irish environment ministry proposed a nationwide ban on the sale of bituminous coal, the type of coal that produces copious amounts of smoke when it burns. Coal burning is already forbidden in Dublin and 10 other cities. The new regulation would extend the ban to the rest of the country. It would also ban the burning of coke—nowadays made from petroleum—as an alternative. The ministry estimated that the ban would reduce annual emissions of sulfur dioxide by 7,700 tons (7,000 tonnes). In 1999 Ireland emitted 173,000 tons (157,000 tonnes), and like all EU members it is required to reduce this—in Ireland's case to 46,200 tons (42,000 tonnes) a year by 2010.

In June 2000 the Washington, D.C., Circuit Court of Appeals issued a final ruling upholding an EPA plan to improve air quality over the eastern United States. The regulations would allow the EPA and the 37 affected states to develop a fixed schedule aimed at reducing nitrogen oxide emissions from 392 coal-burning power plants and factories located in 22 of the states. Emissions are required to start falling by the summer of 2003, and the cuts will eventually amount to 1.5 million tons (1.36 million tonnes) a year.

When people suffering from the effects of polluted air learn that in another city in another country the air is clean, they start asking why this should be. They may travel abroad or talk with friends who have traveled, and those who stay at home see pictures of clean cities on TV. Before long they demand improvements, and eventually their demands are heard and translated into laws and regulations designed to satisfy them. Modern communications make it easier to convince people of the need for improvements and of the benefits those improvements will bring.

Will the world of tomorrow have cleaner or dirtier air?

A century ago it was only the experts who worried about air pollution. Doctors could see its effects on the health of their patients. Chemists could measure the extent to which air was contaminated. Meteorologists could compare city and rural air and shake their heads sadly. Other people took it for granted.

If you grow up in a city that lies permanently beneath a pall of smoke, and if every other city you see lies beneath a similar pall, then the smoke seems inevitable, even natural. Some of the factories may produce truly obnoxious smells, but you learn to put up with it. After all, what can you or anyone else do about it? It may not even occur to you that any alternative is possible.

People may go further and actually approve of the smoke. "Lang may yer lum reek" is an old Edinburgh expression of good will. It means "Long may your chimney smoke." If smoke comes from the chimney, all is well at home. Think of the many stories in which a traveler at the end of a long, arduous journey sees the welcoming sight of a village nestled in a valley, with smoke curling peacefully from the chimneys.

Smoke implies a hearth, which implies a warm, safe home, but it implies more. It implies work and wages coming into the house to put food on the table. The sight of hundreds of factory chimneys belching smoke by night and day used to be a happy sight. It spelled full employment and prosperity. People did tend to cough rather a lot, but they also ate and paid the rent. They also made jokes about the smoke—about waking up to the sound of the birds coughing, for example.

Today attitudes are different. Many of the old heavy industries—steel making, shipbuilding, heavy engineering—have left our cities. Their disappearance has allowed the air quality to improve. At the same time, national laws and intergovernmental treaties have imposed curbs on pollution (see "Laws and Treaties," page 185). Air has improved partly because we have required it to improve and partly because the industries that once polluted it have failed and gone.

Those industries have not gone entirely, of course. Some large factories still survive in our industrial cities, where they are now required to obey the antipollution laws. We continue to use as many industrial products as ever, of course, but nowadays most of these are made in one of the rapidly industrializing nations. The industries have not so much vanished as relocated.

On the face of it, transferring polluting industries from one part of the world to another simply shifts the pollution. Clean air over New York, Manchester, and the Ruhr is paid for by dirty air over Beijing and Djakarta. Many cities in the industrializing world are seriously polluted—by the rise in road traffic as well as by manufacturing industry. This is only part of the story, however.

Our increasing awareness of the dangers of pollution, especially to our own health, has stimulated research into technological ways to reduce the problem (see "Trapping Pollutants," page 150; "New Cars for Old," page 157; "Heat without Fire," page 166; and "Sun and Wind," page 176). Industries have been encouraged—and compelled when encouragement proved inadequate—to reduce their polluting emissions by installing more advanced equipment. Consequently, the heavy industrial factories of today are markedly different from those of a century ago. Indeed, it is partly the difficulty they experienced in modernizing that led to their demise. Industrialists in newly industrializing countries were able to install modern plants from the start, allowing them to produce commodities more cleanly than did their competitors in the old industrialized countries—and also more cheaply, because installing a more technologically advanced plant improves efficiency as well as reduces pollution.

Industrialization does not necessarily imply the kind of pollution that was typical of America and Europe in the 19th and early 20th centuries. Of course, there will be pollution. The pollution in Europe and America was made worse by the rapidity of industrial expansion, and that rate of expansion is now occurring in Latin America and Asia. Competition is fierce, companies appear and fail overnight, and no one has the time or resources to deal properly with the pollution the factories cause.

Countries that are industrializing today are reliving some of the experiences of America and Europe during their industrialization. They are not reliving all of it, because despite the haste with which they are rushing to attain higher levels of prosperity, their peoples are aware of the health hazards. Their industrialists also have access to technologies for controlling pollution. Consequently, the governments of these countries are taking steps to improve air quality at a much earlier stage in the process of industrialization than was possible a century ago.

It is impossible to predict the future. We cannot know what life will be like decades from now, let alone a century from now. All we can do is observe what is happening now and make an educated guess.

The expectation is that the quality of the air will continue to improve over the industrialized countries of America, Europe, Australasia, and Japan. Already it is much better than it has been in the past, and in some countries, such as Great Britain, city air is cleaner than it has been for centuries. Further improvements will come from cleaner methods for generating power, products that use energy more efficiently and therefore use less energy, and radical changes in transportation. Eventually, cars, buses, and trucks will cease to be powered by gasoline or diesel engines.

For a time air quality will deteriorate over the cities of Latin America and Asia as those regions continue to industrialize. Then, and probably within a few decades, their air quality will start to improve rapidly as they introduce technologies and laws to reduce pollution. The countries of Africa south of the Sahara are likely to follow the same path a little later.

So will the world of tomorrow have cleaner or dirtier air? Eventually there can be little doubt that it will have much cleaner air. Until then, the condition of air will be patchy. We may expect it to improve first over the cities of America, Europe, Japan, and Australasia, but at the same time it may continue to deteriorate over the cities of Latin America, China, and southern Asia. Then the improvements will begin to be felt in those regions and, once they begin, they are likely to be rapid. By the end of this century, and perhaps much sooner, they will have caught up with the West.

This is a guess, of course, but it is an educated guess. Despite the appalling smogs over so many cities, despite the factories that are thrown up in haste and that burn the dirtiest fuels, and despite the countless millions of poor homes where low-grade coal is the only fuel obtainable, the future is bright. It is bright because we are aware of the problems, and we know how to solve them. That is what we will do. We will solve them.

Bibliography and further reading

Air Info Now. Pima County Department of Environmental Quality and U.S. Environmental Protection Agency. "What Is Particulate Matter?" Available online. URL: www.airinfonow.org/html/ed_particulate.html. Accessed October 22, 2002.

"Air Pollution." Fact Sheet No. 187. Geneva: World Health Organization, September 2000. www.who.int/inf-fs/en/fact187.html.

"The Air Quality Index." Available on-line. URL: www.apcd.org/aq/aqi.html. Revised September 6, 2002.

Aldous, Scott. "How Solar Cells Work." *How Stuff Works.* Available on-line. URL: www.howstuffworks.com/solar-cell.htm. Accessed October 22, 2002.

Allaby, Michael. *Basics of Environmental Science.* 2d ed. New York: Routledge, 2000.

———. *Deserts.* New York: Facts On File, 2001.

———. *Elements: Fire.* New York: Facts On File, 1993.

———. *Encyclopedia of Weather and Climate.* 2 vols. New York: Facts On File, 2001.

———. *The Facts On File Weather and Climate Handbook.* New York: Facts On File, 2002.

———. *Temperate Forests.* New York: Facts On File, 1999.

American Lung Association. "Major Air Pollutants." *State of the Air 2002.* Available on-line. URL: www.lungusa.org/air/envmajairpro.html. October 22, 2002.

American Wind Energy Association. Available on-line. URL: www.awea.org. Updated September 13, 2002.

An Chartlann Náisiúnta (The National Archives of Ireland). "The Great Famine 1845–1850—Introduction." Available on-line. URL: www.nationalarchives.ie/famine.html. Updated August 8, 2002.

"Ash Wednesday, February 1983." *Climate Eduction.* Bureau of Meteorology, Australia. www.bom.gov.au/lam/climate/levelthree/c20thc/fire5.htm.

"Ash Wednesday Fires, February 16, 1983: Situation Overview." Available on-line. URL: sres.anu.edu.au/associated/fire/IUFRO/CONFLAG/ASHWED83/AW83.HTM. Accessed October 22, 2002.

Baird, Stuart. "Ocean Energy Systems." Energy Fact Sheet. Energy Educators of Ontario. Available on-line. URL: www.iclei.org/efacts/ocean.htm. Accessed October 22, 2002.

———. "Wind Energy." Energy Fact Sheet. Energy Educators of Ontario. Available on-line. URL: www.iclei.org/efacts/wind.htm. Accessed October 22, 2002.

Barry, Roger G., and Richard J. Chorley. *Atmosphere, Weather & Climate.* 7th ed. New York: Routledge, 1998.

Button, Don. "The Smell of Christmas." Article #852. Alaska Science Forum. Available online. URL: www.gi.alaska.edu/ScienceForum/ASF8/852.html. December 21, 1987.

Campbell, Todd. "What About the Wankel?" Available on-line. URL: abcnews.go.com/sections/tech/Geek/geek000302.html. Accessed October 21, 2002.

Cecilioni, V. A. "Lung Cancer in a Steel City: A Personal Historical Perspective." *Fluoride* 23, no. 3 (July 1990): 101–103. Available on-line. URL: www.fluoridealert.org/hamilton.htm.

CFA (Country Fire Authority). "Ash Wednesday." Available on-line. URL: www.cfa.vic.gov.au/info_ash.htm. October 30, 2000.

Climate Education, Bureau of Meteorology, Australia. "Ash Wednesday, February 1983." Available on-line. URL: www.bom.gov.au/lam/climate/levelthree/c20thc/fire5.htm. Accessed October 22, 2002.

"Climate Effects of Volcanic Eruptions." Available on-line. URL: www.geology.sdsu.edu/how_volcanoes_work/climate_effects.html. Accessed October 21, 2002.

CNN Interactive. "Deadly Smog 50 Years Ago in Donora Spurred Clean Air Movement." Available on-line. URL: www.dep.state.pa.us/dep/Rachel_Carson/clean_air.htm. October 27, 1998.

Colbeck, I., and A. R. MacKenzie. "Chemistry and Pollution of the Stratosphere." In *Pollution: Causes, Effects and Control.* 2d ed. Ed. Roy M. Harrison. London: Royal Society of Chemistry, 1990.

"Columbia River Flood Basalt Province, Idaho, Washington, Oregon, USA." Available on-line. URL: volcano/und.nodak.edu/vwdocs/volc_images/north_america/crb.html. Accessed October 21, 2002.

Danish Wind Industry Association. "Wind Energy: Frequently Asked Questions." Available on-line. URL: www.windpower.org/faqs.htm. April 17, 2002.

Doddridge, Bruce. "Urban Photochemical Smog." Available on-line. URL: www.meto.umd.edu/~bruce/m1239701.html. February 6, 1997.

DOE, Fossil Energy Techline. "Converting Emissions into Energy—Three Companies to Develop Technologies for Tapping Coal Mine Methane," Available on-line. URL: www.netl.doe.gov/publications/press/2000/tl_coalmine1.html. September 14, 2000.

"Early Cars." Available on-line. URL: www.cybersteering.com/trimain/history/ecars.html. Accessed October 21, 2002.

Eberlee, John. "Investigating an Environmental Disaster: Lessons from the Indonesian Fires and Haze." *Reports: Science from the Developing World*, International Development Research Centre, October 9, 1998. Available on-line. URL: www.idrc.ca/reports/read_article_english.cfm?article_num=283.

Ecological Society of America. "Acid Rain Revisited: What has happened since the 1990 Clear Air Act Amendments?" Available on-line. URL: esa.sdsc.edu/acidrainfactsheet.htm. Accessed October 21, 2002.

Emiliani, Cesare. *Planet Earth: Cosmology, Geology, and the Evolution of Life and Environment.* Cambridge, U.K.: Cambridge University Press, 1992.

Energy Efficiency and Renewable Energy Network. "Hydropower Topics." January 25, 2002. Available on-line. URL: www.eren.doe.gov/RE/hydropower.html.

Engels, Andre. "Juan Rodríguez Cabrillo." Available on-line. URL: www.win.tue.nl/cs/fm/engels/discovery/cabrillo.html. Accessed October 21, 2002.

"Factors Influencing Air Pollution." Available on-line. URL: www.marama.org/atlas/factors.html. Updated November 17, 1998.

"The Famine 1: Potato Blight." Available on-line. URL: www.wesleyjohnston.com/users/ireland/past/famine/blight.html. Accessed October 21, 2002.

Faoro, Margaret. "HEVs (Hybrid Electric Vehicles)." University of California, Irvine, February 2002. Available on-line. URL: darwin.bio.uci.edu/~sustain/global/sensem/Faoro202.htm.

"Flue Gas Desulfurization (FGD) for SO_2 Control." Available on-line. URL: www.iea-coal.org.uk/CCT database/fgd.htm. Accessed October 22, 2002.

Friberg, L. *Inorganic Mercury—Summary and Conclusions*, Environmental Health Criteria 118. Geneva: World Health Organization, 1991. Available on-line. URL: www.iaomt.nu/who118.htm.

"Fuel Cells 2000: The On-line Fuel Cell Information Center." Available on-line. URL: www.fuelcells.org/. Updated October 21, 2002.

Fuelcellstore.com. "Hydrogen Storage". Available on-line. URL: www.fuelcellstore. com/information/hydrogen_storage.html. Accessed October 22, 2002.

Gedney, Larry. "Years without Summers." Article #726. Alaska Science Forum, July 22, 1985. URL: www.gi.alaska.edu/ScienceForum/ASF7/726.html.

Goltz, James, Jan Decker, and Charles Sawthorn. "The Southern California Wildfires of 1993." EQE International. Available on-line. URL: www.eqe.com/ publications/socal_wildfire/scalfire.htm. Accessed October 22, 2002.

Gordon, John, Mark Niles, and LeRoy Schroder. "USGS Tracks Acid Rain." U.S.G.S. Fact Sheet FS-183–95. Available on-line. URL: btdqs.usgs.gov/ precip/arfs.htm. Accessed October 21, 2002.

Green Cross International. "Environmental Legacy in Kuwait." Available on-line. URL: www.gci.ch/GreenCrossPrograms/legacy/Kuwait/kuwait7years.html. October 14, 1998.

Hagenlocher, Klaus G. "A Zeppelin for the 21st Century." *Scientific American*, November 1999. Available on-line. URL: www.sciam.com/1999/1199issue/ 1199hagenlocher.html.

Harrison, Roy M., ed. *Pollution: Causes, Effects and Control.* 3d ed. London: Royal Society of Chemistry, 1996.

Hauglustaine, D. A, G. P. Brasseur, and J. S. Levine. "A Sensitivity Simulation of Tropospheric Ozone Changes due to the 1997 Indonesian Fire Emissions." Available on-line. URL: acd.ucar.edu/models/MOZART/pubs/indonesia-text.doc. Accessed October 22, 2002.

Heck, Walter W. "Assessment of Crop Losses from Air Pollutants in the United States." In *Air Pollution's Toll on Forests & Crops.* Eds. James J. Mackenzie and Mohamed T. El-Ashry. New Haven, Conn.: Yale University Press, 1989.

Helfferich, Carla. "Consequences of Kuwait's Fires." Article #1051. Alaska Science Forum, October 10, 1991. Available on-line. URL: www.gi.alaska.edu/ ScienceForum/ASF10/1051.html.

Henahan, Sean. "The Great Famine: Gone, But Not Forgotten." Available online. URL: www.accessexcellence.org/WN/SUA03/great_famine.html. Accessed October 21, 2002.

Henderson-Sellers, Ann Robinson, and Peter J. Robinson. *Contemporary Climatology.* Harlow, U.K.: Longman, 1986.

Herring, George D. "Juan Rodríguez Cabrillo—A Voyage of Discovery." Available on-line. URL: www.nps.gov/cabr/juan.html. Updated March 19, 2000.

Holder, Gerald D., and P. R. Bishnoi, eds. *Challenges for the Future: Gas Hydrates.* Vol. 912, *Annals of the New York Academy of Sciences.* New York: New York Academy of Sciences, 2000.

Hybrid Electric Vehicle Program, Dept. of Energy, 2002. "What Is an HEV?" Available on-line. URL: www.ott.doe.gov/hev/what.html. Accessed October 22, 2002.

International Institute for Applied Systems Research. "Cleaner Air for a Cleaner Future: Controlling Transboundary Air Pollution." Available on-line. URL: www.iiasa.ac.at/Admin/INF/OPT/Summer98/negotiations.htm. Accessed October 22, 2002.

Klunne, Wim. "Turbines." Micro Hydropower Basics. December 24, 2000. Available on-line. URL: www.microhydropower.net/turbines.html.

"Lakagígar." Available on-line. URL: www.hi.is/~gunntho/lakagigar.htm. Accessed October 21, 2002.

"The Lakagígar Eruption of 1783." Available on-line. URL: www.volcanotours.com/iceland/fieldguide/lakagigar_eruption.htm. Accessed October 21, 2002.

Latham, R. E., trans. *Marco Polo: The Travels.* Harmondsworth, U.K.: Penguin Books, 1958.

"Leather Working." Available on-line. URL: www.regia.org/leatwork.htm. Updated March 20, 2002.

Lomborg, Bjørn. *The Skeptical Environmentalist.* Cambridge, U.K.: Cambridge University Press, 2001.

Lovelock, James E. *The Ages of Gaia.* New York: Oxford University Press, 1989.

———. *Gaia: A New Look at Life on Earth.* 2d ed. New York: Oxford University Press, 2000.

Lutgens, Frederick K., and Edward J. Tarbuck. *The Atmosphere.* 7th ed. Upper Saddle River, N.J.: Prentice Hall, 1998.

"Manchester: History." Available on-line. URL: www.lonelyplanet.com/destinations/europe/manchester/history.htm. Accessed October 21, 2002.

Marr, Alan. "Wankel Rotary Combustion Engines." Available on-line. URL: www.monito.com/wankel/. April 7, 2000.

Mason, C. F. *Biology of Freshwater Pollution.* 2d ed. New York: John Wiley, 1991.

Mellanby, Kenneth. *Waste and Pollution: The Problem for Britain.* London: Harper-Collins, 1992.

"The Microbial World: Potato blight: *Phytophthora infestans.*" Available on-line. URL: helios.bto.ed.ac.uk/bto/microbes/blight.htm. Accessed October 21, 2002.

Miller, Paul R. "Concept of Forest Decline in Relation to Western U.S. Forests." In MacKenzie, James J., and Mohamed T. El-Ashry, eds. *Air Pollution's Toll on Forests & Crops,* New Haven, Conn.: Yale University Press, 1989.

National Wildlife Federation. "Mercury Pollution." Available on-line URL: www.nwf.org/cleantherain/mercuryQandA.html. March 22, 2001.

"Natural Air Pollution." Available on-line. URL: www.doc.mmu.ac.uk/aric/eae/Air_Quality/Older/Natural_Air_Pollution.html. Accessed October 21, 2002.

Nice, Karim. "How Catalytic Converters Work." *How Stuff Works.* Available on-line. URL: www.howstuffworks.com/catalytic-converter1.htm. Accessed October 22, 2002.

———. "How Rotary Engines Work." *How Stuff Works.* Available on-line. URL: www.howstuffworks.com/rotary-engine.htm. Accessed October 21, 2002.

"No Room to Breathe: Photochemical Smog and Ground-Level Ozone." Ministry of Environment, Lands and Parks of the Government of British Columbia, Air Resources Branch. Available on-line. URL: wlapwww.gov/bc.ca/air/vehicle/nrtbpsag.html. August 1992.

Norwegian Institute of Air Research. "Acid Rain—Can we see improvements?" Available on-line. URL: www.nilu.no/informasjon/beretning96-begge/english/acid-txt.html. Accessed October 21, 2002.

"Nuclear Fusion Basics." Available on-line. URL: www.jet.efda.org/pages/content/fusion1.html. Accessed October 22, 2002.

Ohio State University Fact Sheet. Coal Combustion Products. Available on-line. URL: ohioline.osu.edu/aex-fact/0330.html. Accessed October 21, 2002.

Oke, T. R. *Boundary Layer Climates.* 2d ed. New York: Routledge, 1987.

Oliver, John E., and John J. Hidore. *Climatology: An Atmospheric Science.* 2d ed. Upper Saddle River, N.J.: Prentice Hall, 2002.

O'Mara, Katrina, and Philip Jennings. "Ocean Thermal Energy Conversion." Australian CRC for Renewable Energy Ltd., June 1999. Available on-line. URL: acre.murdoch.edu.au/refiles/ocean/text.html.

Patel, Trupti. "Bhopal Disaster." The On-line Ethics Center for Engineering and Science at Case Western Reserve University. Available on-line. URL: onlineethics.org/environment/bhopal.html. Updated September 6, 2001.

Pennsylvania State University. "Aerobiological Engineering: Electrostatic Precipitation." Available on-line. URL: www.engr.psu.edu/ae/wjk/electro.html. Accessed October 22, 2002.

Peterken, George F. *Natural Woodland.* Cambridge, U.K.: Cambridge University Press, 1996.

"Potato Production and Management." Available on-line. URL: www.rec.udel.edu/class/kee/oct4.html. Accessed October 21, 2002.

Rosen, Harold A., and Deborah R. Castleman. "Flywheels in Hybrid Vehicles." *Scientific American* (October 1997). Available on-line. URL: www.sciam.com/1097issue/1097rosen.html.

Sloan, E. Dendy, Jr., John Happel, and Miguel A. Hnatow, eds. *International Conference on Natural Gas Hydrates.* Vol. 715, *Annals of the New York Academy of Sciences.* New York: New York Academy of Sciences, 1994.

"Solar Chimney." Available on-line. URL: seecl.mae.ufl.edu/solar/chimney.html. Updated September 2000.

Taggart, Stewart. "Creating New, Sky-High Power." *Wired News,* September 18, 2001. Available on-line. URL: www.wired.com/news.print/0,1294,46814,00.html.

Thomas, Keith. *Man and the Natural World: Changing Attitudes in England 1500–1800.* Harmondsworth, U.K.: Penguin Books, 1984.

"The Trail of Destruction: A Chronology of the Fires." *Down to Earth* 35, November 1997, Forest Fires Special Supplement. Available on-line. URL: dte.gn.apc.org/35sul.htm.

Transport Action: Powershift. "Clean Fuels—Summary of UK Situation." Available on-line. URL: www.clean-vehicles.com/cleanv/fuel/about.html. Accessed October 22, 2002.

"Trees and Air Pollution." *ScienceDaily Magazine.* Available on-line. URL: www.sciencedaily.com/releases/2001/01/010109223032.htm. November 1, 2001.

UCAR Quarterly, summer 1998. "Fire and Rain: Indonesian Fires Ignite Cloud Study." Available on-line. URL: www.ucar.edu/communications/quarterly/summer98/fires.html. Updated April 4, 2000.

U.N. Environment Program. "The State of the Environment—Regional synthesis," chapter 2 of *GEO–2000: Global Environment Outlook.* Available on-line. URL: www.unep.org/geo2000/english/0048.htm. Accessed October 21, 2002.

———. "Montreal Protocol." Available on-line. URL: www.unep.ch/ozone/mont_t.shtml and www.unep.ch/treaties.shtml. Accessed October 21, 2002.

Union of Concerned Scientists. "Farming the Wind: Wind Power and Agriculture." December 7, 2000. Available on-line. URL: www.ucusa.org/energy/fact_wind.html.

University of California Cooperative Extension. "Tree Selection Could Have an Effect on Air Quality." Available on-line. URL: www.uckac.edu/press/pressreleases98/treestudy.htm. July 27, 1998.

USA Today. "Understanding clouds and fog." Available on-line. URL: www.usatoday.com/weather/wfog.htm. Updated April 22, 2002.

U.S. Environmental Protection Agency. "About EPA." Available on-line. URL: www.epa.gov/epahome/aboutepa.htm. Updated August 8, 2002.

———. "Acid Rain." Available on-line. URL: www.epa.gov/airmarkets/acidrain/. Updated October 17, 2002.

———. "Air." Available on-line. URL: www.epa.gov/ebtpages/air.html. Updated October 21, 2002.

———. "Air Toxics from Motor Vehicles." Fact Sheet OMS-2. Available on-line. URL: www.epa.gov/otaq/02-toxic.htm. Updated July 20, 1998.

———. "Anaconda." Available on-line. URL: www.epa.gov/region08/superfund/sites/mt/anacon.html. Updated October 8, 2002.

———. "Automobile Emissions: An Overview." Available on-line. URL: www.epa.gov/OMSWWW/05-autos.htm. August 1994.

———. "Clean Air Act." Available on-line. URL: www.epa.gov/oar/oaq_caa.html. Updated March 29, 2002.

———. Coalbed Methane Outreach Program. Available on-line. URL: www.epa.gov/coalbed/. Accessed October 21, 2002.

———. "Emissions Summary." Office of Air Quality Planning and Standards. Available on-line. URL: www.epa.gov/oar/emtrnd94/em_summ.html. August 1, 2002.

———. "Environmental Laws That Establish the EPA's Authority." Available on-line. URL: www.epa.gov/history/org/origins/laws.htm. Updated August 12, 2002.

———. "Radioactive Waste Disposal: An Environmental Perspective." Available on-line. URL: www.epa.gov/radiation/radwaste/index.html. Updated October 21, 2002.

U.S. Geological Survey. "The Cataclysmic 1991 Eruption of Mount Pinatubo, Philippines." U.S.G.S. Fact Sheet 113-97. Available on-line. URL: http://geopubs.wr.usgs.gov/fact-sheet/fs113-97/. January 12, 2002.

van Ravenswaay, Eileen O. "Iron and Steel Industry." Available on-line. URL: www.msu.edu/course/prm/255/Iron&SteelIndustryCase.htm. February 7, 2000.

Volk, Tyler, *Gaia's Body: Towards a Physiology of Earth*. New York: Copernicus, 1998.

Walton, Marsha. "Could Hydrogen Be the Fuel of the Future?" *CNN Sci-Tech*, March 16, 2001. Available on-line. URL: www.cnn.com/2001/TECH/science/03/16/hydrogen.cars/.

"Wankel Car Engine—The Rotary Design." Available on-line. URL: www.cybersteering.com/cruise/feature/engine/wankel.html. Accessed October 21, 2002.

"Wildland Fire." Available on-line. URL: www.nps.gov/yell/nature/fire/index.htm. Updated October 3, 2001.

"Wildland Fire in Yellowstone." Available on-line. URL: www.nps.gov/yell/technical/fire/. Updated September 16, 2002.

World Health Organization. "Air Pollution." *Fact Sheet No. 187*. Available on-line. URL: www.who.int/inf-fs/en/fact187.html. Revised September 2000.

World Nuclear Association. "Safety of Nuclear Power Reactors." Available on-line. URL: www.world-nuclear.org/info/inf06apprint.htm. July 2002.

Wouk, Victor. "Hybrid Electric Vehicles." *Scientific American*, October 1997. Available on-line. URL: www.sciam.com/1097issue/1097wouk.html.

Zeppelin Luftschifftechnik GmbH, Airship and Blimp Resources. Available on-line. URL: hotairship.com/database/zeppelin.html. Accessed October 22, 2002.

SI UNITS AND CONVERSIONS

Unit	Quantity	Symbol	Conversion
Base units			
meter	length	m	1 m = 3.2808 inches
kilogram	mass	kg	1 kg = 2.205 pounds
second	time	s	
ampere	electric current	A	
kelvin	thermodynamic temperature	K	1 K = 1°C = 1.8°F
candela	luminous intensity	cd	
mole	amount of substance	mol	
Supplementary units			
radian	plane angle	rad	$\pi/2$ rad = 90°
steradian	solid angle	sr	
Derived units			
coulomb	quantity of electricity	C	
cubic meter	volume	m^3	1 m^3 = 1.308 yards^3
farad	capacitance	F	
henry	inductance	H	
hertz	frequency	H_z	
joule	energy	J	1 J = 0.2389 calories
kilogram per cubic meter	density	kg m^{-3}	1 kg m^{-3} = 0.0624 lb. ft.$^{-3}$
lumen	luminous flux	lm	
lux	illuminance	lx	
meter per second squared	speed acceleration	m s^{-1} m s^{-2}	1 m s^{-1} = 3.281 ft. s^{-1}
mole per cubic meter	concentration	mol m^{-3}	
newton	force	N	1 N = 7.218 lb. force
ohm	electric resistance	Ω	

SI UNITS AND CONVERSIONS (*continued*)

Unit	Quantity	Symbol	Conversion
Derived units			
pascal	pressure	Pa	1 Pa = 0.145 lb. in.$^{-2}$
radian per second	angular velocity	rad s^{-1}	
radian per second squared	angular acceleration	rad s^{-2}	
square meter	area	m^2	1 m^2 = 1.196 yards^2
tesla	magnetic flux density	T	
volt	electromotive force	V	
watt	power	W	1 W = 3.412 Btu h^{-1}
weber	magnetic flux	Wb	

PREFIXES USED WITH SI UNITS

Prefixes attached to SI units alter their value.

Prefix	Symbol	Value
atto	a	$\times 10^{-18}$
femto	f	$\times 10^{-15}$
pico	p	$\times 10^{-12}$
nano	n	$\times 10^{-9}$
micro	μ	$\times 10^{-6}$
milli	m	$\times 10^{-3}$
centi	c	$\times 10^{-2}$
deci	d	$\times 10^{-1}$
deca	da	$\times 10$
hecto	h	$\times 10^{2}$
kilo	k	$\times 10^{3}$
mega	M	$\times 10^{6}$
giga	G	$\times 10^{9}$
tera	T	$\times 10^{12}$

Index

Page numbers in *italic* refer to illustrations.